SPEAKING OUT:

Gifts of Ministering
Undeterred by Disabilities

Edited by Robert Walker

CreateSpace, Inc.
7290 B Investment Drive
Charleston, SC 29418
Toll Free: 1-866-308-6235

Library of Congress Control Number: 2006910139
Publisher: CreateSpace, Inc.
North Charleston, South Carolina

Table of Contents

Biographical Statements about Each Contributing Author

1. **Anonymous.** At the request of the writer, neither a name nor a biographical statement is published.

2. **Helen Betenbaugh** was the first Episcopal priest who used a wheelchair to be called as the Rector of a parish in the history of the Episcopal Church. Now retired, she lives in suburban Dallas near her two daughters and two grandchildren. Helen earned the Master of Divinity degree from Perkins School of Theology, Southern Methodist University (SMU), in 1993, and the Doctor of Ministry degree in 1997. Her project was on *Disability in the Canon*. During Helen's first seminary year, a faculty member suggested that she contact The Rev. John Miller, a disabled Colorado minister, who was organizing what turned out to be the founding meeting of the Association of Physically Challenged Ministers. He, in turn, asked her to write a hymn for the organization. Her "We Celebrate Challenge" was adopted as the official hymn of the APCM at that 1990 founding meeting in Nashville. Helen also holds two degrees in church music and had 30 years experience leading some of the country's most celebrated music ministries. She has taught courses in church music in three colleges and universities. Helen served in a variety of offices for the aforementioned association, including being a Co-Chairperson with The Rev. Mickey Stringfield, and presiding over the first national meeting that included a presence on a United Methodist seminary campus. Helen's publications include more than two dozen articles on various aspects of church music and another two dozen on disability and the Church. She has taught disability-related graduate courses at the University of Dayton and at Perkins, SMU and has lectured throughout the country on a wide variety of disability topics.

3. **Kathy Black, Ph.D.**, is the Gerald Kennedy Professor of Homiletics and Liturgics at the Claremont School of Theology in Southern Cali-

fornia. An ordained elder in the United Methodist Church, and prior to her current position, Kathy has served as a local church pastor in Maryland and California. She is the author of "A Healing Homiletic; Preaching and Persons with Disabilities." Raised on a toxic waste dump, Kathy has dealt with her own issues of living with temporary episodes of paralysis.

4. **Brian Burch** is a pastor with a physical disability. At the time of this writing, he and DeAnne have been married for 23 years and have three sons attending college and high school respectively. Brian finds great enjoyment in tending his 2,000 gallon "portable" water garden. On many nights you will find him trying to defeat his sons in some computer game; usually unsuccessfully. While earning his Chemical Engineering degree at Georgia Tech, God called him to "feed the flock" in the United Methodist Church, where he has—at the time of this writing—served for 24 years as a local pastor in the Holston Conference.

5. **Jonathan Campbell** has the cerebral palsy condition, along with a learning disability. He holds degrees of Master of Divinity (M.Div.) and Master of Theology (TH.M.) from Princeton Theological Seminary. Jonathan is a strong advocate for creating theological frameworks that can help the Church support and strengthen people with disabilities; also aided are their families. He has served as a student chaplain at Matheny Medical and Educational Center in Peapack, New Jersey. Additionally, he has worked as an advocate focused on issues of affordable and accessible housing, along with job issues. At the time of this writing, Jonathan serves as the pastor for two United Methodist Churches in Stony Point, New York. He is married to Jessica who is also an ordained Elder in the United Methodist Church. They have three sons.

6. **John A. Carr** was born in 1932 with the congenital absence of both hands and with the absence of his left foot, with his left leg approximately two inches shorter than his right. In 1953, John graduated from Ohio Wesleyan University and entered Yale Divinity School on a three-year pastoral track. John applied for an annual conference scholarship, but with funds unavailable, he was offered a position with a summer camping program as manager of a children's camp, allowing him to meet church clergypersons, laity, and children from all around the annual conference. In 1956, John was offered a position as associ-

ate pastor at Westbury, Long Island Methodist Church. He then served for five years as pastor of the Hauppauge, Long Island United Methodist Church. In 1963, John was appointed pastor of Faith United Methodist Church in North Haven, CT, where he served for three years before becoming a chaplain-in-training at Yale New Haven Hospital in the Department of Religious Ministry. Starting in 1970, John was a CPE supervisor, preparing divinity students and laity for hospital ministry, serving until retirement in 1997. During a portion of this time, John chaired a COCU task force on disability concerns. He also chaired the annual conference accessibility committee and a Connecticut-wide group of advocates called the Connecticut Coalition of Citizens with Disabilities. Upon retirement, John accepted a part-time position as executive director of the Association of Physically Challenged Ministers and helped to lead the former organization into the current United Methodist Association of Ministers with Disabilities.

7. **Paul Crikelair** was born profoundly hearing-impaired, but with lip-reading training and speech therapy through his elementary school years, he was graduated from Ridgewood (N.J.) High School, Franklin & Marshall College (B.A., Religious Studies and Government), and Gordon-Conwell Theological Seminary (M.Div., Magna Cum Laude). Paul experienced God's call to ordained ministry while serving in student ministries at Yellowstone and Glacier National Parks during his college years. He has served as a United Methodist Pastor in the Eastern Pennsylvania Conference in three appointments over the past thirty years in Upper Darby, Elverson and Stroudsburg, PA. Married to Janet, the couple has seven children: Jesse, Heidi, Emily, Jody, Peter, Nathan and Stephen.

8. **Gary L. Lake Dillensnyder** is an ordained elder in the Eastern Pennsylvania Conference of the United Methodist Church. At the time of this writing, Gary has served in parish ministry for 30 years in Pennsylvania and North Carolina. His undergraduate degrees are from Lebanon Valley College, Annville, PA in psychology and religion. His graduate degrees have included study at Duke University Divinity School and the Theological School of Drew University. He is a life member of the Order of St. Luke. His wife, Mary, is an ordained pastor in both the Christian Church (The Disciples of Christ) and the United Church of Christ. They reside in the Philadelphia, Pennsylva-

nia Area with their two dogs, Mollie (a Bichon Frise) and Webster (a Weshighland Terrier).

9. **William Downing** entered the United Methodist Church ministry in June of 1973. He earned his psychology degree from Carolina University in Belmont, North Carolina, and his Master of Divinity degree from Wesley Theological Seminary in Washington, D.C. Prior to his severe injuries in an auto accident, Bill served in the following Maryland parishes: Powellville Charge consisting of five churches, Girdletree, Stockton Charge, Oriole Charge, and Cecilton Parish. In Delaware, he served the Georgetown Circuit, Frederica Charge and Ewells-St. Paul and Kenton Churches. In 1978 Bill worked for United Methodist Bishop James K. Mathews in researching for his book "Deeper Furrows." At the time of this writing, Bill serves as a volunteer Chaplain for the Intervention Crisis Ministry of Alexandria, Pennsylvania. Married to Martha "Marty," the couple has two children—Helen and Linda Lee—and two grandchildren. Their son, Charles Edward, is deceased.

10. **Mitchell M. Galloway** was born in 1952 in York, Pennsylvania. His journey through education includes a 1970 graduation from York Central High School, four years later from Lebanon Valley College, and in 1980 from United Theological Seminary in Dayton, Ohio. Mitchell has served the following churches in the Susquehanna Conference of the United Methodist Church in Pennsylvania: St. Johns UMC, Chambersburg, Watts Memorial in Belleville, and the Trinity and Adamsville charge in Dallastown. As of this writing, Mitchell is in his tenth year as the lead pastor at Fourth UMC, an urban congregation located in York. Married in 1977 to Carol, the two are parents of a son and a daughter.

11. **Nancy Jill Hale** entered pastoral ministry in 1998 as a local pastor in the former Wyoming Conference. Prior to receiving her call to ministry, she lived in New Jersey and on Long Island and worked at various times as a race horse groom, a sign painter, and a church sexton. Nancy received her Bachelor of Arts degree from Binghamton University in 2005 and her Master of Divinity degree from Boston University School of Theology in 2008, where she is currently pursuing a Doctor of Theology degree (Th.D.) in liturgy and theology. She was ordained in 2010 and serves as an Associate Pastor in the Upper New

York Conference. Currently, Nancy is the senior pastor for the Broad Street United Methodist Church in Norwich, New York. She is married to Jeff Hale, who is also a United Methodist ordained minister. Nancy has been active in the United Methodist Committee on Ministries with Deaf and Hard-of-Hearing People, most recently serving as the Chairperson of the Grants Committee. She has authored several articles on disability, including "Spiritual Guidance and Disability," (*Presence: An International Journal of Spiritual Direction* - in publication), and "Was Blind but Now I See: Challenging Metaphors of Disability," (*Doxology* #27, 2010).

12. **Thomas Hudspeth** serves as the executive pastor and pastor of Deaf ministries at Lovers Lane United Methodist Church in Dallas, Texas. He is a graduate of Lon Morris Junior College, Southwestern University and Southern Methodist University's Perkins School of Theology. Tom has a postgraduate diploma from the University of Otago, New Zealand and a Doctor of Ministry degree (D.Min.) from Wesley Theological Seminary, where he wrote his thesis on "American Sign Language as a Means of Grace." Tom has served on the General Board of Church and Society (1992-1995), the United Methodist Committee on Deaf, Late-Deafened, Hard of Hearing and Deaf-Blind People (2000-2008), and as an officer of the United Methodist Congress of the Deaf. He has served on the boards of the Methodist Mission Home of San Antonio, Texas, New Life Deaf Ministry of Honduras, and Lovers Lane Academy for the Deaf of Dallas. In 2009 at the 2nd Global Missions Conference of Deaf Methodists, held in South Korea, he was elected General Secretary of the World Federation of Deaf Methodists. At the time of this writing, Tom is the consultant for the United Methodist Committee of Deaf and Hard of Hearing Ministries. He and his wife Mary Kay, who he met through her father's sign language class in Midwest City, Oklahoma, have two children, Lossie, who is hearing and Christian, who is deaf.

13. **Donna Fado Ivery** is the painter of "Circle Dance", pictured on the front cover of this book. She is a disabled minister and artist who is called to the Art of Healing. She sells original paintings, prints, cards, and Scarf of Tears from her home business website, www.AdventuresInHealing.com. Donna describes her artistic process as "an exhilarating experience and a celebration of Spirituality and Healing." Graduating with honors from the University of California

at Davis and Boston University School of Theology, Donna was ordained as a United Methodist minister in the California-Nevada Annual Conference of the United Methodist Church, and served churches in Livermore, Hayward, and Madera, California. In 1994, her eighth year of pastoral ministry was shut down by a disabling head and neck injury. For Donna, spirituality and painting became an alternative form of expression and understanding, and has helped her to live well with chronic pain. After the onset of her disability, Donna has taught silk painting and the Art of Healing across the United States. As keynote speaker, conference painter, preacher, and writer, she distills the clutter down to an amazingly articulate and resilient breath of fresh air which has been well received by secular, interfaith, and Christian audiences. Donna lives with her husband, the Rev. Dr. Hubert Ivery, also a United Methodist minister, and her daughters, Aisha and Imani, in Richmond, California. Donna welcomes your feedback. She can be reached via her website or e-mail at Donna@AdventuresInHealing.com.

14. **Bishop Peggy A. Johnson** is a native of Baltimore, Maryland. She received her Bachelor of Science degree in music education from Lebanon Valley College, a Master of Divinity degree from Asbury Theological Seminary, and a Doctor of Ministry degree from Wesley Theological Seminary. She was ordained a Deacon in 1979 and an Elder in 1981 in the United Methodist Church. She served a 4-point country charge in Frederick, Maryland, was a co-pastor with her husband in a suburban church in Baltimore, MD, and served as the pastor of an all-deaf congregation in Baltimore, MD. She is married to Rev. Michael C. Johnson, an ordained United Methodist Pastor. The Johnsons have two adult sons: Peter and Gabriel.

15. **Cheryl T. Magrini** is an ordained Deacon in the Northern Illinois Conference of the United Methodist Church with her pastoral appointments having been primarily in the local church setting. With a Ph.D. in Christian Education and Congregational Development from Garrett-Evangelical Theological Seminary in Evanston, Illinois, her loves are Christian education—using the "Out of the Box" approaches—and guiding congregations in mission and spiritual development. Cheryl often speaks in academic settings at conferences on topics such as the Daily Meal as a Sacrament and the Lament of Children. She has published in journals in the Christian education area, and about the

sacramental life. In June of 2011, Cheryl was the clergy keynote speaker on the bipolar disorder at the Naomi Ruth Cohen Conference in Illinois. Reaching into the Chicago area, Cheryl developed and directed the Tutoring Center of the Chicago Temple United Methodist Church serving a Chicago Public school with a focus on tutor-student relationships and reading comprehension. In June of 2011, she was appointed to the presidency and Peer-to-Peer Certified Specialist of the Depression and Bipolar Support Alliance Chicago Loop Chapter for support groups and educational events. Cheryl is the resource person for mental illness in the Northern Illinois Conference of the United Methodist Church.

16. **Evelyn R. McDonald** had a career outside of the church before entering the United Methodist ministry. She holds Bachelor and Master degrees in Nursing, was the Director of Intensive Care, Coronary Care, and Director of Education at Hillhaven Hospice, one of only three hospices at that time in the United States. With three colleagues, she began a nonprofit business named the "New Road Map Foundation;" it was a charitable and educational foundation focusing on giving people new symbolic road maps in two key areas of life; namely, money and health. In 1998, Evelyn answered the call to ordained ministry, and was graduated in 2001 with a Master of Divinity degree from Union Theological Seminary in New York City. In 2010, she earned a Doctor of Ministry degree from Drew University in Madison, New Jersey. At the time of this writing, Evelyn served at Grace UMC in Newburgh, New York. Evelyn is also president of the Greater Newburgh Ministerial Association, vice-president of Project Life, a transitional housing program, and is a board member of the Rural and Migrant Ministry agency. Evelyn is a Co-founder of Abraham's Table, a ministry to feed the children and youth of Newburgh in the summer months when there is no school lunch program. Evelyn is a member of and has been chairperson of her District Council on Ministries, and her District Committee of Ordained Ministry. She also serves with her conference's Connectional Table, has been the Assistant to the Conference Secretary at the Annual Conference sessions, served on the Frontier Foundation and a conference merger committee. She was a delegate to the 2008 General and Jurisdictional Conferences; in 2012, Evelyn was an alternate delegate to the General Conference, and a delegate to the Northeast Jurisdictional Confer-

ence. Evelyn is the co-chairperson of the United Methodist Association of Ministers with Disabilities.

17. **Lisa Lavelle McKee** was born two months prematurely, and weighed (as she puts it) "a whopping three pounds and seven ounces" when she came into the world. When she was two and a half years old she was diagnosed with cerebral palsy, a neuromuscular disability that has multiple presentations and outcomes. She received intensive therapy from the Easter Seal Society, and attended public school. Lisa holds bachelor and master degrees in Rehabilitation Counseling, along with a Master's degree in Parks and Recreation Administration with a Therapeutic emphasis. In 1996, she received her Master of Divinity degree from Wesley Theological Seminary in Washington, D.C., and is an ordained Elder in The United Methodist Church. Lisa and her husband, John, also an Elder, live and serve in the West Virginia Annual Conference. They have a Welsh Corgi named Chloe.

18. **Michael W. McKinney Sr.** is a United Methodist Local Pastor currently on Incapacity Leave due to the bipolar disorder and skeletal problems. He served for 9 years as a full-time pastor, and 4 years as a half-time staff member for the Rome City United Methodist Church in the Indiana Conference. After graduating with a business degree at Indiana Wesleyan University in Marion, IN, he worked for 25 years in manufacturing management in Indiana and Wisconsin. Married to Connie, the couple lives in Columbia City, IN. At the time of this writing, their son, Michael Jr., was a student at Indiana University in Bloomington, Indiana.

19. **J. Eric Pridmore** at the time of this writing with his wife Lisa was serving as co-pastor for the First United Methodist Church of Poplarville, MS. He holds a Bachelor of Arts degree in sociology from Mississippi State University, a Master of Divinity degree in theology from Candler School of Theology at Emory University, and a Doctor of Philosophy degree in the sociology of religion with an emphasis on religion and disability from Drew University. Eric has served churches in New Jersey and Mississippi. At the time of this writing, he is a co-chairperson for the United Methodist Association of Ministers with Disabilities, and is a member of the United Methodist Task Force on Disability Ministries. Eric is also matched with a beautiful male Golden Retriever guide dog named Atlas.

20. **Victoria Schlintz**, RN, MA, M.Div., and her husband Gerald were raised in Wisconsin but have lived during their adult years in California. Victoria has undergraduate degrees in Registered Nursing and Communications, and Master's Degrees in Education and Divinity. Before entering the pastoral ministry, Vitoria worked as an emergency nurse, a hospital education director, and a college-level educator. She has published several dozen written works and photographs. Victoria is an ordained elder in the California-Nevada Annual Conference of the United Methodist Church, and served in three churches in California before entering into disability retirement.

21. **David T. Seymour** was graduated in 1973 from St. Michaels Senior High School in St. Michaels, Maryland. Four years later, he was graduated from Salisbury State College in Salisbury, Maryland with a Bachelor of Arts degree in history. In 1985, David was graduated from Wesley Theological Seminary in Washington, D.C. with a Master of Divinity degree. From 1988 to 1990, David was appointed as Associate Pastor for the "Bayview Cluster," a group of local United Methodist churches that stretch from St. Michaels to Tilghman Island in Maryland. In 1990, he was ordained as an elder in the Peninsula-Delaware Conference of the United Methodist Church. Placed on retirement in 1990, David has spent many years teaching adult Sunday School classes and Bible studies groups in churches in St. Michaels, Maryland and Easton, Maryland. He has at times supplied pulpits in the absence of a pastor, and has taught at Shore Harvest Presbyterian Church in Easton, Maryland. As of this writing, David is the chairperson of the Disability Coalition in Talbot County in Maryland. He has made presentations about the former President Franklin Delano Roosevelt as a role model for those who cope with disabilities.

22. **Ruthann H. Simpson** is an ordained Elder in the United Methodist Church. As of this writing, she has been a pastor for 20 years. In 1996 she married George and they have a daughter named Abigail. Ruthann grew up in Langhorne, PA (about 25 miles northeast of Philadelphia), and attended Wake Forest University and Eastern Baptist Theological Seminary (now Palmer Seminary). Her passion is to be a worshipper of Jesus and to glorify Him in all that she does, and she refers to her story as an act of worship in that she willingly joins others in their vulnerability as disabled individuals, totally dependent upon God.

23. **Kirk Van Gilder**, Ph.D., was born hard of hearing before losing more hearing in late adolescence and transitioning into the Deaf world. He currently teaches in the Department of Philosophy and Religion at Gallaudet University in Washington, DC. He is an ordained United Methodist clergyperson, and has served as a minister in Deaf churches in Baltimore and Pasadena, MD, as well as being a campus minister to Gallaudet University from 1997-2002. Kirk has also traveled to Kenya, Zimbabwe, and Turkey to work with Deaf community development and support. Kirk hopes to continue his travels and research in other countries as well as present his findings and experiences to a wide variety of scholarly and non-scholarly audiences.

24. **Tim Vermande** worked in the photography field for several years before returning to graduate school at United Theological Seminary in Dayton, OH and Southern Methodist University in Dallas, TX. He teaches anthropology and history at a private art college. He is also secretary of the United Methodist Association of Ministers with Disabilities and webmaster for the United Methodist Task Force on Disability Ministries and the United Methodist Committee on Deaf and Hard of Hearing Ministries. His photographs appear in several publications, and he is a contributor to the *Dictionary of the Bible and Western Culture*, edited by Mary Ann Beavis and Michael Gilmour. Tim's wife, Sherrie, is an accountant who was brought up in the Evangelical United Brethren church, now merged within the United Methodist Church. They have two cats, Blaze and Chessie, who have their own fan page on Facebook.

25. **Robert Leroy Walker** was born in Portland, Oregon on Thanksgiving Day in 1931, the second child of the Rev. Leroy Hilton Walker and Catherine Alene (Ritchie) Walker, living in nearby Hillsboro. Tragically, Bob's mother died in 1934. The bereaved family moved to southern Idaho where the father served in four pastoral appointments over a 16-year span in the Idaho Conference of the Methodist Episcopal Church that, in the 1939 merger, became The Methodist Church. Bob's public schooling in Idaho included one year at Idaho State University in Pocatello, before transferring to the University of Washington in Seattle. Graduating in 1953 with a Bachelor of Arts degree in Journalism and a minor in sociology, Bob entered what today is the Garrett-Evangelical Theological Seminary in Evanston, Illinois. In 1954, he and Marjorie Mardy Gamon were married in Seattle. In 1957, he was graduated from Garrett with a Master of Divinity de-

gree; in 1982 at Saint Paul School of Theology in Kansas City, Missouri, he earned a Doctor of Ministry degree in the theology of preaching. In 1957, having transferred from the Pacific Northwest Conference to the California-Nevada Conference of The Methodist Church, Bob served in two separate pastoral appointments. In 1966, the couple and their first two children returned to the Pacific Northwest Conference, where Bob served in six different pastoral appointments, retiring in 1995. Throughout his ministry, he participated—often in leadership roles—in the denomination's district, conference and global committees, boards, and special ministries, along with service in local, county, and state agencies for social justice for all people. Beginning in 1952, he wrote articles for the denomination's several magazines, "op-ed" pieces for local newspapers, was a contributing author for two manuals on accessibility for people with hearing and/or seeing losses, is the co-author to Bishop Peggy A. Johnson in their book, titled as *Deaf Ministry: Make a Joyful Silence*, and is the editor of this book. In 1991 and as a "deaf-blind" person, he was one of three physically-challenged clergypersons featured in a UMCOM-produced video titled "Claim the Promise." Mardy, his wife of 49 years, died in 2003, due to non-Hodgkin's lymphoma; he has three children, four grandchildren, and one great-grandchild. Currently, Bob resides in the independent living section of the Panorama Retirement Community, located in Lacey, Washington.

26. **Nancy Jarrell Webb** was, at the time of this writing, entering her seventh year under appointment as one of the pastors at the Grace United Methodist Church in Baltimore, Maryland. As of this writing, Nancy has served for 34 years as an ordained minister under appointment in the Baltimore-Washington Conference. Nancy has lived with macular degeneration since the age of 6. She does not read regular-sized print but has had reader-service throughout her high school years, undergraduate college education, and earning two master's degrees. Volunteers in the congregation read for her to this day. She does not drive, and for that reality, Nancy says, "Thanks be to God!" Her limited eyesight, however, never stops her from doing pastoral calls or getting anywhere she needs to be.

Dedicated to all who have had to work against the odds as servants of God and the church to respond to God's call for the dream in their lives

Introduction

In the aftermath of the 6th century, B.C.E., when freed by the intervening Persians from their half-century Babylonian exile, the biblical Judeans developed what modern day scholars call the "Purity Code." The Code was based on the belief that God had sent the Judeans into exile as punishment for their sins; therefore, it was decreed that being cleansed of sins was paramount for the restored nation's future security.

In the Code, the Hebraic people were ranked from top to bottom, with religious leaders adjudged as clean, and placed at the top of the Code. At the bottom, adjudged as unclean, were Gentiles—including their Samaritan neighbors—along with women, children, impoverished people, and those who were either ill or disabled in mind or body.

Tragically, physically or mentally-challenged people were often separated from or abandoned by their families and neighbors in what was otherwise a communal society. Inhumanly, some have read the Book of Leviticus to specify a collection of cruelties that they ought to inflict on those marginalized people whom they viewed as contemptible in God's sight.

This view of the Purity Code was still dominant during Jesus' era; however, he viewed the Code, not the marginalized people, as being contemptible. Repeatedly, as the Gospel stories tell us, he violated the Purity Code. He treated children and women equally as first-class citizens, brushed aside ethnocentrism, let a constantly menstruating woman touch his garment, welcomed lepers, and pronounced that the truly deaf and blind were those who did not see, hear, or practice God's compassion toward the poor, ill, or otherwise disabled people—reminding them that all people are unmistakably precious to God. Not surprisingly, Jesus was likewise seen as "unclean," contaminated by his brotherly care for the "impure" Judeans. Furthermore, in one account of Jesus' ministry, he was regarded as an ill or disabled "'doctor" who could not cure himself, therefore "unclean."

Disappointingly, in the United Methodist Church and other religious denominations, there still resides a semblance to the ancient Purity Code, for people coping with a physical or mental disability are frequently denied full acceptance within the church as either lay or ordained agents of Christ in local and global ministries.

At the 1984 General Conference of the United Methodist Church, the Health and Welfare Ministries department of the General Board of Global Ministries successfully petitioned the conference to state that a physical or mental disability cannot be the sole cause for rejecting a lay or ordained ministerial candidate. Also established by that General Conference were the principles of fully accessible church facilities and ministries, including church-owned parsonages.

As you will learn from this book, despite the 1984 General Conference action, the ancient, but erroneous understanding of the Purity Code still serves as a prejudicial wall that leads to unfounded discriminatory actions against candidates or ordained ministers who—despite their injuries, incurable illnesses, genetically-caused sensory or physical disability, or birth-created conditions—possess the gifts and graces for ministry within the church as Christ's ongoing earthly body.

So it is that with this book, we bring you greetings from the United Methodist Association of Ministers with Disabilities. The Association is an official caucus of the United Methodist Church which advocates for the concerns of ministers who live with a disability, and offers support all persons with a disability in their call to service wherever it may be. As such, we are ecumenical and include all kinds of ministry, whether as ordained, professional service, or lay ministers.

The Association was founded in 1990 as the Association of Physically Challenged Ministers. We changed our name in 2009 to reflect a wider mission that would encompass all disabilities and ministries. This book is a result of that meeting. Our members felt that we need to tell our stories, both good and problematic, for the benefit and enlightenment of the church at large.

Our caucus's theological statement emphasizes trust in God's creation as good, rather than equating disabilities with fear or sin. Therefore, we do not see the minister with a disability as a liability, but as a person with different and unique gifts, called by God. That stance is parallel to our view that all members of the church are God's people who work together in ministry. As one of our members, Thomas Hudspeth stated, "the church is blessed when people with disabilities are seen as partners in ministry, rather than liabilities or objects of ministry. It is the church learning how to be truly a church." In the lives of many of our members, however, hurtful ignorance about the cause and nature of disabilities has led too many churches, their pastors, and the conference officials to be prejudiced to the extent of discriminating against both the candidates and the established ministers who cope with disabilities. As a result, the United Methodist policy of not using a physical or mental condition be the sole cause for denying one's call to ministry, is too often forgotten. In order for the church to learn and change and become truly inclusive of all God's people, we must bring truth to light. It is to spread the light that has led us to write and publish this book.

The authors of these chapters represent a variety of experiences, as well as many different theological stances and points of view. Some have grown up with disabilities and some became disabled later in life; subsequently, these stories tell of many ways of adaptation and coping with a disabling condition. Some welcome technologically-based assistive devices and some do not. Some are active in ordained or licensed ministry and some have found other ways to fulfill their calling, albeit not always doing so perfectly. Some are practically-oriented, some are highly philosophical. But in their diversity, they testify to the care of an all-loving God who calls us to be one. While the book has a specific focus—the lives of clergy dealing with disabling conditions—these stories are applicable to all. It is a call for change throughout the church, whose foundation is the lay person, and both groups deal with the effects of the prejudice that leads to discrimination when a church facility or its ministries are inaccessible or otherwise not inclusive

We invite anyone who is interested to join in our work. Our website is www.umdisabledministers.org. We work closely with the United Methodist Task Force on Disability Ministries, whose web site is www.umdisabilityministries.org.

We have many people to thank for their role in this effort, and to attempt a list runs the risk of accidentally forgetting someone. We start with all of those who took the time to share their stories, which are often highly personal. Several members of our caucus were unable to contribute due to time constraints, and we wish to thank them as well, for they often contributed insights into the process. Patricia Magyar of UMCOR Health has offered unfailing support for the project and for our caucus, along with the disability ministries of the church in general. Bishop Peggy Johnson recruited and encouraged many of our writers.

Tim Vermande, Secretary of UMAMD and project manager

Eric Pridmore and Evelyn McDonald, Co-chairpersons, UMAMD

Bob Walker, Editor

Foreword

I remember a moment in time when I thought, "This is truly the Body of Christ on earth!" It was 1990 and I was attending a meeting at the Scarritt Bennett Center in Nashville, Tennessee. About 15 clergy and seminary students who lived with a wide variety of disabilities had gathered to get to know each other, study together, and share our stories. Our sessions were very meaningful, but it was the "in between" times that true community happened when we were getting from one session to the next, or getting our food in the cafeteria line. Ray used a wheelchair to get around, and while he could push himself, it helped Clare, who was blind, if she could hold on to the wheelchair so that Ray could guide her since she was unfamiliar with navigating the Scarritt Bennett campus. Consequently, Clare was pushing Ray who was giving verbal instructions about when to turn in which direction. In the dining hall, Helen—who used an electric cart to get around—put Greg's tray of food on her lap to carry to the table since he had cerebral palsy that made it hard to steady a tray while walking. Harold, who didn't have any arms, was telling those who couldn't see what food was available at the salad bar.

Everyone was a very competent, well adjusted individual, and when we lived interdependently, we were a true community. We could not say to any part of our body collective, "I have no need of you" (I Corinthians 12:21). Interdependence was not considered a weakness, but rather a sign of the Kingdom of God on earth, a community of the faithful depending on God as our source of strength.

The stories found in this book include the testimonies of some of those clergypersons who were at that first meeting in Nashville when the Association of Physically Challenged ministers—now named as the Association of Ministers with Disabilities—was established within the United Methodist Church. It is this Association that has compiled the narratives for this book. These stories are faith-strong and hope-filled.

They are also pain-full and soul-wrenching. They are stories of acceptance by boards of ordained ministry and local churches, but also stories of one rejection after another. There are testimonies of self doubt and insecurity; they are clergypersons who feel they must hide their disability because of society's tendency to judge and shun such individuals. Yet, there are also testimonies of clergy who believe that God has used their disability as an avenue for reaching those on the margins of our society. Found in these narratives are depictions of the church at its best as communities that value the worth of all people because of who each one is, regardless of any disability; however, they also testify to the fact that the church can be cruel and harsh.

As we read through these stories, the life journeys of these clergy cause us to examine our own responses to persons with disabilities. They force us to ask whether we first see the God-given gifts and graces these clergy have for ministry, or see only their disabilities. As a starting point for faithful hospitality, these testimonies also challenge us to educate our congregations and our denominations about Jesus' inclusion of persons with disabilities; and, what is most important is that they beg us to take seriously the full accessibility of persons with disabilities for ministry within the church.

Kathy Black, Ph.D., Claremont, California, March 1, 2012

Donna Fado Ivery

Adventures in Healing
by Donna Fado Ivery, MDiv.

So Many Changes

In January of 1994, my husband Hubert and I were celebrating. We had weathered a year with so many changes. The birth in March of our second daughter, whom we named Imani, was followed during my maternity leave by a telephone call from the bishop's cabinet for the California-Nevada Conference of the United Methodist Church, an interview for a new parish appointment, and a subsequent move on July 1 into our first ever purchased home. What a whirlwind! There I was, at the age of 32, the Senior Pastor of a multi-staffed church, and my husband was not only my half-time Associate Pastor, but also the half-time Pastor of a small United Methodist Black Church in nearby Fresno, California. We had found a part-time preschool program for Aisha, our three year old daughter, and were able to coordinate infant care for Imani between us. We had joined an athletic club with free childcare, located a half mile between the church and our home, and regular racquetball, step aerobics, and healthy eating were melting off my "baby pounds."

In that January of 1994, Grandma and Grandpa Ivery arrived from Florida; together, we journeyed to the High Sierra mountains for a vacation in a friend of a friend's cabin. We felt warm and blessed. Do you know how things just fall into place miraculously when we're riding on the wings of the Spirit? We felt assured that the many threads of our life-changes in that year were woven seamlessly by the direction of the Holy Spirit. Yes, we had every cause to be celebrating!

After an afternoon of sledding with Aisha, we journeyed through the falling snow to Lake Tahoe—nestled between California and Nevada—for a $5.99 prime rib dinner at a popular casino. As I scooted into the booth, Hubert placed Imani in the high chair. Impressive glass partitions were perched between the back of the booths and the ceiling so that diners could have an unobstructed view of Lake Tahoe. With a sound of warbling thunder, that five by seven foot glass partition—somehow loosened from its ceiling moorings—fell and hit me directly on the back of my head, just above my neck. Immediately the partition rebounded to smash the water glasses on the table, and then whacked me on the left-hand side of my head, pinning me down. Surprisingly, the two hundred pound glass partition didn't shatter when it crashed on me, but parts of my brain did. All of a sudden I was disabled by the brain injury that compromised my speech, memory, vision, left-side, balance, endurance, and blanketed my daily life with a sodden covering of chronic pain.

With a door-splitting slam, my beloved work as a pastor had ended. Full time childcare was quickly found for my nine month old and four year old daughters. Hubert became the primary caregiver for our family, and he even figured out how to write a Ph.D. dissertation with a baby on his lap during the midnight hours. Pre-injury, a big day for me was step-aerobics and high energy work on into the late evening. In the first months post-injury, a big day for me was sitting in a recliner on my driveway, watching Aisha roller skate, and then napping to recover from exhaustion. Three months in bed, eleven months of physical therapy, five years of rehabilitation with what seemed to be a full-time occupation of going to doctors, all of whom confirmed the fact that I would never "get back to normal."

Creating Space for Healing

Looking back now, and after some eighteen years of living as a disabled person, there was much for me to learn; most prominently, I learned how the rooting of my faith has allowed me access to an abundant life beyond what is expected and accepted. My disability has pressed me into relying upon the Holy Spirit, and she has come through brilliantly beyond my wildest imagination.

In the earlier years of injury, dressing, showering, and riding in the car exhausted my brain to the point of not being able to speak, find words, or negotiate my way through doorways. If I did speak when my brain was worn out, consonants were hard to pronounce—as if my mouth were full of peanut butter—and finding words felt like going through the library stacks looking for a certain book that I knew was there, but it just took too much work to locate it; words evaded me, and even writing a sentence was a toil and trouble, often resulting in bazaar spelling and misplaced synonyms. But when my brain was freshly rested, I could then understand more and speak more for awhile, only to tire again with my disabilities swelling to overflowing. My doctor placed me on a rehabilitation regimen of "one hour down for every hour up", saying that the brain must rest to heal and overtaxing an injured brain makes one susceptible to seizures. I became the ideal patient (e.g. showering the night before and laying out my clothing so that I could go to church in the morning). Hubert served Sunday breakfast to us all, and dressed the girls because I couldn't do that and also have the energy to attend the worship service. I could be at the first part of worshiping, and then leave for about an hour to lie on the floor in Hubert's church office, and get up again to visit folks and make it back home to lie down again. Most people have no idea how much additional work and effort goes into the disabled person getting to church, or to any other event or task. I could handle going out to something only every other day, so that attending the worship service realistically entailed three days of dedication.

While continuing to attend weekly counseling for my emotional health, my therapist noticed that post-injury I would sit silently for most of our time together; she asked whether I could draw or paint a picture of my pain, and then bring it to our next session. Of course I could do that! My brain gears weren't cogitating smoothly in the speaking and writing department, but I could feel and sense color perfectly well. The only television shows that moved slowly and calmly enough for me to follow were the Public Broadcasting System (PBS) how to paint and sew shows. Within three weeks, I received a Bob Ross beginner oil painting set from Hubert for Christmas, my pregnant sister-in-law sent me a full box of oil paints (saying she didn't want the toxicity around her child), and a church family who owned a lumber company in town delivered cut wood panels to my door for about a dollar each. "Everything falling into place" just so felt like a delightful rain in the desert, and my heart rejoiced that the Holy Spirit was at the helm.

During my many "one hour down" spaces in each day, I was in fact exercising my heart, mind, and soul in prayer. I wonder what I would have done, had I not been taught to pray. Many of my friends offered sympathy to me for "doing nothing" for so much of my days, and wondered whether or not they could stand it. But my faith in Jesus Christ taught me differently. My times of stillness were not spent in "doing nothing." My stillness involved hard work at meditation, with me intensely focusing on receiving the life-giving Spirit of God when I inhale, balanced by exhaling whatever my body mind didn't need. It was hard breath-work for me to become entirely empty and still. It was within my own stillness that there was space for the wisdom of my body and mind to have its turn at center stage, directing all of the rebuilding of my injured brain and heart. My disabilities had stripped away my pre-injury comfortable way of praying by linking words and ideas, and talking to Jesus. In my new way of praying, if the breath-work of reaching stillness led to an idea or concern that resisted release, I then knew it was the stuff destined for therapy, and that it was time for me to paint.

Finding a New Language for Expression

One of my early paintings was of the rocking chair that sat in my living room. In that rocking chair, I had rocked and nursed both of my babies; but, after the brain injury, my eyes could no longer tolerate motion, and rocking chairs, cars, and ceiling fans cause me to become instantaneously toppled and nauseated. I could no longer nurse or rock my baby. In my prayer time, I would try to "take your burden to the Lord and leave it there," but would continue to be interrupted by my grief and anger over what I had lost. I would argue with God, saying something like, "I have lost my job, my income, my pain-free days, but you can't take away my ability to soothe and nurture my children!" More than a year after being injured, I was still fuming inside, no matter how many times I tried to "leave it there." Coming face-to-face with that old rocking chair, I scraped oil paint onto a panel with a palette knife, creating a rough image of what the rocking chair looked like. Emotionally, I was inundated by all of the cherished, but stolen moments that this rocking chair represented. For days, I painted its picture. My sister supported my new painting habit by buying me 25 cent frames from garage sales. One such frame was nailed to a dirty and torn canvas that was just about three or four inches too big to fit the 22x28 inch oil painting of the rocking chair.

Tight money pressed me into finding a way to make it work. I took the blanket sleepers worn by Imani at the time of my accident, and sewed an appliqué matte of empty, cradling arms that covered the gap between the panels glued to the torn canvas and the frame. With the painting finished, complete with the lingering touch of blanket sleepers which could never be worn again, the picture felt like a fitting place to lay my sorrows. It wasn't until I stood back and saw the rocking chair with the empty, cradling arms that I named the painting "Rocking Lost."

This painted prayer came with an unexpected answer. When I would feel the regret and anger about not being able to rock my baby—by then a toddler—I would go up and touch the blanket sleepers, remember the loss, and then "leave it there," in the painting. "Rocking Lost" functions as a memorial in my home, so that the loss is remembered and honored, but not belittled or thrown away. When the painting was finished, I was finally able to release my grief over "Rocking Lost," and—most noticeably—my prayerful exercises to find my still center were no longer obscured by its weight. The monkey on my back, clinging to the heaviness of my heart, had found a new home in the painting.

Sharing Spirit-led Imagery

Preaching has been and remains one of my favorite things to do as a minister. About two years after my injury, I was invited to preach on "Creative Healing," and share a few of my paintings. By then words had been flowing a bit more easily, but I still kept to the hour up/hour down regimen. As I prepared for my talk, I searched the scriptures for a few verses that would integrate well with my journey, and offer Good News at the same time. I felt shivers flow through my entire body when I came across these words in Paul's Letter to the Romans: "Likewise the Spirit helps us in our weakness; for we do not know how to pray as we ought, but that very Spirit intercedes with sighs too deep for words. And God, who searches the heart, knows what is the mind of the Spirit, because the Spirit intercedes for the saints according to the will of God" (8:26-27, NRSV).

In all of my painted prayers, when I couldn't find the words to pray, when I honestly "did not know" because words and memory evaded me, the Holy Spirit understood my prayer petitions in the language of sighs too deep, or groans too deep, or pain too deep for words (phrases used in alternate versions of Romans 8:26). The Holy Spirit interceded on my behalf and spoke my prayers to God. In every painting, there was an expression of honesty and answers. My heart smiles when I feel the assurance that the Holy Spirit is able to understand me more deeply than could my thoughts and words, and is able to speak in the language of imagery. With each painting I would consider sharing with others expressed honestly the truth of what was happening to me. Each painting reveals a new benchmark of understanding the way of healing. Each painting is a prayer asked and answered, with the Brushes of the Spirit a part of the process, always pointing me toward healing that is the will of God. Each painting illustrates the give and take dialogue and blessings of Spirituality.

In the Gospel According to John, when Jesus tells his disciples about an Advocate whom he promises God will send to them, Jesus describes the Holy Spirit as "partner to truth" whom we know because the Holy Spirit "abides with you" and "will be in you" (14:17, NRSV). When I finished a painting, and if in that painting I touched the pulse of honesty that is the key to open the way for the Holy Spirit to enter into the equation, only then would a new dimension, a new spark, a creative burst be added to the painting. When the Brushes of the Spirit enter into the image, I always discover a new perspective, a healing motion that I didn't intend to include. In teaching others about the Art of Healing, I use examples of these paintings, each telling the story of another layer of healing being revealed.

A New Vocation Unfolding, on the Wings of the Spirit

Step by step, in the timing led by the Holy Spirit, I now understand myself to be an artist and minister called to the Art of Healing; while my full time job is managing my disabilities, I moonlight by investing my passions into my home business, reached at www.AdventuresInHealing.com; through my business, Adventures in Healing, I teach, paint, write, and sell art works dedicated to the Art of Healing. My home business began when I took what I had learned through the paintings of "Rocking Lost," and "Formed by Tears" (that "Tears are Holy Waters at work"), and created what I call the Scarf of Tears™, "offering comfort and care for the healing process of grief." My good friend, whom I have known since our church youth group days and as a college roommate, had suffered another late miscarriage. Using silk paints, I portrayed holy, moving waters onto a silk scarf that she could use at work or however she wished to care for her tears, to keep in touch with both her own truth and wholeness, and to have a tangible memorial in which her tears could have a home. Working as an oncology nurse, she was amazed by how much the Scarf of Tears helped her; she encouraged me to publish my written reflection about using the Scarf of Tears, and provide it and the hand-painted scarves for others to purchase. More than seven hundred painted and sold Scarf of Tears later, I've had a licensed home business since 1997. I had not planned or even imagined having a business; nevertheless, that possibility opened itself to me through the work of the Holy Spirit. The Brushes of the Spirit are always leading me to new Adventures in Healing.

I often say that the Holy Spirit is my manager. Through the years, I've become more in tune with the workings and promptings of the Spirit. After the 2000 General Conference of the United Methodist Church, my still center/empty space, was interrupted by a call from God to build a communion table portraying healing for a church body that is in pain. For about a month, God chased me down, with the constant image of building this table and telling the story in "Spirit and Truth." Discouraged by disabilities getting in the way of my progressing in the traditional process of pulling things together (such as being able to look up names and make phone calls in the afternoon—all very difficult to do), I asked for the Holy Spirit to take the lead and manage the whole thing. The next morning, Ellie Charlton, a friend, telephoned me and asked when she could come to work on the table; we had spoken about it in passing some six months earlier. I believe that the Holy Spirit heard my prayers the previous night that I entered into my journal, and then prompted Ellie to phone me the next day. I have learned that the Spirit is more capable in managing our days and affairs than we ever entrust to the Spirit. My disabilities pressed me into depending more upon the Holy One than my old self would ever have allowed to develop.

With the assistance of many people, I completed the communion table that the Brushes of the Spirit and I named the "Table of Tears." It is a six foot diameter stained glass and acrylic table and tells the story of the Art of Healing. It was finished just in time for its inaugural presentation at the 2004 Western Jurisdictional Conference of the United Methodist Church. The Table of Tears' seven 22x38 inch acrylic teardrops with mosaic stained glass portraits of people excluded from churches through-out history forms a table when the Holy Spirit stained glass mosaic and acrylic centrepiece is placed on top and pulls together the teardrops into a blossoming whole. Lit from beneath, the stained glass portraits and Holy Spirit sculpture shine, illustrating beautifully healing brokenness. The Table of Tears easily breaks down for acts of worship and travels with me when I speak and teach what I have learned about the Art of Healing. Expressing our tears honestly invites the Spirit to heal our wounds. By the power of the Holy Spirit, we can become whole (another word for healing). I believe that this promise made by the Christian faith applies to both communal and individual bodies.

The Holy Spirit has continually led me through deep authentic experiences of Adventures in Healing. I have reclaimed a love of painting with a method learned through my disabilities that I call "Spirit Brush Art." Each painting begins with a prayerful process of emptying myself fully so that I can feel the Brushes of the Spirit moving and leading me, and using my brush like a surfboard, I jump on for an exhilarating ride. Many of my paintings are acrylic on silk canvas. Woven of cocoon threads, silk is the stuff of transformation, and its touch reminds me of the sacred space of waiting for unseen healing while upheld by a loving Creator. Just like a drop of water spreading rapidly on a silk blouse, control over painted images is minimal because diluted paint spreads in varying degrees, and the paint continues to move on the silk as it dries! For example, the faces of the people in my painting called "Circle Dance"—found on both the cover of this book—appeared the next day, after the paint had dried. That was my partner, the Brushes of the Spirit, completing the painting. My heart, emotions, faith, and joy are part of my paintings, as well as my "not knowing."

Appearing in community with one another in the "Circle Dance" painting are figures who are of different sizes, shapes and abilities. Here is a very wide and inclusive circle, otherwise, I, as being disabled, and others who don't fit into the perfect round (actually, isn't that all of us?) could not be part of the dance. The Holy Spirit's winds and breath bring the zeal and possibility to our dancing together.

Kirk Van Gilder

A/part From My Church
By The Rev. Dr. Kirk Van Gilder

A Part of, or Apart from the Church?

Praise to the Lord, the Almighty, the King of creation!
O my soul, praise Him, for He is thy health and salvation!
All ye who hear, now to His temple draw near....Praise Him in glad adoration.[1]

I was baptized as an infant in a United Methodist Church (UMC), and attended it with my family until I left home for college. I was your typical "church brat" who was ever-present in worship services, children's church, Sunday school, and youth group activities. To the present day, that congregation of my childhood remains close to my heart. I have been invited to preach there when visiting my parents and still receive their loving support and prayers. In many ways, it was and is a home for my soul to feel welcomed and loved. I am a part of that church who has been called and sent into ministry with the world.

Yet, as I reflect upon being a young boy in a mid-sized UMC in the Midwest during the 1970s, I recall a lingering unease even in the midst of a congregation who did so much to love and support me. I was born hard of hearing and required the use of a hearing aid in one ear at the age

---

[1] *United Methodist Hymnal Book of United Methodist Worship* (Nashville: Untied Methodist Publishing House, 1989), 139.

of five. My father is hard of hearing, and a hearing aid user as well. My mother and sister, however, do not require any adaptations to hear and participate in the world around them. I remember singing the above hymn one Sunday, and when we reached, "all ye who hear, now to His temple draw near," I lost my will to sing that hymn, because a thought came entirely unbidden into my mind. That thought was, "I don't hear right. That invitation to draw near doesn't include me." I may have been a part of that church, but at that moment, I was also kept apart from the congregation that loved me. The use of "A/partness"—as I did in this chapter's title—is a visual way of showing this tension of living in between being a part of the church and kept apart from the church. A/partness remains a powerful influence in how I experience The United Methodist Church.

For some readers, it might seem easy to dismiss my childhood intuition that somehow that hymn was implying that I was not welcome to approach the temple of God as the type of overly concrete thinking reflective of immature thought processes. After all, the hymn doesn't mention those who don't hear at all, and "all ye who hear" is a metaphorical phrase about the call of God that is not an audiological phenomenon. I simply needed to develop the intellectual skill to recognize metaphor and I'd realize this hymn wasn't excluding me at all.

But, Bonnie Miller-McLemore reminds us that respecting children as moral agents in our churches and society means recognizing the plain truths about injustice and unfairness they articulate that adults have learned to overlook and rationalize.[2] Like the child who remains baffled at even the most subtle changes in behavior and attitude in their parents when they express a desire to play with children of a race other than their own, my internal realization about this hymn and the ambiguous nature of my welcome in the church has an authenticity that pokes through the rationalizations we learn to make in our later years. The reality is, despite all the loving care shown to me by the congregation of my childhood, we all still lived in a society that would label me as different, and will—at times—hold me at arm's length.

---

[2] Bonnie J. Miller-McLemore, *Let the Children Come: Reimagining Childhood from a Christian Perspective* (San Francisco, CA: Jossey-Bass, 2003), 150-151.

The bluntness of children that makes them astute observers of injustice can occasionally make them unintentionally cruel when they begin to adopt the behaviors of their parents that once baffled them. It was in the first grade when playing a board game with a classmate during a rainy day recess break that he looked at me suddenly and asked, "What's that tube going into your ear?" I explained that it was a hearing aid, and that I needed it to hear him and others. The next day, it rained again, and I got the board game off the shelf and went over to ask him if he wanted to play it again; after all, it was our favorite game. He didn't want to play with me, and no one else did that day. Because the children at school are often the same children who are at church, the social distance that developed in one social environment often carries over to other settings. A failure to examine how the practices and habits of our lives as congregations overlook, or even at times affirm this type of social dislocation remains a theological failure to reflect on our purpose as communities of disciples of Jesus Christ seeking to enact his radical love for all people.

"There's Something Wrong"

When I was ready to enter kindergarten class, I underwent the standard hearing test the school district put all students through. I was flagged in the screen and told we needed to go see a specialist downtown. Being five years old, a trip downtown to see a specialist sounded like fun. After all, I must be special to get to see a specialist. Arriving at the audiologist's office, I remember being seated in a small soundproof room, something I would get used to in future years, but at that age, it was intimidating. Despite all the colorful posters and toys in the room, the air around me went strangely still when that big thick door closed. I was fitted with a large set of headphones and began to take my first formal hearing test. As a five year old child with an older sibling, I already knew a "test" was something you either passed or failed-- and I realized that I wasn't passing this test as I struggled to hear the barely audible beeps. When the test was finished, I remember the audiologist talking to my parents with a less cheerful voice; otherwise, I was more interested in the things on his desk than I was in listening to him. Soon he turned to me and said, "Kirk, there's something wrong with you. You need a hearing aid."

This was the phrase that stuck in my head whenever I gave thought to my hearing loss. Despite my father being someone who used hearing aids, I was the only child I knew who wore one, and the only vocabulary I had to explain it were the words of that audiologist; that "there's something wrong with me." Despite this nagging thought, the hearing aid worked well for the most part. Aside from times when it had to come off for swimming, which made swimming lessons all the more difficult for me, I was able to use the aid to understand people talking directly to me in most cases. There remained, however, that lingering sense of "something wrong with me" that I couldn't quite articulate. At the age of seven or so, my mother and I went to sign language classes at another nearby United Methodist Church where they had an interpreted worship service with a handful of deaf people in attendance. I did well in those classes, but since I didn't need sign language to communicate at home, it never really became anything more for me at that point than an activity to do with mom. I never really saw myself as being like the teacher or other deaf people who came to the classes.

Adolescence brings challenges to anyone, but for a shy kid who is already significantly different in some way, and thus far set apart by his peers, it has its own unique struggles. In addition, my hearing loss was worsening during this period in my life, but at a gradual enough pace so that my increasing deafness wasn't obvious. I continued to get honor roll grades in all my classes thanks to a deeply ingrained love for reading. Reading everything I could find was a survival habit formed for a student who knew he wasn't hearing everything in class. But this habit was also the product of having a mother who was a preschool teacher, and knew the importance of reading for young children. No one questions how you're doing when you get A's and B's on your report card, lead the church youth group, and have a circle of friends that comes automatically with being in the marching band. Everyone—including me—assumed everything was going fine for me.

College in Stereo: Learning A New Vocabulary

When it came time for college, someone suggested that I apply at the state Vocational Rehabilitation Department, as it could be a source for financial aid. This meant yet another hearing evaluation, this time with the department's affiliated medical staff. I remember one doctor, after learning that my father was hard of hearing, asking me if I was interested in genetic testing to determine the cause of my deafness. I saw no reason to bother with genetic testing because it wouldn't change anything. What troubled me more was the result of that hearing test. I had lost a significant amount of hearing, and would now be best off with two hearing aids. The vocabulary I learned when I was five came back to haunt me as I reflected on this reality. If there was something wrong with me that required a hearing aid, there must be something going more wrong with me now that I require two aids. I masked the pain of this changing reality with my usual humor when I attended a "get to know you" retreat with the Wesley Foundation United Methodist Campus ministry at Ball State University where I would be enrolled in a few weeks. There were a few Deaf education majors at the retreat who knew some American Sign Language (ASL)—far more than I then did. As they were asking me about my family and education, I awkwardly confessed the recent discovery that I'd lost more hearing and laughed it off with a joke. This was about the time when stereo TV sound was being introduced and so I borrowed the ubiquitous tagline that I would soon be, "in stereo where available." Yet the fears behind my joking must have shown through my feeble attempt at humor as instead of laughter, I got looks from my peers that they were concerned with how I was handling this new reality.

Arriving at Ball State, I immersed myself in college life with the support of a great community of friends I was getting to know as an active participant in the Wesley Foundation. Unlike any local church could have ever done, the Wesley Foundation campus ministry was a circle of fellow college students, and our entire ministry and life together was shaped by our experience as college students without competing with any other ministerial needs or programs. This allowed us a unique place within the United Methodist Church to be ourselves, and explore our faith in a stage of life when as young people, we needed to redefine ourselves and what we believed as we became independent from the structures of family and church in which we grew up. While active in the Wesley Foundation program, I intentionally resisted taking up any leadership positions as I had done in my high school church youth group. My disinterest in leadership roles was largely a result of my being enrolled in the highly time consuming architecture program. Also, I had decided at that point, that while church and faith would remain an important part of my life, I wasn't going to make them be my entire life since I had other plans for my future.

While at Ball State, I also began socializing with other Deaf and hard of hearing students. Most of us were refugees from mainstreaming educational backgrounds like myself, but one was a transfer student from Gallaudet University-- the only four year liberal arts University in the world designed for Deaf and hard of hearing students. This student became our "mother hen" as she taught us American Sign Language, and what it meant to be a part of a Deaf culture and community. The 1988 "Deaf President Now protest" movement had just been completed at Gallaudet which resulted in the first Deaf president of that University since its founding in 1864. It was both a moment of Deaf cultural pride and a renaissance of awareness and creative thought about what being Deaf meant.[3] The capitalization of the word Deaf was adopted to signify the difference between the view of Deaf people as a unique cultural and linguistic community and the medical definition of deafness as a state of hearing loss.

All of this was completely new to me as a young man who had spent most of his life with nothing but the vocabulary of, "There's something wrong with you. You need a hearing aid." I began to read books, watch videos, learn American Sign Language as a second language of my own, and talk with other Deaf people on the same journey of self-discovery. I found my closest parallel in another young woman who attended the Wesley Foundation for a short time. She was an African-American woman who was adopted by white parents. She had spent almost all of her life as the only African-American child in her school and church. Upon entering college, she now had avenues open up to discover the cultural values of African-American community, culture, and church. She ultimately made the decision to leave the Wesley Foundation to pursue her own journey of self-discovery with an African-American church. The lack of a Deaf church nearby meant I was not afforded that opportunity to immerse entirely into a new outlook and community.

Through reading books and talking with others, I learned that her journey and my own were not all that different. As we Deaf people began to articulate our own views of the world and our community after the Deaf President Now protest movement, there was recognition that while

---

[3] Jack R. Gannon. *The Week The World Heard Gallaudet*. (Washington, DC: Gallaudet University Press, 1989).

the larger society viewed deafness as primarily a physical disability in need of being changed or cured, Deaf people have rejected this view. Rather than being disabled, Deaf people who rely on American Sign Language, and identify themselves with the Deaf community, see our difference as being primarily one of language and culture, thus an ethnicity. To be sure, for those who lose their ability to hear later in their life-experience, that loss as a true deprivation of physical capabilities, and they often want to regain their ability to hear. On the other hand, for those who grow up Deaf, and especially for the 10 per cent of Deaf people who are born to Deaf parents, being Deaf is a state of normalcy, not an abnormal state in need of curing.

So, where do I fit into this picture? I could have easily continued to use my hearing aids, eschew sign language, and socialize primarily or even exclusively with hearing people. To answer my own question, when reading about Deaf culture, experiences, and lives, I recognized my own experience growing up as fundamentally different from those around me. I began to learn a new vocabulary to describe myself. I wasn't a broken hearing person who had something wrong with him, and therefore needed a hearing aid. Instead, I might view myself as a Deaf person who never had the opportunity to socialize with those like me. Learning a new vocabulary to describe oneself is, of course, as difficult as learning a new language. Since the sign language lessons of my childhood must have stuck in my head somewhere, I learned the basics of understanding ASL quickly; however, my expressive skills developed slowly, making the integration into Deaf communities difficult. Consequently, I continued to be neither fully here nor there in the social categories and labels that society likes to imagine are real.

Called to Plans That Were Not Mine

The changing vocabulary about my identity was not the only transformation taking place in my years at Ball State University. During my sophomore year, my campus minister was recruiting people to go to something called Exploration '90, the first convocation held by the General Board of Higher Education and Ministry to encourage young adults to consider ordained ministry as a vocation. At first, I wasn't interested; as I said earlier, I had other plans for my life. Ultimately, however, I agreed to go with the intention of skipping out on sessions and exploring the St. Louis waterfront for an urban planning project. While I had my plans, little did I know, God had other plans for me.

Arriving at the convention center in St. Louis after nightfall meant my friends and I experienced the interesting opportunity to buy watches and jewelry directly from the coats of people we passed by outside. I made the decision to stick with the group for the first evening's speakers with the rationale that I could then at least say, "It doesn't interest me," and take my leave in the morning. The keynote speaker that night was the Rev. Shelly Matthews from the Dakotas Annual Conference. She spoke of the honor it was to be an ordained minister and be present for her congregation. The honor of representing the presence of a community of faith during the highs and lows of people's lives. The honor of being there when a baby was born. The honor of being there when someone breathed his or her last breath and a family needed comfort. The honor of leading worship services that gathered a community together each week. As she went through this litany of humbling honors, it hit me, "Oh, that's what I'm supposed to do with my life!" I never did do that project on the St. Louis waterfront, and I never did leave the convention center that weekend.

Later, I found myself negotiating with God between my own plans and these radically unexpected plans God had dumped in my lap through the person of Rev. Shelly Matthews. God eventually won out in that struggle despite my reservations that I, a young person in the midst of some big identity changes, could not possibly become a minister in The United Methodist Church. I remained involved in the Wesley Foundation at Ball State, and I represented us at the 1992 Student Forum in Tulsa, Oklahoma. The Student Forum was another program of the General Board of Higher Education and Ministry, and became the forerunner to the rebirth of the United Methodist Student Movement a few years later, in part due to the energy of my cohort of college aged United Methodists. I found my calling and community affirmed in a supportive way by the Student Forum. At the same time, I found my difference and alterity as a Deaf person affirmed in a less than supportive way. By then, my confidence in understanding American Sign Language was strong enough to feel I could benefit from the use of interpreters to understand what was being spoken in large and small group settings. So it was that along with my Student Forum registration I sent for ASL interpreters, although I had not used them much except for some large campus wide events at Ball

State where they were already present for other Deaf students. This was not the only interpreting request made of the General Board of Higher Education for the Student Forum, since we had some visiting students from Africa joining us whose primary language for educational purposes was French. These requests were addressed by having someone stand up at the first meeting and ask, "Does anyone here know sign language or French?" Of course, this resulted in two timid people raising their hands. One who had taken two semesters of French and one who had taken a semester of ASL. Neither of these students could serve as an interpreter, and asking them to do so would have robbed them of being a participant in the Student Forum. Despite this irresponsible gaffe by the General Board sponsoring the forum, I enjoyed my time at the event, and found good friends who were willing to sit by me and fill me in on what was going on when it wasn't clear to me. My frustrations were largely worked out on the sand lot volleyball courts during recreation time as I dove for digs and set up teammates for volleyball "kills." However, upon returning home, I drafted a letter to the staff of the General Board of Higher Education and Ministry expressing my frustrations and experience. It was here that I first articulated the idea of being a/part as the odd experience of being simultaneously a part of the church around me and apart from it. Little did I realize, this would be my first foray into the articulation of a vocabulary of Deaf theology.

Called to Be Deaf as a Minister

As a student at the Iliff School of Theology, I began classes in much the same mainstreamed way as I had at Ball State. However, I quickly realized that many classes depended far more on group-based conversations than lectures, making them harder for me to follow from my usual seat in the front row where I could do a lip-reading of the professor. After my first quarter, the wife of one of my classmates struck up a conversation with me. She was a certified interpreter, and was curious about how I handled communication access in the classroom. She volunteered to interpret the very last session of Theological Imagination and Construction taught by Dr. Sheila Greeve Davaney who was famous for packing as much as she could into every class lecture and discussion. Again, no one questions how you're doing when you get A's and B's, so I was stunned to discover how much more there was going on in the classroom that I was unaware of until I had an interpreter. I thirsted for this information and experience as I continually sought to raise the bar of my educational expectations out of a love for scholarship and learning.

It was also here that I began to journey deeper into the Deaf world. Summer courses at the School of Theology at Claremont in California with Dr. Kathy Black, who had been a minister with the Magothy United Methodist Church of the Deaf in Maryland, led to an internship at Christ United Methodist Church of the Deaf in Baltimore, MD. It was during this nine-month internship that I arrived at a milestone that connected my personal journey into Deafhood and my calling to ordained ministry. I transferred my ordination candidacy to the Baltimore-Washington Conference after being asked by a member of the District Board of Ordained Ministry in my home conference if my expression of a calling to Deaf ministry was an attempt to control the Bishop's authority to appoint me anywhere in the Conference. In working as a minister in Deaf congregations, a new church start for Deaf people, and the Gallaudet University campus ministry in the Baltimore Washington Conference, I continued to find the same odd mixture of being a/part of the Conference. I was very much a part of the Annual Conference's ministry as my several ministries were well supported financially. Yet I was also apart from the conference. That actuality was revealed when my attempt to found a new church failed, and I was told that a part time appointment to a hearing church was not a possibility for me.

Baptized to Serve

In the midst of all this, a new facet of my calling began to emerge. While serving as associate minister at Christ United Methodist Church of the Deaf, I was recruited to help lead a team of Deaf and hearing people on a short term mission trip to Kenya to work with Deaf schools and church workers. This led to similar trip to Zimbabwe two years later, and was followed by many more trips to Kenya, Zimbabwe, Turkey, and Puerto Rico. I found myself fascinated—and strangely comfortable—when I crossed cultural and linguistic boundaries in mission work. In part, my personal experience with boundary-crossings had prepared me for such a ministry. On my first mission trip to Kenya, I found myself in a society where deaf people were even more strongly marginalized than is the case in the United States. On one very long and frustrating day, and while I was teaching Deaf children, I had been literally pushed aside by a hearing woman who had felt herself to be a more appropriate person than I was to communicate with the children. That evening, our team met to debrief one another on the various places we had worked that day. I was physically and emotionally exhausted, and had never before experienced the intensity of marginalization and rejection as a Deaf person as I had that day. As I recounted my experience, I broke down in tears. Not wanting to embarrass myself further by having the Deaf members of the team see their pastor fall apart, I tried to leave the room. Instead, I was encircled by the Deaf members of the team—but no one else—as they embraced me, and prayed together with tears of pain in their own eyes. It was a truly holy moment of grace as God's redemption and liberation bound us together. Hearing people on that team, who had never before encountered the Deaf culture, also remember the power of that profound moment. Consequently, the hearing team members realized that they needed to step aside and let things happen among us Deaf people. Looking back, that encircling remains one of the most cherished experiences of my life. Having been baptized as an infant, I don't recall it and although I had spiritually powerful moments in my confirmation and ordination as a minister, being fully encircled and accepted by Deaf people who knew my pain in the midst of my brokenness was a new baptism of its own as I encountered what God was doing among Deaf people around the world.

The World as My Parish

Mission, scholarship, and teaching were what continued to sustain ministry as I began to realize that God was calling me to a form of ministry beyond the usual setting of the local church. After a period of discernment, I came to a decision to return to theological training and work toward a Doctor of Philosophy (Ph.D.) degree in practical theology and missions at the Boston University School of Theology. It was there that I encountered another rebirth of my calling, Deafhood, and scholarship as I tackled theological and social questions with the maturity and development of thought tempered by my experiences as a minister in mission to the world. I'm happy to say other scholars in various places who have encountered the intersections between Christianity, the churches, and Deaf culture accompany my work in theology. Mary Weir articulates her theological understanding of deafness by saying,

> "It has been in my adulthood that I have come to claim my deafness as a banner over my life and a blessing which I am called to honor and use for God's greater glory. I chose and choose to be deaf, even though this particular gift of God has not always been to my liking. Deaf is who I am, and where I come from, deaf is more than not hearing—it is being a person of vision and touch. Perhaps it is that all deaf people need to come to choose their deafness—as a calling, a gift, and as essentially good creation."[4]

Although Weir's experience is one of a deaf non-signing Canadian, she adopts the same acceptance of her being that I do as someone who transitioned into a Deaf cultural vocabulary for expressing my being. Deafness is not a curse, it is not something wrong with me, and it is not a disability. My existence as a Deaf person is a divine blessing, a unique contribution to human variety, and gain rather than a loss. Instead of signing a song that dredges up mixed feelings of being a/part from the church that I both love and struggle with, I begin to sign the living Word of God into being as I watch and learn what God is doing in the world around me.

---

[4] International Ecumenical Working Group, *The Place of Deaf People in the Church: The Canterbury 1994 Conference Papers* (Northampton, UK: Visible Communications for the International Ecumenical Working Group, 1996), 2.

Works Cited

Gannon, Jack R. *The Week the World Heard Gallaudet*. Washington, DC: Gallaudet University Press, 1989.

International Ecumenical Working Group. *The Place of Deaf People in the Church: The Canterbury 1994 Conference Papers*. Northampton, UK: Visible Communications for the International Ecumenical Working Group, 1996.

Miller-McLemore, Bonnie J. *Let the Children Come: Reimagining Childhood from a Christian Perspective*. San Francisco, CA: Jossey-Bass, 2003.

United Methodist Hymnal: Book of United Methodist Worship. Nashville: United Methodist Publishing House, 1989.

Peggy A. Johnson

Be Thou My Vision
By Bishop Peggy A. Johnson

Growing Up without a Second Eye

One of my earliest memories as a child is that of taking the bus to Baltimore City with my mother to visit the "Bowen and King" office. I was born with an underdeveloped left eye, medically known as micro-opthalmia, and since the age of two I have worn an artificial eye. "Bowen and King" was a company that sold glasses and prosthetic eyes. It was located in one of the upscale buildings on North Charles Street. The words "Bowen and King" were carved into the marble slab above the front door. The door was made of heavy glass and ornate gold fixtures. Once inside the building we had to take the elevator up to the top floor, where they sold the prosthetic eyes. In the elevator was an African American woman whose job was to operate it all day. It had two sets of doors: one that was in the front and a cage-like inside door. "Going up" was all she would say.

These trips to visit the "Bowen and King" office felt very important, but there was something tense about it too. I could feel that my prosthetic eye was a source of concern and sadness for my mother, and I sensed early on that it was best not to ask questions about it. In the office there was a room where many patients were reading magazines while waiting to be seen. When I was very young I would dance in the middle of the room to offer some entertainment for the waiting people. I would receive smiles from some of the clients, but most of them would not look up from their magazines. I reasoned it was because this was a sad place where not even my dancing could cheer them up.

After what seemed like hours of waiting we would be called into a back room where there was a tall man wearing a white lab coat. The room smelled like rubbing alcohol. I would be hoisted into a gigantic black leather examining chair that could be raised and lowered with a foot pedal. It was like a very quick amusement park ride. The man in the lab coat would look intently at my plastic eye and then lift it out of the socket with a little red rubber stopper. Then he would open these amazing medal drawers that held many plastic eyes. They appeared to be like a hundred dismembered people crowded into a drawer. The brown-eyed people were in one drawer, the green-eyed ones in the second drawer and my new eye would be chosen from the blue-eyed drawer. My eye was something of a blue gray color. Mother would get involved in the selection of the eye and between her and the doctor the right color was chosen from the drawer and the same red rubber stopper would put the new eye in place. It always felt cold and strange at first. The new eye would be polished and adjusted several times. When the doctor and my mother were finally satisfied, we were sent on our way, back down the big elevator with the same woman inside who would say "going down."I wondered if she lived permanently inside that elevator.

Coping with Reality

Years have passed since those early days of growing up with an artificial eye. It was always a part of me. I never knew what it was like to see with two eyes and sometimes wondered why people needed two eyes, or how it was that the two eyes could actually work together to create a single image. I was told that my condition with only one eye as a birth defect was really quite remarkable. Usually a person with that kind of condition is blind in both eyes. I had one good eye, an eye that I never took for granted.

When I was a school-aged child a few of my classmates knew about my condition. They asked curious and sometimes rude questions. At other times children would tell me I looked cross-eyed, and I really did because an artificial eye does not move like a natural eye. Comments like that made me feel ugly, and I tried hard to look straight ahead when I talked to people. I felt I was a little "different," because of this prosthetic eye, but everything else in my life was normal. I was surrounded by a loving family, and a supportive church community as well since all of them knew me from the time of my birth.

I remember one Sunday morning as a child I arrived at church, and I had forgotten to put in my plastic eye. (I always took it out at night to give it a rest). Without my prosthesis my left eye looked shrunken and odd, but no one at church said a word. I was shocked when I came home and looked in the mirror. I wondered greatly about their silence.

One day in high school I rubbed my left eye the wrong way and the prosthesis popped out and bounced down the hall. The hall was full of students rushing to class, but somehow I found this little sliver of plastic, covered with dust from the floor, and popped it back in place. I did not want anyone to see me without my artificial eye.

For all of my life I felt an affinity with anyone who had a disability because of this curious little eye of mine. My best friend was a classmate who had polio as a baby and wore orthopedic shoes. I sought out the loners and the outcast types to make friends with them. Deeply inside, people are the same, and the outcasts had great insights into life that most of the world does not take the time to experience. Not surprisingly, at an early age I valued an association with the underdogs; after all "they" were "me." It was from this unique community that I drew a kind of strength and comfort zone.

The Hurtful Healers

Sometimes I wondered why I was born this way. When I was a young adult I attended a Christian Bible study group that emphasized the gifts of the Holy Spirit. One of those gifts of course was healing, and I began to ask God if my eye could actually be healed. It happened that a few of us from the Bible study group went on a Christian Camping trip in eastern Pennsylvania, and known as "Jesus '76." It was like a sanctified version of "Woodstock," the infamous hippie rock festival of the late sixties. A makeshift stage featured daily worship services, Christian rock concerts, and heart-warming testimonies about the miraculous works of God. Former drug addicts and members of motor cycle gangs spoke of their evil lives that had been transformed by God's amazing grace. There was a pond at the camp where new believers were baptized by immersion, and there was a healing tent where the elders prayed for people to be healed of every kind of infirmity.

Three of us from the Bible study group had physical handicaps. My friend Stu was extremely myopic and wore glasses that looked like the bottom of a coke bottle. My friend Arlene had polio as a child and she still wore a back brace. I had my prosthetic eye. We decided to go to the healing tent to be healed.

The people in charge (known as "elders") told everyone who wanted to be healed to come forward to surrender those things on which they depended for mobility or other kinds of assistance, doing so as a sign of their faith. On the altar were crutches that a man no longer needed because his legs had been healed. There was also a hearing aid left by a woman who was now able to hear. My friend Stu went forward and clunked down his heavy horn-rimmed glasses on the altar and asked to be healed of his near-sightedness. Arlene put her back brace on the altar and said she wanted to be free of back pain. But there were audible gasps when I went forward and plucked out my plastic eye and laid it on the altar. "I would like to see in my left eye" I said. The elders laid hands on the three of us and prayed but they prayed the longest and the hardest for me. It was a hot, humid mid-summer night and swamp frogs outside were making croaking noises that seemed to mix with the many prayers in a peculiar chorus. After a very long prayer they slowly lifted their hands, and I was still blind in my left eye. Likewise Stu and Arlene were not healed. One of the elders said the failure was due to our lack of faith. Quoting the Apostle Paul from Romans 10, he lectured us by saying "Faith comes from hearing and hearing from the Word." He encouraged us to read the Bible more often as a way of increasing our faith so that we could eventually be healed. I wondered greatly over that line of reasoning. Another elder said that God may yet heal us if we left our things on the altar, and that would be a sign of our faith.

I ventured a glance over at Stu and Arlene and they were nodding their heads in agreement, and they did leave their respective glasses and brace on the altar. I, however, was not buying into this notion. Maybe it was vanity, maybe it was a lack of faith, maybe it was a moment of common sense, but I marched up to that altar, took my little plastic eye and popped it back in place. Every real eye in the tent was on me as I walked back up the center aisle and left the healing service. I drew a deep breath as I escaped into the dark, dark country night with the smell of grass and hay and a canopy of a million stars over my head. I wondered, "Why didn't God heal me?" Somehow that night, I came to the realization that I was born this way for a reason; namely, God had a plan for me and the disability community.

God's New Plan

It is no wonder that I fell madly in love with American Sign Language (ASL) when I first saw it in action, because it was connected to a group of left out people, and I was convinced that ministry among Deaf people was God's call on my life. What initially attracted me was the gracefulness of signed music. At that time I was a music teacher in the public school system after graduating from college, and the signed songs came alive in a powerfully new way for me. With great enthusiasm I registered for a sign language class at a Deaf Church in East Baltimore. I was fascinated with the language, and those charming silent people who spoke with their hands and had very intense eyes.

Sign language, however, did not come easily for me; especially difficult was the receptive part of the language. When one sees with only one eye it is more or less monocular vision, and that did not lend itself well to the three dimensional aspect of this visual language. For ten years, I practiced the art of signing as much as I could while I was busy going to seminary, getting married, preparing for ordination, starting a family and serving as a pastor in a 4-point country charge. All the while, it was a relentless passion for me to be constantly finding ways to connect with the Deaf community with whom I could practice the sign language. Even when I was up all night with crying babies, and overwhelmed with church work, I would get out my sign language textbook and practice a few signs every morning. As far as I was concerned, I had to learn this language no matter how difficult it was.

Eventually it happened that the Deaf Church that first taught me those early sign language classes in East Baltimore had lost their pastor, and I was appointed to serve this church. With barely usable signing skills, I began preaching there each Sunday even though I was frustrated most of the time with my linguistic inadequacies. As grace would have it, the Deaf people were patient, and what I did not have in the way of skill, I tried to make up for it with kindness and careful attention to their needs. Serving the Deaf Church was a great source of joy for me as I felt as if I had arrived at home.

Touched by Deaf Blind People

After a few years at the church for Deaf people, I had the opportunity to teach an after school religious education class for Deaf-Blind students at the state school for blind children. When I met these Deaf Blind young people, who read sign language with their hands and fingers and had eyes that looked like mine, I was smitten once again. This time it was even more personal. They were MY people. I felt a deep sense of identity with this community, and I grieved over their debilitating condition that blocked them from so much of what make life meaningful and interesting. Communication and mobility was severely hampered with this dual sensory loss. I found in the Deaf-Blind community yet another group of amazing people with insightfulness and grace in the midst of their isolation from the sight and sound world. They were like buried treasure deep in the sea.

While I was serving the Deaf Church I went back to school part-time and got a Doctor of Ministry degree in which the topic of my doctoral thesis was "How Deaf-Blind People Experience God." I traveled around the country interviewing such people about their experiences with God. Some of the interviews moved me to tears as they shared their heart-felt sense of the presence of God's Spirit. I also felt grief and indignation when they revealed the many times they had been ignored or abused because of their disabilities.

As a direct result of the writing of my doctoral thesis, the first Deaf-Blind camp was born. It started with 6 campers and 10 brave sign language assistants. For 6 glorious days the Deaf-Blind campers experienced the love of God in Christian community at a church camp out in the Maryland countryside. We had tactile arts and crafts, lots of snacks, massage therapy, aroma therapy, line dancing, swimming, boating, and a field trip to a local farm. The campers' joys and spirits were overwhelming, and once again I was touched by the tenacity and resourcefulness of this precious Deaf-Blind community.

Deaf and Deaf-Blind ministry has taught me everything that we need to know about life; namely, faith, community, compassion, grace and God's amazing way of using the talents of all people. Deaf ministry took me to Africa, Cuba, the Dominican Republic, and around the United States. I found myself working with Deaf people in the margins of life in mental hospitals, prisons, group homes, hospitals and tenements. The ministry was always about being a bridge between the hearing and the deaf worlds and finding a common humanity between them.

Elected to the Episcopacy

I am not quite sure how I ended up as a bishop. It is not the normal turn of events for a pastor in a Deaf church to be elected to serve as the CEO of 900 churches in a large mainline Protestant denomination. Nevertheless, after serving for 20 years in the Deaf community, I felt a strong call to put my name up to be considered for election as a bishop. On July 17, 2008, and on the 10th ballot of the Northeast Jurisdictional Conference of the United Methodist Church held in Harrisburg, Pennsylvania, I was elected. At the consecration service following my election, the Deaf Church members and not a few Deaf-Blind people participated in the event. Hands were flying, the Deaf choir sang, there were wheelchairs and canes being employed, and multiple levels of interpreting in use during the service. Leaving the Deaf and deaf-blind people was an incredible sadness for me, but I felt an overwhelming assurance that it was God's plan for my life.

Bishops can set the tone for the churches that they oversee, and it has been my goal from the beginning—quietly, but deliberately—to interject people with disabilities and disability awareness into as many places as I can. Just about everything provided in church life is exclusively for the able-bodied people of the world. With the exception of the usual wheel chair ramp in the front of the church, most buildings are totally inaccessible. Most churches provide no sign language interpreters, and only a few churches on the planet earth make a place for Deaf-Blind people. Also too often neglected is the purchase and promoted use of an Assistive Listening Systems (ALS) for the benefit of hard of hearing worshipers. I pray for the day when the church will not only provide accessibility for people with disabilities, but also for their empowerment. May people with disabilities be allowed to have full participation in all aspects of the church's life and work, including the professional ministry. Through it all I have found my calling, my life's work, and my true healing as one with only one eye. God has been my source of spiritual vision. Now you know why for the title of this chapter I borrowed the opening words of the hymn, "Be thou my vision." Let that be true for you, sighted or not.

Tim Vermande

A Call Deterred
By Tim Vermande

He who planted the ear, does he not hear?
He who formed the eye, does he not see?
(Psalm 94.9, NRSV)

Differentness

Individuation is a psychological term that names the process of learning to see oneself as separate from others. As part of this process, a person finds the true self along the way of growing into life. As a professor whose classes include cultural anthropology, I teach my students that individuation is also a cultural and social property. The process includes learning that the way each person sees the world is different from the way others see it. It also means that the way others see us is different from the way we see others, and sometimes that difference is profound.

When I did not begin to walk at the expected age, my parents took me to a doctor who diagnosed the condition as cerebral palsy. The doctor suggested institutionalization, stating that in addition to being unable to walk, I would be unable to learn to read or communicate. This was the first in a series of incidents where my parents refused to go along with the then-current attitudes toward disabilities—an attitude which they passed on to me in the individuation process.

As I entered school, I did not think of myself as greatly different from others, but I quickly learned that I should have done so. I have memories of being forced to compete in sports with responses of laughter. And, while I did not know what was happening at the time, I was often removed from classes in elementary school to take tests that evaluated my learning abilities. Later research on common ideas of those early years taught me that my parents had engaged in a long and difficult argument for "mainstreaming" in the public school system. Sadly, I often hear from others who have similar problems today. I honor the memory of my parents and others who have been through and continue this struggle.

Another struggle, increasingly my own, was fitting in elsewhere in society. My junior high school had outdoor portable classrooms, approached by stairs. As I struggled with these barriers, especially during a series of surgeries that sought to improve my mobility, some students accepted accommodations made for my differences, but others did not. Today, there are still people who regard accessible parking spaces and ramps as "special favors" to a privileged few.

At this age, as have so many, I also went to summer camp. It soon became obvious that I could not climb the hills and stairs in a wonderfully rustic and hilly setting. It was arranged that a retired pastor, who was one of the camp teachers, would drive me around. This was no problem, because he had a disability similar to mine. It was from talking with him that I came to realize the extent of God's love for all people, and that disabilities are not punishment for anyone's sin. He became a continuing role model who encouraged me to use my gifts to fulfill God's call to service in the ordained ministry.

As that sense of call developed, I also began to confront a dilemma. I realized I could no longer belong to the church in which I had been brought up; troubling me was that whatever that church proclaimed, its practice reflected a reprehensible belief that disabilities are God's punishment for sins.

With the end of high school, I received a state scholarship. That was fine with me, for the branch of our state university was reasonably accessible, certainly far more so that the church college to which many were pointing me. I also found other doors opened at the university. One of these doors was acceptance; that is, here was a place where people were judged far more by their ability than by what they could not do. I was able to study arts, languages and history. Learning more about the wide experiences of humankind, thinking about the meaning of progress and the process of change brought me to the United Methodist Church. In a directed study, I read Luther, Calvin, and Wesley. All were interesting, but it was John Wesley who spoke to both my heart and reason, and I responded by joining a United Methodist church that was near the campus.

As college graduation came near, I received several awards and encouragement to pursue graduate work; however, I found—like many others—that being in a world of adults would not mean that discrimination would cease. In those pre-ADA days, my university was one of a very few facilities that featured level entrances, elevators, and close-in parking.

The short form of the story is that neither graduate school nor appropriate employment was open in a pre-ADA world suffering from an economic slump. However, God didn't give up. My hobby of photography became a job, one that meant learning the then-new world of personal computers and early forms of electronic information transfer. It was, however, a job that took me away from regular church attendance.

I do not believe that God brings disaster into our lives. God calls us backed with knowledge far beyond what is available to humans, but God is not a micro-manager of every step and event in human life. If we listen and respond, God can thereby use good as well as bad events to bring about what is good for us and the world. Several years later, and after I had renewed my church commitment, I was asked to speak to a Sunday school class. I wrestled with what to say. The week before, I visited my family home, and found that our former neighbor, who was the age of one of my sisters, and who had started her own taxicab company, had been found dead after a robbery a day before. Her life was worth less than $25. She had a sister who had a mental disability. As had her family and mine, I likewise talked with the mentally disabled sister about what happened, and it was clear that she did not understand that her sister had been murdered. But she remembered that a few years before, when she won a medal at Special Olympics, that I had been there to take photographs, and that she had pointed to me and told the crowd, "that's my neighbor there, taking the pictures."

As it did for the disabled sister, one event can bring a flood of memories. In my case, that day reminded me of my own exclusion, but also finding acceptance in various places along the way. And that, in turn, recalled the joy of learning, thinking about human progress, and sharing those findings. As have so many others, I found strength in the Psalter, especially Psalm 94. It gave me a topic to speak to the Sunday school class about how the church needs to lead, reach out, and speak to the world about the love that Jesus has brought us. Conversion without commitment to a transformed life and world is indeed the "cheap grace" that Dietrich Bonhoeffer disdained in his book *The Cost of Discipleship*. Because people have a deep need for change that only God can meet, other attempts to satisfy the need will fail. That need may be met, fleetingly, in a set of rules, doctrines, or other counterfeits that create a false holiness of separation and walls from other. But in the long-term, only the often-misunderstood experience of uniting in divine love that John Wesley called "Christian perfection" will last. It is not freedom from errors or mistakes, or even from physical distress, but it is a long-term process of loving each other that mirrors the absolutely free gift of divine grace that we so often try to subvert into a reward for holiness. That love upends social standards and creates radically new demands for the disciple of Christ as he or she shares it freely in gratitude for God's freely given grace.

Rerouting

I consider that Sunday school class presentation to be the first serious step in my recommitment to the call I had felt many years before. Other steps came quickly. The class asked me to continue speaking; and teaching that one meant absence from my regular class. Soon one of its members, named Sherrie, asked where I had been. Before we left the building, we had talked about the college degree she was finishing, the chronological order of the book of Jeremiah, Beethoven's music, missions, and a plan to visit the local zoo. The crisis point in our relationship came when Sherrie interviewed for a job in a city several hours away, and we realized that we didn't want to be apart from each other. From there, we entered pre-marital counseling with our pastor. He was satisfied that we belonged together, and suggested that the most important aspect of our marriage would be how we dealt with my call to ministry. I had not discussed this call with him before, but apparently he had been hearing something from the Sunday school class.

Sherrie and I were married on May 22, 1993. While waiting for an airplane the next day, she suggested that I should quit my job and enter graduate school after she found full-time employment. On our return, moving into a house and getting settled as a couple occupied much of our time. But the call to ordained ministry remained, and after exploring several educational options, I enrolled at United Theological Seminary in Dayton, Ohio. It was there that we celebrated our first wedding anniversary, and the end of my first semester at the seminary.

Physically, the old United seminary campus was the product of a vision that took "higher learning" literally: the former Evangelical United Brethren (EUB) facility, which became a United Methodist seminary in the 1968 merger of the EUB with the former Methodist Church, had massive stairways into its oldest buildings. Three newer buildings had elevators. A circuitous route led to the back door of the library, where one could traverse the length of the building again to get into an elevator. A nice ramp led into the chapel that ended at a locked door and again required traversing its length to find an elevator that, at first, required a key that wasn't kept in the elevator. And, after an initial assignment to an old dormitory with stairs, we were moved to a newer building with an elevator, as well as a single classroom in the basement. This classroom, small and crowded, became the point of a few snide remarks over the next three years as I and two professors, one who used a scooter, and another with a prosthetic leg, jockeyed with each other to fit our respective schedules in the use of that room.

In my first year, my community placement had me developing one of the first databases and electronic outreach systems for Dayton's ecumenical agency. In addition, after a church history course in my first semester, I became that history professor's assistant. Along with that work, in my second and third years I was the associate pastor in a local church. An important part of that experience came when the senior pastor was hospitalized during Holy Week of my second year. With two days notice, I preached on Easter Sunday. For the rest of that semester, and much of my final year, while the senior pastor recovered, the congregation chose to trust me with pastoral leadership in a plan that included developing the gifts of its members who were considering ministry as their calling.

In the summer before my final year, United (as the seminary was called by us students) required a two-week trip involving a ministry context different from one's own. Typically, these programs centered on traipsing along the Mexico-Texas border, or working in inner cities. Seeking something I could handle physically, Sherrie and I went to Erie, Pennsylvania, where we lived for two weeks in a L'Arche community. In several group homes, best-known through Henri Nouwen's writings, people with mental disabilities live in a place of acceptance and mutual respect. Although often unable to read or write, discriminated against, and faced with seemingly impossible governmental demands to receive basic sustenance, these people radiated a joy that showed the love of God in their acceptance of everyone, simply for being who they were.

During my third year at the seminary, as the senior pastor recovered and slowly returned to work, I began to consider my future. My seminary experience convinced me that I was gifted not only as a pastor, but also as a teacher. However, my superintendent, while being generally supportive, had, in response to a question I raised about accessibility in potential appointments, sent a very out-of-character message to the effect that if I placed restrictions on the kind of appointments that I would accept, then the Board of Ordained Ministry would consider this as an indication that I wasn't a serious candidate for ordination. It would also limit opportunity for advancement and continued appointment. At the advice of my candidacy mentor (who was also the professor I assisted), I investigated several graduate schools. Although it was late in the academic year to be applying for entrance, and after being placed on several waiting lists, I was accepted outright by the Dallas, Texas Southern Methodist University in its Graduate Program in Religious Studies, with the intent of becoming a teacher in that field.

Graduate school added further added to the chain of learning that began in my early days. Drawing from university and seminary teachings, I found the tools to more fully understand and speak about biblical stories such as John 9 and articulate a theological stance on disability and inclusion. The process of healing described in that gospel includes not only how Jesus completely disowned so many of the beliefs about disability and sin that I had run across, but also how the healed man spoke for himself and others—and how both were driven out by the religious and political authorities.

The struggle to come to terms with a physical disability, in the light of John 9, has been definitive for me and my ideas of the church.

Old injuries were aggravated by parking problems as I went through graduate school. As a result, I needed back surgery. An agonizingly slow recovery of motion and ability have led to a battery of still incomplete tests in an effort to define my condition better, as well as needing to use a wheelchair for mobility. The religious authorities responded, but not with acceptance. When I returned to my home conference, no replies came to my messages and applications. Eventually, a confidential message indicated that the conference, concerned about insurance costs, was not willing to consider any candidate coping with a disability. It was in the recital of that confidential information that I learned I was not alone in being rejected. An individual, I was told and later got to meet, had—for similar reasons—been denied the journey toward ordination as an Elder in the United Methodist Church.

Professor as Pastor

As a result of the conference's blatant prejudice, I am not an ordained Elder, but a professor teaching history at a college. It is not the church, but as a history teacher I am not content with seeing history as a series of dates. Rather, it is a conversation about where we have been, and that exploration can open the doors for needful changes as we meet the future. The teacher of history is ultimately a pastor who shepherds students to a greater understanding of themselves and God's role in their lives. It was a history teacher who first opened my mind to the wider world of ministry. Perhaps I will someday do the same for another student. Ah, but I must change that sentence! In fact, I have helped some of my students to open the doors of their minds to the wider world of possibilities that so need their single and collective actions.

My understanding of God and ministry as developed by this experience is inclusive. People, especially those who ought to know better, spend great amounts of time and effort categorizing other people, and then use those mistaken distinctions to judge them as unacceptable. God, however, accepts us as we are, and then proceeds with change in the heart that comes to be seen outside. Jesus told his followers that he came to give abundant life to everyone. Yet we stay with, or even create social models that lead to unemployment, underemployment, poverty, and lost lives. The church all too often mirrors those human values, not God's: we blaspheme God by wasting the diverse gifts and talents God has given everyone.

My heart breaks for the church, and especially for the United Methodist Church as it continues to create articles of exclusion in many categories. While there are signs of acceptance coming down the road for those who live with disabilities, there are many problems yet to be named and resolved. We still hear phrases such as "there aren't any of *them* in our church, so why worry about accessibility?" Too many churches refuse to let anyone know that their facilities are accessible when that's the case, or extend attitudinal barriers.

"Man proposes, God disposes" goes an old (and non-inclusive) adage. It is God who calls us to ministry; the church is God's agent. When God calls, the call does not end simply because the church looks away. So God continues to work through a different form of ministry in which I and others engage. Aside from the ministry of teaching, I assist several organizations with their on-line presence, which is growing to include using technology and social media to bring people together, and this is especially the case for those who are isolated by the "physical" nature of the world that is too often inaccessible.

In Wesleyan theology, salvation is not only about "going to heaven." It is also about living a life of joy and purpose here and now in a new community of all God's people. For many among us, technology has opened new doors in the drive for inclusion and acceptance. It has also opened new doors for awareness of those who are hindered by blatant prejudices and discrimination. As a person with a body in which pain is part of existence, I feel a responsibility to speak out on behalf of those in many kinds of pain, most of whom are disadvantaged and unable to speak for themselves. With modern technological tools, the words of Charles Wesley, John Wesley's younger brother, take on a new level of meaning:

1. O for a thousand tongues to sing

My dear Redeemer's praise!

The glories of my God and King,

The triumphs of his grace!

5. Hear him, ye deaf; his praise, ye mute*,

Your loosened tongues employ;

Ye blind, behold your Saviour come,

And leap, ye lame, for joy!

9. Anticipate your heaven below,

And own that love is heaven.[5]

The discerning reader will note that the original word in verse five is not "mute," but is "dumb." I have changed this because "dumb" has become a disparaging term in our society. This action is symbolic of the change from being mute, deaf, blind, and paralyzed that the church needs to engage in becoming an inclusive body, living the metaphorical challenge of Hebrews 13:2 of "being open to those you don't know is something you shouldn't overlook, because by doing that, some have had angels as guests without knowing it."[6]

---

[5] Taken from "A Collection of Hymns, For the Use of the People Called Methodists, #1, The Bicentennial Edition of the Works of John Wesley.

[6] Author's translation from the original Greek version of this New Testament call for radical hospitality toward all people.

Cheryl Magrini

Your Story Matters!
By The Rev. Cheryl T. Magrini, Ph.D.

I have an art-deco piece of art with large black letters on the foreground saying, "Your Story Matters." While it is not a cross or a Bible, I call this piece of art one of my sacred reminders of how much I am created "just a little lower than the angels" (Psalm 8:5, Hebrews 2:5-8).[7] I am reminded every day that, indeed, my story matters. While on the phone with my sister, she asked me, "So, what are you going to write about? You know, your story has a lot of parts to it." I thought to myself, "She has a point." In telling my story, it is hard to know where to begin. I say that because the beginning is really the middle and the ending never ends. Laughing, crying, and saying, "Ah…now I get it," are all stirrings of the heart that I hope you will experience as we journey together through this chapter.

Identity Unleashed

Let me introduce myself. I am Cheryl, an ordained Deacon in the Northern Illinois Conference of the United Methodist Church. Now you have my "official" clergy designation. Here is the other part of who I am: I am a person with a mental illness called bipolar disorder. My diagnosis does not define my identity. I live in recovery on the other side of my diagnosis, and I take responsibility for remembering that every day is about hope and recovery. When I was first told that I had the "bipolar

---

[7] All Scriptural passages in this chapter are from the New International Version (NIV).

disorder type I," I then asked the therapist, "What is that?"[8] I had never before heard of bipolar disorder. At that time I was in my mid-forties. It is not unusual for the symptoms to go undiagnosed, to be misdiagnosed, or for a person to diagnose him or herself. In my case, I thought that was how I had grown up, how I was functioning as a successful clergyperson, even earning a Ph.D., and all of that was perfectly normal. In other words, I have excellent coping skills. One day, however, those skills were no longer enough. That is how I ended up hearing a diagnosis of bipolar disorder at the age of 40-something.

Now I begin my day with gratitude. The contemporarily designed angel on the cover of my small writing book has her angelic dress decorated with these aphorisms:

> Embrace Change; **Love** **with Abandon; Speak of Your Gratitude;** Believe in Healing; Be Positive; Wear Yellow Shoes (my favorite aphorism); Dance in the Moonlight (my second favorite aphorism)

I call this notebook my Gratitude Book. Just about every morning I date and write a list of things for which I am thankful. Knowing "if anyone is in Christ, the new creation has come: the new is here! (2 Corinthians 5:17)" takes on a whole new meaning for me. The foundation of faith is what has got me this far, and I know it will get me to the next day and beyond. I have faith in the wisdom of the Spirit of God manifested through my doctors, my family, and through the pastors who have helped me along this path. They have touched my life in a way that leads to my being a new creation every day! The organization named the Depression and Bipolar Support Alliance (DBSA) is the leading national source of education for those who are newly diagnosed with the condition, their peers and families trying to understand this illness; I can testify that this organization has been a constant source of support and encouragement for me and my family. What is especially important to understand is that the illness of bipolar disorder is hard to diagnose, difficult to stabilize, and demands that the affected person focus every waking day on self-care for living in hope and recovery.

---

[8] The "I" in "bipolar I" is the Roman numeral for the Arabic numeral one.

Erasing the Stigmas of Mental Illnesses

I am not going to bother you with the whole story of how I came to "have" bipolar disorder. Every person's story is unique *and matters!* What I do want to share with you are some of my personal struggles around the stigma of mental illness, and the triumphs that have led me to hope and to "living" into recovery every day. You see, there is never an end to living with a mental illness. Bipolar disorder does not magically disappear by swallowing a pill, or by having an epiphany during a session with a therapist. A person lives with a mental illness just like a person lives with diabetes or any other disabling illness or disability. Living with the bipolar disorder takes hard work every single day.

Stigma, unfortunately, is one cruelly unsympathetic part of the battle. "Just get over it." "How come you can't get out of bed?" "You are just a lazy person." "You are fired. You aren't doing your job." "How could you spend so much money?" "You are crazy." "This marriage is over." "You are turning into a drug addict." "If you would just take your medication then things like this wouldn't happen." "You are a bad, lazy, no good person." There are more scathing and derogatory remarks that I have personally heard, but not recorded here.

By means of speaking about my own illness of bipolar disorder in public forums and ministry settings, I hope to help break the silence and shatter the dark despair of stigma surrounding any mental illness. What makes bipolar disorder particularly hard to diagnose is that symptoms can overlap with other illnesses. Some people self-diagnose their condition, but will not even see a doctor, thereby going untreated. Other illnesses like Post Traumatic Stress Disorder, (PTSD), anxiety, panic attack, and clinical depression can also make bipolar difficult to diagnose. Many people may go untreated for years. My experience was that I had all the symptoms of bipolar I, including psychotic episodes from childhood on, but the symptoms were never recognized as having anything possibly related to a mental illness.

I am also a long time severe migraine sufferer. I have seen my same top rated doctor in the country for several years; he is Dr. Lawrence Robbins, board certified as both a neurologist and psycho-pharmacologist. Dr. Robbins practices at the Robbins Headache Clinic in

Northbrook, Illinois, a northern suburb of Chicago. The doctor has explained to me that I have a connection with migraine and bipolar disorder, and other individuals can also have this dual possibility. Both conditions are genetically inherited.

From Dr. Robbins, I quote the following explanation of the connection between migraine and bipolar disorder:

> "Bipolar and migraine are each inherited, genetic chemical differences in the brain. Serotonin and dopamine levels are genetically determined. Bipolar disorder is a spectrum. Eight to nine percent of migrainers have bipolar disorder; 30% of bipolar disorder people have migraine. A mood disorder often begins before the headaches. In bipolar disorder there is often earlier depression and anxiety by the age of thirteen to fifteen. The family history in those with the bipolar spectrum may include substance abuse, mood disorders, and psychiatric hospitalization. Depression may fuel headaches, and headaches fuel depression. Both must be addressed and treated."[9]

I asked Dr. Robbins why it was not until my mid forties that I had a "crash" as the lingo goes. He replied: "Brain chemistry changes throughout our life. You were able to cope, and at some point nothing works any more, particularly with stresses. Your coping mechanisms worked for a long time, and one day they were not enough anymore."

At the time of this writing in the year of 2011, I have been married twenty-nine years to a husband who has the fortitude of a mountain. In the early part of working on finding the new "normal" between depression and mania, he was the mainstay of how I kept going every day. I longed for the new normality. I can tell you that functioning as a public persona as a clergyperson was filled with familial, personal, and—of

---

[9] Dr. Lawrence Robbins, Robbins Headache Clinic, 60 Revere Drive, Suite 330, Northbrook, Illinois

course—pastoral stress. Despite those hindrances, and for most of the time, I somehow was able to put on that pastoral public persona.

Allow me to share with you a personal and vulnerable glimpse into the parts of my life that are not those of a clergyperson's public face:

> Crying on the floor wrapped in a blanket with the cell phone just waiting for my therapist to call me back; staying in bed and not being able to put a foot on the floor; severe reactions to a medicine causing a seizure, vision distortions, vertigo, nausea and stomach problems; not feeling hungry; spending a lot of money; throwing all my clothes out of the closet onto the bedroom floor and walking on them for a week before I had the energy to put them away –, and then doing the same thing with my hundreds of books. I am an expert at crying without a sound. I have flushed my whole "cocktail" of meds down the toilet three times, thinking I was feeling so well that I did not need them. Then there is the side effect of weight gain. Lithium, the long time mainstay drug prescribed to control the disorder, added at least twenty pounds to my petite five-foot frame. Once I got off lithium it took me a year and a half to lose the weight.

Every Day Self-Care

Now you know about the person of Cheryl who has bipolar disorder. If there is a "best part" of this illness, then it is that I have learned how to take care of myself that I must manage to do every day. I call this life-management process "My Self-care Checklist." I have spelled out the list below, and I believe everyone should use it, or something like it: "Brief quiet time during the day (I have this as my devotional morning time). Eat healthily. Exercise. Take medication on time. Learn breathing and relaxation skills. Talk to someone every day. Remember gratitude, and express thankfulness. Sleep for 7 hours. Nap for no more than 30 minutes. Read an inspirational book. Be positive even when it is hard to be so. Keep a support person and doctor phone list. Talk with people who are living with bipolar disorder, and are in recovery. Give back to the world. Reduce stress, even if only in a small way. Keep a suicide prevention number at reach."

Did that seem like a long list? Nevertheless, it is akin to the daily practices of many people through the previous centuries, including Jesus. When Jesus got up early and went to pray, he taught us the need pray and commune with God in solitude. Even then Jesus had to get up early to do so! Relying not on myself, but on the faith that Jesus had in God gets me through the day in gratitude in the tough as well as good times.

> "Very early in the morning, while it was still dark, Jesus got up, left the house and went off to a solitary place, where he prayed. Simon and his companions went to look for him, and when they found him, they exclaimed: 'Everyone is looking for you!'" (Mark 1:35-37).

When Jesus fed the more than five thousand people on the grassy hillside, we learned about all the ways we are to be in community with one another in the Kingdom of God today and in the fullness of the Kingdom yet to come. Providing a support group, and going to a support group, doctor, or therapist are parts of a person's treatment that creates a supportive community. When Jesus is said to have cast out demons, we learned that in his era the sources of illnesses were not understood. Currently, and in sharp contrast to the two millennia ago belief, what a difference treatment can make in a mentally-ill person's life today. When Jesus prayed to God in the Garden of Gethsemane, we learned that we can pray the hardest prayers from our deepest pain. "Father, if you are willing, take this cup from me; yet not my will, but yours be done" (Luke 22:42).

Heartbreak and Hope

My story and your story are intertwined as the brothers and sisters that we are in Christ. If I can get anything across to you, it is to take care of your brothers and sisters along with yourself. Bipolar disorder is genetic, although it is not always passed on to the children, depending on the formation of the gene.

Here is a bit of the story of our young adult son Dan, who was clinically depressed, had severe panic attacks, highly manic episodes with two attempted suicides. He was in intense treatment for about four years.

He died in June of 2011 at the age of 23, due to a completed suicide from bipolar disorder. As his therapist told me, "Bipolar disorder is a terminal illness." We who have the disorder live with that illness forever. Dan's death came as a complete shock to my husband Pete and Dan's brother John, age 21, and to me; it even came as a shock to the professionals treating him. Dan had been accepted at two colleges, and was trying to decide which to attend. He had been living successfully more and more on his own. He had a good support group of friends. Our hearts were and are still broken at the shock of his death. There is not one moment that I do not think about how much *"Dan's Story Matters!"* Irrefutably, bipolar disorder is a serious mental illness.

There are no words that can express the pain of losing the life of a child. The words of Psalm 91 give me hope, particularly verses 9-12:

> "If you say, 'The LORD is my refuge,' and you make the Most High your dwelling, no harm will overtake you, no disaster will come near your tent. For he will command his angels concerning you to guard you in all your ways, they will lift you up in their hands, so that you will not strike your foot against a stone."

Months before Dan's death, and living in recovery from my own illness for some time, I sought out the DBSA training to become a Certified Specialist to lead Peer-to-Peer support groups. DBSA did not have a Chapter in the Chicago Loop, and that unmet need was just my kind of challenge! I passed the Certification examination, and completed all of the requirements for establishing the DBSA Chicago Loop Chapter. On the same date of my relinquishment of my Deacon appointment from First United Methodist Church at Chicago Temple in the Chicago Loop, I was given a new appointment as the President and Certified Specialist of the non-profit DBSA Chicago Loop Chapter. I provide educational programs and facilitate Peer-to-Peer Support Groups. Through the wisdom of Bishop Hee-Soo Jung, I am now living within a new calling from God. It is in tune with the calling of the Deacon – to go where the world's needs are found, all the while connecting the world and the church for the work of justice and mercy in the name of Christ.

Life is experienced one day at a time. Hope and recovery are my watchwords. The words of Jesus from Matthew 11:28-29 are my comfort and strength: "Come to me, all you who are weary and burdened, and I will give you rest. Take my yoke upon you and learn from me, for I am gentle and humble in heart, and you will find rest for your souls. For my yoke is easy and my burden is light."

Throughout my life I have been challenged and inspired by the writings of the late Henri J.M. Nouwen. In the edited book by Michael Ford called, *The Dance of Life: Weaving Sorrows and Blessings into One Joyful Step*, there are selections from Nouwen's writings. Here is one of my favorite Nouwen sayings on Divine love: "When St. John says that fear is driven out by perfect love, he points to a love that comes from God, a divine love. He does not speak about human affection, psychological compatibility, mutual attraction, or deep interpersonal feelings. All of that has its value and beauty, but the perfect love about which St. John speaks embraces and transcends all feelings, emotions, and passions. The perfect love that drives out all fear is the divine love in which we are invited to participate"

With a mental illness—particularly bipolar disorder—the fear of no one being present in the darkness is frightening beyond description. The light of life just might be a spark that can begin to dispel the darkness. My hope lies in John 1:5: "The light shines in the darkness, and the darkness has not overcome it."

Reaching out to someone in depression or to someone who is working up into what I call being "revved up," can make all the difference between life and death for that person. As I live into recovery it takes hard work every day, and sometimes the needed energy becomes too draining for me. What I do have are support people who understand the illness of bipolar disorder and the peace that passes all understanding through faith. I pray that I can be a vessel of God's grace in sharing with others through support and education on bipolar disorder that can lead to healthier lives for us all.

A Cry for Communal Support

There are difficult questions we must face in breaking down the barriers of stigma and silence; consider these questions: How can faith communities work together to break the silence and dispel the stigma and myths about mental illness? Are you willing to be educated and to educate others? Will you be the catalyst wherever you are in community to begin a ministry that focuses on hope and recovery?

No one person can break down these barriers. One individual, however, can be the ray of hope while holding someone's hand, and merely sitting in silence with him or her. Bipolar disorder does not have to be a mystery. I hope that by sharing my story, and the faith that holds me up each day, you will likewise take into your heart how much *Your Story Matters*. I tell people that no one can ever put a period after recovery in one's life. Living in recovery takes place in every day, every step, self-care, faith, hope, and love. I know that *My Story Matters* as I sing the words from *"Be Thou My Vision,"* an Eighth century Irish poem: "Waking or sleeping, Thy presence my light." May we work together in educating faith communities about mental illness in general, and bipolar disorder in particular, to establish outreach ministries of support and providing education. Why? Because *"Everyone's Story Matters!"*

John Carr

Of Course I Can Write
By The Rev. John A. Carr, B.A., B.D., S.T.M.

The Pain of Prejudice

I am a retired United Methodist elder who has been blessed with a rich and rewarding ministry that includes ten years of serving churches and thirty years as a hospital chaplain, with most of those chaplaincy years being spent as a clinical pastoral education (CPE) supervisor. My process in entering the ordained ministry, however, was made somewhat challenging because of the way the leadership of my annual conference reacted to my disability.

My initial call to pastoral ministry came while I was an undergraduate student at Ohio Wesleyan University (OWU). I had given a lot of thought to my future before I entered college. In high school, most of my vocational research had led me to aspire to a career as a lawyer; consequently, when I entered OWU, my plan was to follow the pre-law track of studies. It was, however, while I was home for the Christmas vacation that a change in career goals was launched. Our pastor, the Rev. Matthew "Mattie" Gates, invited me to join him on the hunt for our church's Christmas tree. While looking for a tree, we had what for me was an unexpected conversation. Mattie said, "John, when are you going into the ministry?" I said, "Mattie, I'm not sure what I'm going to do, but I can't be a minister." Mattie replied by asking, "Why not?" I said that I had too many doubts. Mattie then said, "You show me a minister who doesn't have some doubts, and I will show you someone who won't be a good minister."

That conversation was an important breakthrough that started me thinking anew about my vocational options. I had considered the law profession because I wanted to work with people in a helpful way. As I thought and prayed about my future, I realized that I had a faith, grew up in the church, and had some wonderful ministerial role-models to guide me. Also, I realized that as a minister in a local church, I would probably be working with a wider range of people than I would as an attorney. It was not too long after my conversation with Rev. Gates that I returned to college and changed my major from pre-law studies to pre-theological studies.

As I reflect back on my call to the ministry, I am struck by two things. One is my readiness to realize that my pastor had a better understanding of God's call on my life than I did as a very young adult. The second reflection is that I was much more concerned about the strength of my faith than I was about the fact that I had been born without hands or a left forefoot. My disability was not something that I considered a serious obstacle.

Overcoming the Presumed Obstacles

It was during my years at Ohio Wesleyan University that I had two key experiences that were to have an influence on my early ministry. First, I met Sammy, the young woman who I dated seriously through my last two years of college, and who would become my wife for twenty-five years. Also, I had been active in scouting from my Cub Scout through high school scouting days; it was in the latter years that I attained the rank of Eagle Scout. During my Ohio Wesleyan summers, I worked at Boy Scout Camp, first serving as a counselor, then a unit leader, and finally as program director and cooking counselor. My passion for playing ping pong in my spare time eventually played a role in my ministry.

Since I had accepted my call to ministry, the arrival of my senior year in college meant it was time to find a seminary. I wanted to be closer to my home in Connecticut during that schooling. I had also decided that I preferred to be among a greater diversity of students than I would encounter at a Methodist school like Drew or Boston seminaries, even though I knew both of them to be excellent. So, I decided to risk it all by applying solely to Yale Divinity School (YDS), located in New Haven, Connecticut.

Until my dying day, I will never forget the impact of the last question put to me during my interview at the seminary. Professor Hugh Hartshaw was the one who met with me, and his final question was "What right do you think you have to be a minister? Don't you know that the symbol of the pastor is to shake hands with people after the service? Why -- you don't even have any hands to shake."

I don't know how I responded to the professor's sharp and painful thrust, but I do know that I went back to college very bitter and disappointed. That dark mood lasted until the next week when I received the letter of acceptance from YDS. It was then that I realized that I had been put through the fire to see what I could take, and how I would respond to such attacks. Despite my initial shock and disappointment, I had passed the test!

So it came to be that in the fall of 1953, I entered Yale Divinity School (YDS) on a three-year track for pastoral ministry. During my first year there, I met a clergyperson who would help me to accept an important turning point in my life; he was the Rev. Mr. Lattimer Neale who was in charge of our New York East Annual Conference education and camping program. After I had requested some scholarship help, Rev. Neale came to meet with me to say two things. He couldn't offer me scholarship money because it was all spoken for, but he would rather do something else. He had learned about my extensive summer experience working at scout camp, and he wanted to offer me a job in the conference camping program. The position was as camp manager of Camp Epworth, a children's camp for fourth, fifth, and sixth graders. Lattimer told me that some people were questioning my ability to be accepted as a parish minister; I inferred from his words that my taking the job could change their minds.   Camp Epworth would be having several turnovers of campers over the summer with different clergypersons, lay people, youth, and children from all over the conference coming for different programmed weeks. As the manager, Lattimer said I would be in charge of the permanent staff, and also work in liaison with the different program directors and their staff. The permanent staff included a camp nurse, a housekeeper, a maintenance worker, a cook, and kitchen staff. On the grounds we had two large wooden buildings that were almost like Army-style barracks; however, the counselors and kids did not live in the buildings, but in pyramid tents. That management position was a wonderful experience for me, and I got to meet a lot of people from around the conference.

One of my experiences during that summer of 1954 exposed me to my own vulnerability and ambivalence as a person coping with a physical challenge. One of the clergypersons had made several educational filmstrips (a still slide show on 16 mm film), and wanted to make one of me. I emphatically refused, since the filming would be focused on my disability. Many years later, when I had become highly active in advocacy for disability issues within the church, as well as in the secular community, I regretted not aiding and advancing the cause earlier in my life.

In June 1955, I was married and a few weeks later I returned to Camp Epworth with along with my wife, Sammy. Once again, I enjoyed the camp experience and the opportunity to meet so many people. I had the privilege of accepting a great honor in that I was invited to bring the opening message at the new outdoor worship center at our conference's neighboring Camp Quinipet. Although Camp Epworth has changed and moved to a different location, the neighboring camp and the outdoor worship center still stand today.

After I returned to YDS, early in the school year, I was faced with a serious attitudinal obstacle to my plans to pursue parish ministry. The obstacle appeared when I was visited by Barton Bove, District Superintendent of the New Haven District where I was officially connected; not surprisingly, it was the old, old storyline: "We don't think you should plan on entering a parish ministry because we don't think it can happen. Why don't you plan for another type of ministry, such as becoming a chaplain?"

Although I didn't agree with his reasoning, I also knew that it was the voicing of some individuals in their conference leadership roles, and I had better take it seriously. Feeling that I had no other choice, I made several unwanted decisions. I changed from the three-year to the four-year track so that I would have more time to complete the studies. I also applied for a summer training program in chaplaincy, and really wanting to get away for the summer, I was accepted by a program in North Dakota. They even offered my wife a summer job; however, the getaway opportunity never happened.

74

Breaking the Parish Ministry Barrier

In the spring of 1956, my phone rang, and the voice of a man who was a complete stranger to me said, "Is this John Carr? I am Homer Kern Rhinesmith from Westbury, Long Island. I am about to hire my first associate, and some of our members who have known you at Camp Epworth suggested that I interview you. Would you like to come down for an interview? "

Once we ascertained that this was a legitimate call from a real pastor, Sammy and I arranged to drive down to Long Island. We met Homer and then his wife Winifred. The only time we lied was when they asked us if we liked cheesecake for dessert and, despite never having eaten cheesecake before, we both said, "yes." Homer offered me the position to begin in July, the start of the conference year.

The only problem was that I was supposed to take another year at YDS, but this was an opportunity for parish ministry that I could not turn down. I was able to make changes in my studies. I cancelled out of the chaplaincy training program in North Dakota, and I consulted with the administrators at YDS where—because of my change to a four year program—I had two required courses remaining. Arrangements were made for me to take the two courses at Union Seminary in Manhattan, New York, and return to YDS in June to graduate with the class of 1957. I greatly appreciated the cooperation between the two seminaries that allowed this important change.

The two years at Westbury were exceedingly valuable. I had an excellent role-model in Homer, and his wife Winifred was very helpful to Sammy. It was an added blessing that Homer offered me the opportunity to replace him as a counselor at our Camp Quinipet at the High School Methodist Youth Fellowship Week. This began a pattern that I followed from 1956 through 1962, enabling me to continue my connection to camping. In 1963, I left the Assembly Week staff to become the program director for a junior high camp. The return to camping afforded me a chance to improve my ping pong game, and for many summers everyone who challenged me lost. I still run into people who say they remember how they couldn't beat me in ping pong at Camp Quinipet. I like to think they also remember to be careful about the kinds of prejudices and assumptions that they make when they meet a person with a disability.

I can't think about my tenure at Westbury UMC without remembering my "Beth story" that took place when Sunday school began in my first autumn at that church. I had recently been visited by a young couple who said they were having some concerns for their little girl, named Beth. It seems she was very upset that God would let me be born with no hands. About a week later, I was asked to speak to one of the children's Sunday school classes, and Beth happened to be in that class. I knew this would be an important time to connect with all of the kids and specifically with her. So I shared some of the things that I could do, and brought a ball to throw back and forth. One of the things I told the children was that I didn't know if I first stopped asking either God or Santa Claus about giving me hands. Whichever it was, I then decided that since I wasn't going to get hands, I better ask God to help me use my arms better. I remember Beth intently watching me and taking it all in.

A few days later, I was out driving to do some parish visiting when I found myself in Beth's neighborhood; although her home was not my destination. She spotted me and I heard her running toward her house saying, "Mommy, Daddy, Rev. Carr is coming!" So of course I had to go in. We had a very interesting visit, and I believe Beth told me every story there was to tell about her family, including some that her parents would have preferred to keep within the family. Many years later, my wife and I returned to Westbury for Homer's retirement party, and a lovely young woman came up to me and said, "Hello, Rev. Carr. It is so good to see you. I am Beth." I learned that Beth had become a practicing lawyer, and we had a wonderful reunion.

As rewarding as it was to serve as the associate pastor in Westbury, when the time came for my full ordination, I was anxious to have a church of my own. So it was that at the Annual Conference session when I was ordained as an Elder, I was appointed to serve in Hauppauge, Long Island.

Denouncing Bigotries and Discriminations

After five years in Hauppauge, we moved on to Faith United Methodist Church in North Haven, Connecticut. While there, I had the opportunity of witnessing Martin Luther King, Jr. in his marvelously prophetic "I Have A Dream" speech delivered on the National Mall in Washington, D.C., followed by joining with the Rev. Don Rackliffe in responding to the call to go to Selma, Alabama to prepare for the historic and seminal "March to Montgomery," also in Alabama. It was an experience that I call one of the most thrilling, but also one of the scariest times of our lives. Among the good events, there was the opportunity to talk for the first time with a Catholic nun and to find some of my fraternity brothers. Coming back from one of the marches, we were invited by the principal of the black high school to join him in drinking iced tea, and all of us heard President Lyndon Baines Johnson say for the first time that, "We shall overcome." For me, the "I Have a Dream" speech and the March on Montgomery were the first time the Christian churches had truly come alive.

It was about that momentous period in my life when I began to realize that I might be called to a different form of ministry. When Chaplain Ed Dobihal initiated the Department of Religious Ministries at Yale New Haven Hospital, he offered me the opportunity to take the first unit of clinical pastoral education (CPE). The training that I received convinced me that although I greatly enjoyed parish ministry, I did want to move into hospital chaplaincy. I started to look around the country for a place to take further training when I learned that Ed Dobihal was going to offer his second unit of CPE. I applied and was accepted as his first staff person and part of the second CPE unit.

Before leaving my third and last year at North Haven, we had our tenth anniversary of the life of Faith United Methodist Church. The church dignitaries who helped Faith UMC get started were invited back for the special celebration. It was an interesting experience for me as the host pastor to welcome back Barton Bove; he was the District Superintendent who urged me to discontinue my preparations for parish ministry, and become a chaplain instead. That account rounds out this part of my story.

Hospital Chaplain and Advocate for Equal Rights for People with Disabilities

I continued my preparations for teaching chaplaincy with additional units of CPE, and in 1970 I was approved as a full supervisor by the Association for Clinical Pastoral Education (ACPE). In my interview with the ACPE's Certification Committee, it was noted that only in Ed Dobihal's first evaluation was there any mention of my disability. I think part of our process in that interview was my affirming and confirming with them that my disability was a reality, but not a hindrance to my becoming a full supervisor.

During my early years in the chaplaincy, I returned to Yale Divinity School, and in 1977 earned my Masters in Sacred Theology degree, my second advanced one from the seminary.

I served as a CPE supervisor until my retirement in 1997, providing training to clergy, seminary students and interested laity. Throughout that time I was employed by Yale New Haven Hospital, and worked not only there, but also at the Connecticut Mental Health Center, Yale Psychiatric Institute, and Gaylord Hospital, a rehabilitation facility where I supervised nearly 100 CPE students. Additionally, I supervised CPE students in the other settings.

My early interest in civil rights and racial justice issues expanded as I realized that at the same time as I was questioning the motivation of African American people who were not involved in the struggle for equal civil rights, I had to confess that as a person with a disability I was not engaged in the issues of disability rights. Once I did become an advocate, I went on to co-chair the Consultation on Church Union (COCU) Disability Task Force for several years. I also chaired our annual conference accessibility committee, and served as president of the Connecticut Coalition for Citizens with Disabilities. For the first ten years of my retirement, I was the part-time paid executive director of the Association for Physically Challenged Ministers of the United Methodist Church, the forerunner to the current United Methodist Association of Ministers with Disabilities (UMAMD). Most recently I have been President of the Connecticut Disability Advocacy Collaborative.

On a personal note, my first wife, Sammy, and I raised a son David and a daughter Karen, and after 25 years of marriage, we were divorced at her initiative in 1982. It was while I was serving on the board of the Connecticut Coalition of Citizens with Disabilities that I met Maggie who became my second wife; her interest in disability rights had been heightened by her employment in the Connecticut's Council on Developmental Disabilities. At the time of this writing, Maggie and I have been married for more than 25 years, and my family has expanded to include a son-in-law, daughter-in law, and five grandchildren.

I have learned in my later years that people still make assumptions about what I can or cannot do, rather than checking out the accuracy or inaccuracy of their suppositions. In a current situation, people who are meeting me for the first time see me without hands and assume that I cannot write, while in actuality I write very well!

Victoria Schlintz

Thorns and More than Sufficient Grace

By The Rev. Victoria Schlintz, R.N., M.A., M.Div.

A Thorn in the Flesh

Is there no balm in Gilead? Is there no physician there? Why then has the health of my poor people not been restored (Jeremiah 8:22, NRSV)?

...a thorn was given to me in the flesh... Three times I appealed to the Lord about this, that it would leave me, but he said to me, My grace is sufficient for you, for power is made perfect in weakness (2 Corinthians 12:7b-9a, NRSV).

If the blind see or the deaf hear, and if the lame walk or the mute speak, then there are evidences and witnesses to testify to miracles, awe and wonder over amazing grace at work. My testimony, however, is of God's grace in either the presence *or* absence of cures. I declare that God is good all of the time.

God's grace is more than sufficient; indeed, I claim it to be amazing and abundant. Let me share with you my testimony of grace in the midst of life's many trials, in my case having been diagnosed with a degenerative and fatal disease. I pray that my testimony will help you see the grace of God in the midst of any life-challenging experience through which you might go.

I have what the Apostle Paul would call a thorn in the flesh. We don't know what his thorn was. Countless explanations for Paul's thorn have been offered, ranging from temptation to opponents to speech impediment to limited eyesight to maladies such as migraines headaches, epilepsy, or malaria. I, however, do know that my thorn is Amyotrophic Lateral Sclerosis (ALS), or Lou Gehrig's Disease because he, as a former and celebrated New York Yankees baseball player, was the most famous person to have the illness. ALS is a degenerative neuromuscular disease that causes progressive demise to voluntary muscles until death comes when breathing muscles are terminally affected.

At the time of writing this chapter, I have lived for nine years with symptoms of a disease with a textbook life expectancy of two-to-five years, although I wouldn't put those textbook boundaries on God's grace; therefore, I'm living as though I have no tomorrows and as if I have every tomorrow. This attitude of "living with dying" is one of the many paradoxes in which I can live still more fully, all the while my life and ministry is being deeply enriched.

The Apostle Paul says that God reminded him by saying, "My grace is sufficient for every need." Paul knew that incredible, amazing, and outlandish grace in the midst of whatever difficulties he had to suffer, and I know it too. May you as a reader of this book likewise know and live in the midst of God's grace that is for everyone without exception.

I also know that you are no stranger to metaphorical thorns. We all have them because they are part of living. All of us have some kind of thorn, be it a disease, condition, malady, or another "issue" of some sort. Every treasure has thorns in the sense of the prickling aspect that we don't totally understand or know how to handle.

Life, we must say, has its thorns. Even Jesus in the Garden of Gethsemane prayed for the thorn to be taken from him, but then had to wear a crown of thorns up the hill to Calvary. Paul says he was traveling life's journey in awe and wonder, and then there came the unwelcome and life-hampering thorn.

The final diagnosis of my big thorn was made just six days before the bishop moved my pastoral appointment from Fairfield, California to Atwater, California. That event didn't seem like good timing. Of course, when is there ever a good time to hear that you have a terminal disease? During the same week of moving from my home of 20 years, my church, friends, and community resources, I discovered what I thought was merely a back problem causing a foot problem, turned out to be a disease with no known cause or cure—not even a hope for chemotherapy or radiation to treat the disease.

In many ways, however, I felt the grace of God defying what could be expected of this incurable disease. For instance, the doctor assured me that I would have at least a year as a pastor in Atwater; instead, I made it over halfway through my fourth year in that parish ministry, for which I praise God. Prior to ending my ministry there, however, I had to give up walking. I missed that activity, but not the tremendous energy consumed by the effort to walk, because of my muscle loss. Nevertheless, I saw God's grace at work to extend my full time ministry. This was made possible, in part, by a parishioner-carpenter who constructed a fine wheelchair-accessible pulpit and ramp. What a blessing that was!

For a long while I was experiencing the daily disabilities caused by my ALS condition. Showering and dressing are among the most difficult things I do. Despite the thorn, God has been faithful through it all with more than "sufficient grace." I have been able to serve and love God, finish the long United Methodist ordination process, and even maintain my Registered Nursing license. How's that for positive thinking?! I believe in miracles, and even though they may not come through healing my body, the Lord has already performed miracles in my life and the lives of others.

Four Gifts from ALS

My testimony is that all of life in Christ can be a witness to amazing grace. Let me share four specific gifts for which I praise God; for me, they are ways in which God has written grace on my soul that go beyond the ALS disease to impact the ministry to which I have been called.

PERSPECTIVE is the first gift of God that came through this disease. How easy it would be to go through life day by day with very little perspective so that we see narrowly through our momentary feelings, past experiences, or reactions to the insignificant matters of life. Living with dying, however, can make one's perspective less narrow, less tempo-rary, less self-centered – and possibly drawing us closer to God's perspective on life's matters. Clearly the phrase—"don't sweat the small stuff"—has new meaning. So what if something wasn't fair, or someone was rude, or a minor tragedy occurred? In the realistic light of my eventual dying, I can live more fully, because the "little things" have less power over me.

All of us can realize our mortality and renew our perspective. We can be aware of where there is pettiness and insignificant indignation. We can stop if we start in on something that "pushes our buttons," and pause long enough to say "it doesn't really matter, does it?" As the perspective changes, relationships can be blessed or restored, and the work of God through us can be kingdom-building. As we either transform or renew our perspective to be more like God's perspective, we become more loving, more forgiving, and more disciples for our Lord to use to transform, renew or heal—for ourselves and others.

So, "let go and let God" is one of the works of our Lord's more than "sufficient grace" in the midst of life's numerous trials.

VALUES CLARIFICATION has been the second gift that came through this disease. When the doctor gave me the inescapable diagnosis of my disease being ALS, she said, "Consider what you want to do with the rest of your life, because this is it." She added that it would be perfectly justifiable for me to go immediately on disability leave, and write my memoirs, or get my scrapbooks in order. I was blessed to be able to say I was doing what I need to be doing with the rest of my life; namely, sharing the gospel of Jesus Christ throughout all of my days. Furthermore, my husband graciously supports me in this ministry. My life has been about fulfilling that purpose, and I believe God has honored my commitment to continue in ministry for as long as possible.

Turning to you as a reader of this chapter, I ask what you are doing with the rest of your life. Do you also feel like the biblical Esther, alive in the "here and now" for such a challenging time as this? Are you making a difference for others and honoring God by doing what you are currently doing with your life? As we clarify our values, we may come to the realization that time itself is precious, and it should be used to bless us and others in honor of God. How we use our lifetime is important. What we choose to do is significant, because our choices can edify or distract, build up or tear down ourselves and others. It is always a good and right thing for each of us to examine our own lives, and ask how does what we say and do reflect our values within us—especially those values acclaimed by Christ.

A third gift received through this disease has been a clearer development of a **THEOLOGY OF SUFFERING**. I have preached sermons—even a sermon series having to do with a theology of suffering; however, for clarity's sake let me give you my four-word summary of such a theology: "**God didn't do it.**" An all too common, but questionable theology of suffering shows itself when someone—usually a nonbeliever—comes upon a crisis and blames God. "Why?" he or she asks, and then goes on to declare that there must not be a God because a good God wouldn't let this terrible event happen. There are also those who believe in a sovereignty-based theology, meaning a sovereign God's control of life includes punishing sinners by means of a disability-causing tragedy or disease; supposedly that traumatic threat will refine or get us in line with God's commands, thereby avoiding a Godly punishment. The Pharisees asked Jesus, "Who sinned, the blind man or his parents, that he has this affliction?" "Neither," Jesus responded and added that God could, however, be glorified through this loss of vision (John 9). I don't believe God did it. God is sovereign, but allows free will and natural law, so we can be in relationship with God and all of humankind. By means of our free will, we can bring on lifestyle-caused diseases because of choices we make as humans. Other free will decisions can result in suicides, homicides, abuse, and other consequences of evil deeds. Turning to the principle of natural law, we are provided with nature's incredible beauty, such as the ocean and sustaining life by water, yet we also have hurricanes, floods, wind, and rain that cause damage. We can also have tragedies brought on by airplane and automobile crashes. I was very young when I learned of the first natural law of physics informing us that two masses cannot occupy the same space at the same time; and if they try to do so, there will be a calamity. God *can* intervene, God *does* intervene, but normally God sees us *through* rather than *around* our trials.

God didn't do it. God didn't say, "I'll give you ALS to grow you." God doesn't need to do that; furthermore, I don't believe it was God's desire for me to have ALS, but God can work mightily in the midst of the disease. God, I maintain, can use the disease that is in my life, and do the same with other people in their lives.

85

Not everyone "gets" that insight, but the kids at our church "got it." One day there was a mix up about where the youth were to meet, resulting in eight kids sitting in my office. Five neighbor kids came by, and I asked if they wanted to join the youth group that night. As they waited in my office, a neighbor asked one of our kids, "Does your pastor have a broken leg?" She answered: "No, she has a disease." Astonished, the neighbor youth asked "Does God do that to pastors?" She responded, saying "God didn't do it to her, sometimes things happen, but God will help her deal with it." I thought the church's youth were handling it well, so I stayed quiet, gladly realizing how well they had listened to the theology of suffering and grace that comes about naturally in the course of our life together. After receiving the answer, one of the neighbor kids said, "Oh, I get it--like getting hurt on your bike, nobody makes it happen, but you still get hurt." They looked at me and asked if it hurt. "No," I said, "it just doesn't work." The oldest asked, "Is that grace that it doesn't hurt?" "Yes," I replied, "one of the many graces God gives you when you need it most." (As an aside comment, sometimes the grace isn't without pain, but in this case the ALS itself isn't painful.) Then the youngest youth pointed to the candy and asked, "Can we have one?" It was a matter of fact shift to a new subject since clarity was achieved.

The fourth gift with which ALS has reached the depths of my soul—and the lives of others—is a clearer understanding of **GOD'S GRACE AS MORE THAN SUFFICIENT**. Paul says the thorn in his flesh was never removed, but he soon realized God's grace was sufficient (*2 Corinthians 12:9a*).

Grace, mentioned 170 times in the Bible, is especially spoken of in two ways. One is God's unmerited favor of salvation. I've heard it described that justice is getting what we deserve, mercy is not getting what we deserve, and grace is getting what we don't deserve; namely, eternal life.

The other way grace is used in the Bible emphasizes God's freely given and unrestricted love that leads to fullness in the life of the believer. God's generosity or sufficiency of love for one and all enabled and empowered Paul in his weakness. I am weak in my suffering, you may be weak in your own trials, but God can use our acknowledged brokenness *or* blessings for God's glory to equip us and others for ordained or lay ministry. That reality—along with its possibilities—shows us our supportive need for one another; furthermore, we can use our sufferings to reveal God's sufficiently abundant grace for everyone.

I, unashamedly, ask you to pray for me, because I need it; but also because you need to pray; and I need to pray for you. We weren't made for isolation. We need God, and we need each other. Unquestionably, those who come alongside us are in themselves powerful gifts of grace in our midst.

At a community event at our church when I was still able to walk, one of our members introduced me to a neighbor, who looked down at my leg to see what was wrong. The parishioner said, "Our pastor has a disability, but we use our gifts so she can use hers," and then she offered her arm so that I could walk alongside her. A great act of grace is that we each use our gifts, so others can use theirs.

Even the children understood that essential maxim. For a Children's Sabbath, after rehearsal for the youth-led worship service I said, "Okay, I think every kid has a part and all parts are covered." A 7-year-old child raised her hand, asking, "Who gets to help the pastor walk?" She had seen the lay liturgist do that and thought it was an important role in our worship service; she was right, I had forgotten that important aspect. The child, fortunately, "got it" -- that the grace of God within us enables us to use our gifts so others can use theirs.

Additionally, God uses people to grant grace to others in lovely and unexpected ways as we commit ourselves to continue on the journey of discipleship for Jesus' sake. The California-Nevada Conference of the United Methodist Church clergy offered a blessing after I preached at annual conference in 2006, followed by a beautiful stole signed by hundreds of colleagues, and a certificate saying, "Victoria Schlintz is called by God and claimed as a colleague..." That unexpected tribute meant so much to me. Still more, in 2007, folks from throughout the conference helped with the conversion of a wheelchair vehicle, which enables me to continue in ministry. I am overwhelmed by the grace—pure grace— poured on me. God, we can say, uses you and me to bestow grace on others.

Such grace came from my congregation as well. One instance involved a child again, and left me with no wonder why Jesus calls us to be like children when it comes to being Christ's eager followers. After a confirmation class discussion on grace, the children and I went out for pizza. While the squirming kids waited for the pizza, one of them—from out of the blue—asked, "Pastor Victoria, is there a cure for your disease, or are you going to die?" The young people got quiet, awaiting my answer. I prayed quickly, and then began to talk about God's grace available for us in all that we might be going through, for me in this ALS disease, and for whatever else any of us might encounter in our lives.

The next day, I received a handmade card from a 12-year-old child that said on its cover, "The grace of God is always with you." Inside the card was this message: "Dear Pastor Victoria, Thank you for all the things you have taught me. Whenever I'm around you, I feel safe. Whenever I feel bad, you turn my frown into a smile. You have been an awesome pastor to me! I will never forget your beautiful smile and wonderful spirit. I know that you have a great gift, and I'm very happy for you sharing it with me, my family, and our congregation. You are awesome! I love you very much!"

Living with Dying

God's grace is more than sufficient. It is abundant and amazing. The Jewish Seder, celebrated by Jesus with his disciples in what we remember as the Last Supper, has a moving litany of blessing and thanksgiving. It lifts up God's gifts to the people, and goes like this:

"O Lord, our God... if you had [done nothing more than] delivered us from Egypt,

Dayenu, it would have been enough.

If you had given us [nothing more than] the Torah... the Sabbath... the Temple...

Dayenu, it would have been enough."

We can echo this prayer, by saying ""*Dayenu, it would have been enough."*

If you had given us nothing more than the Gospel of Jesus Christ

88

Dayenu, it would have been enough.

If you had allowed us nothing more than to be ministers for the sake of the Gospel

Dayenu, it would have been enough.

If you had given us nothing more than the privilege of blessed relationship

D*ayenu*, it would have been enough."

Indeed, God's grace is more than enough; it is abundant and amazing!

I Thessalonians 4:13 says we do not grieve as those who have no hope; our Christian faith confesses to this hope, and I am a witness to it as I live with dying. I've always been dying—I'm just more aware of it because of this disease called amyotrophic lateral sclerosis; and I'll always be living since that is the gift of eternal life. Would that we all live as though dying and die as those living eternally? The paradoxes of life are more real because I've been faced with a terminal disease. In living with dying, I can be more alive. As I die to this life, I come more alive to the next life. As I look beyond this life, I gain a perspective for living this life. As I lose my life, I gain it still more.

What I have written in this chapter is my testimony and the source of my great gratitude in the midst of the thorns of life. Will you say "thank you Jesus" with me? God is our creator, redeemer and sustainer, through the past, present, and all the future–in this life and the next, because Jesus Christ is our Lord and Savior, forever and ever.

God, I declare, is good. Not once or occasionally, but all of the time. I invite you to join me in this prayer of gratitude:

Precious Jesus, how grateful we are for the gift of yourself, which would have been enough, and yet you have blessed us with so many other gifts. Almighty God, you are grace sufficient, and that would have been enough, yet you are life abundant for now and eternity. May we always be moved to know, and live in, your outlandish love and amazing grace. In the name of the Lord of the Universe and Lord of our Lives, now and forever, Amen.

William Downing

From this Twisted Wreck
By Rev. Dr. William S. Downing

I contributed my chapter to this book because I believe that the Christian Church in general has laid aside the understanding of what it means to be truly one who has answered the call to the pastoral ministry of the faith. Moreover, my small contribution might help to strengthen the role of those individuals who faithfully answered the call to ministry, despite having to cope with a disability, and are capable of fully performing the duties of ministerial service in the church.

My ministry began in the year of 1973 with a five point charge that covered two counties on the Eastern Shore of Maryland. I preached five times each Sunday and was paid $6,000 per year. On top of that I went to college full time, and earned a Bachelor of Arts degree. I then was appointed to a four point charge, and entered Wesley Theological Seminary in Washington, D.C., and earned my Master of Divinity degree in 1980.

Over the next 23 years I fulfilled my call as a pulpit pastor with several different ministerial appointments on the Delmarva Peninsula Annual Conference that today is known as the Peninsula-Delaware Annual Conference. Along the way, I earned a Doctor of Ministry degree.

On February 10, 2003, my life—in general and as a pastor in particular—was abruptly and horrifically turned upside down. On that day at 7:30 in the morning, I was involved in an auto accident. I suffered a broken neck, and a broken back in two places. My ribs were broken on my right side, along with a crushed clavicle, a broken jaw, and several other facial bones. My heart and lungs were bruised, and severely injured were my right leg and hip.

As the United Methodist Book of Discipline has it, I was incapacitated, unable to continue as a pulpit pastor. Devastated as I was, I was convinced that my ministry had ended. That was because for me "disability" meant "inability" until Bishop Peggy A. Johnson showed me otherwise. At her suggestion, I attended a caucus for ministers with disabilities held in Dallas, Texas. Following are some insights garnered from the caucus that also served to free me from what I call my life's twisted wreck:

Thus, my assertion is that being disabled doesn't mean stopping or losing one's ability to be a minister; instead, the disabling condition can bring new ways of ministering to the church. Like the rising sun at the break of day, these new ways of ministry are rays of light into the church that might have otherwise remained in darkness. God has used disabilities as a means to increase God's church in strength. With Christ becoming disabled by the cross, he was able to usher in the enlightenment of God's Kingdom, where all people have purpose, a place where we all hope to arrive some day. So, it can be said that pastors and laity alike who have a temporary or permanent disability still have the ability to shine in the light of God's love for all people.

Dr. Bruce Birch, a Wesley Seminary retired dean, said at the Texas event, "Remember, if we live long enough, we will all suffer from some form or type of disability, even if only temporarily." We might have lost physical means but we have not lost our original purpose: To teach and preach the Gospel, and live out God's purpose for human redemption.

Recently I heard it said, "If you are willing to die for your country, you should also be willing to live for it." I believe this to be true to the service of the church by those who are called into its ministry. When the devastating accident occurred, I was on my way to the hospital to visit the sick members in my pastoral charge. It can be said that I almost died in doing the work of my calling to be a pastor. After that accident, I spent many years in a wheelchair; all that while, I was engaged in the hard work of learning to walk again, to speak with clarity, and to overcome twelve reconstruction surgeries.

I feel that it is my obligation to fulfill my calling as a pastor, despite my disabling condition. So why then is the church saying no? While I have no negative feelings about the decision of the cabinet for not returning me to active ministry, I am nevertheless praying that the church will soon realize that my efforts to recover from the injuries, my willingness to meet the educational requirements for us ministers, and my years of faithful service to God's call to the pastorate did not end because I now have some physical disabilities. Let it be thoroughly understood that I am willing to live within the call to ministry, and die—if need be—while fighting for the purpose that God calls us to serve.

After all, isn't that why God summoned us to be ministers in the first place?

Nancy Hale

The Healing of Acceptance
By Rev. Nancy Jill Hale, Th.D. Candidate

The Inescapable Truth

My day of reckoning came in the late fall of 2001. I was serving as a full-time local pastor at a rural two-point charge in upstate New York. One Sunday morning as usual, I was warming up with the choir before our worship service. I sang in the alto section, and for some reason, I was having a difficult time finding my notes. After the choir finished rehearsing, I walked over to the piano and played the alto part, but it still didn't sound right. So I tipped my head closer to the piano and slowly played a few notes in a scale. To my horror, all of them sounded exactly the same. I had lost the ability to discern the pitch of notes that were close together. There was no more denying it: my hearing loss had finally progressed to the point that even my powerful, behind-the-ear hearing aids were not enough to let me keep pretending that I had "normal" hearing.

I think denial is part and parcel of any experience with disability, but in the case of hearing loss, it is easier to pretend that you don't have a disability. Hearing loss is an invisible disabling condition; there's no wheelchair or cane or limp to give you away. In fact, if you are skilled enough in pretending, you can coast right along, fooling people into believing that you don't have any kind of disablement. The inescapable truth, however, is that pretending and living in denial only get you so far, and can cause a lot of grief along the way. That Sunday morning, sitting there in front of the piano, I knew that my days of pretending, along with being dishonest with myself and with others, had come to an end.

The fact is that I have had progressive hearing loss all my life, beginning with a very mild loss as a young child. As I got older, my hearing slowly worsened. But I spent many years – even after getting my first set of hearing aids at the age of 17 – blissfully denying that I had a problem. I learned to live in this kind of denial partly because of my mother's own experience; she also had progressive hearing loss, but spent most of her life feeling angry about it. She steadfastly refused to use hearing aids or any other form of assistance, including the help of well-meaning people. Because of my mother's example and lack of emotional support, I learned to feel ashamed of my hearing loss and to hide it whenever I could. I spent a good deal of time honing my acting skills so I could "fake it" in social situations by pretending I didn't have any trouble hearing.

Disability and the Divine Call

When I was 35 years old and an active lay person in my church, I felt a strong call into pastoral ministry. Although I was excited at first, I began to wonder how on earth I could possibly be a pastor with my hearing loss that by then was severe. To that point in my life, I functioned fairly well by avoiding social situations in which I wouldn't be able to hear. I could also avoid – to a point – people whose voices were hard for me to understand. I could insulate myself from challenging situations and live safely in that web of denial. But a pastor cannot simply choose to avoid certain people or situations! One of the most important tasks of pastoral ministry is that of listening deeply and caringly. How, I worried, could I ever listen the way a pastor should listen to the people in my congregation?

For a few weeks, I did a lot of praying and soul-searching. I talked to a few people, read every book on ministry that I could find, and even tried bargaining with God: if God "fixed" my hearing, I would declare my candidacy for ministry without any hesitation. But my hearing did not improve, and I did not follow my call. I continued my lay ministry, but put the whole idea of ordained pastoral ministry on the shelf.

Later that year, I attended the annual session of the New York Conference. It was my first experience as a lay member, and it was so exciting to see all the people in the conference who had followed God's call to become pastors from every walk of life. But, I said to myself, of course *they* can be pastors; after all, *they* have good hearing. I continued to ignore God's call by hiding behind my receding hearing. One evening during the conference session, the ministerial retirees were being honored, and I sat spellbound as I listened to these retiring pastors as they recounted the joys and the challenges of their years of ministry. Still, it was not enough to convince me that I too could be a pastor with such a severe hearing loss. That was the case until they called the name of the next retiree to be honored: the Rev. John A. Carr. When John walked up to the podium, all my fears, concerns, and ambivalence about my call to ordained ministry fell away in an instant. All my defenses against God's calling were stripped away because John, who had spent a lifetime in pastoral ministry, had been born with no hands. The message could not have been clearer: "If John can do it, so can you!"

I declared my candidacy the following week, and within a couple of months, I was certified and invited to begin my first appointment as a local pastor (in a three-point charge, no less!) in the former Wyoming Conference, now merged into the Upper New York Conference in upstate New York.

Hearing, But Not Understanding

Throughout my candidacy and in my interview for that initial pastoral appointment, I knew I had to be open with people about my hearing loss; open, I was, but I was less than honest in what I said. I told the District Superintendent and the church committee that I wore hearing aids, but I did not divulge the depth of my disability; nor was I honest about specific things that were difficult for me, such as carrying on a conversation in a crowded room or on the phone. I was so thrilled to be starting my vocation as a pastor, and I was convinced that with God's help, I somehow would be able to handle whatever challenges that I faced. But I was only fooling myself. I was *not* able to manage all the difficult situations that came up, and I fell back on my old habits of denying and pretending. At church dinners, where background noise made it almost impossible to carry on a conversation, I would nod my head, smile a lot, and pretend I heard what people were saying; however, this kind of pretending only works to a point, and more than once, I had to scramble to fix a mistake I made because of my inability to understand something someone had told me. I did not make an important hospital visit because I had misunderstood the date of a parishioner's surgery. I failed to respond appropriately to a family's crisis because I did not fully understand what the distraught mother was trying to tell me. And I eventually stopped answering the phone and let the answering machine pick up the call, because I simply couldn't understand what people were saying on the phone. (At least I could replay the machine as often as necessary to get the message.)

I was worried about the effect that my hearing loss – or my denial – was having on my ministry. But I was even more worried about being honest with anyone about the problems I was having, because I was afraid that I would be asked to leave the ministry. So I kept covering up as best I could, and somehow, I managed to squeak by in my ministry for three years.

Finding a New Path

But then came that day at the piano. One of my parishioners told me later that she saw the look of horror on my face when I realized I couldn't distinguish the notes of the scale. In that moment, all the false security I had built up around my hearing loss came crashing down, leaving me face-to-face with the harsh reality of my disability and the emptiness of my denial.

My husband took me to see an audiologist for my first hearing test in several years. (Like most people with hearing loss, I hate hearing tests with a passion!) I had hoped that the audiologist would say that she could fit me with stronger hearing aids so that I could get on with my life and ministry. Instead of granting me my wish, she said, "You need a cochlear implant." I felt as if she had punched me in the stomach. "*Deaf* people use cochlear implants," I thought, "and I'm not deaf!" But as she re-vealed the results of my test, she explained that with a loss as profound as mine, a cochlear implant was really the only solution. As the reality of my situation settled in, I felt devastated.

I went on incapacity leave so that I could focus on learning to hear with the implant. Hearing with a cochlear implant is an entirely different experience, because the sound is actually a digital signal sent directly into the auditory nerve via the cochlea. Some people can make this switch from "acoustic" to "digital" sound very quickly, and I naively assumed that I would be "up and running" soon after my surgery. But for some reason, I was one of the minority among the cochlear implant recipients who are not able to hear well at first. I could hear lots of sounds – more sounds than I had ever heard before! But I couldn't make out what the sounds were. I could hear people talking – even from the next room! I could not, however, understand a word of what they were saying. I spent six months training my brain to process those new digitalized sounds. It was an agonizing time. I started to think I would never be able to return to the ministry, and that I would have to find some kind of job for which being able to hear well was not a requirement.

Because I was afraid I would never be able to hear and communicate even as well as I had before the surgery, I reluctantly decided to take a course in American Sign Language at my local community college. After class one day, the instructor asked me if I knew about the school's Disability Services Office. I said I didn't, and she suggested I visit the office and see how they might be able to help me.

When I met with the Disability Services Coordinator, a new world opened up to me. I learned about all the different accommodations that were available to students, from note-takers to assistive listening systems to CART (real-time captioning). All of those aids were available for free as long as I was a registered student. Suddenly I realized that with this kind of help, I could return to school to complete my education. I had dropped out of college when I was 18 because with no available assistive technology, I simply couldn't hear the professors in those huge lecture halls. But now, with the help of an FM assistive listening system (ALS), I could hear the professors almost as well as could any other student in the room!

I put my ministry on hold and enrolled in the college full-time. I majored in English, figuring that even with my hearing loss I could find a job as a writer or an editor. But my call to ministry was still vying for my attention. So after graduating with a Bachelors of Arts degree, I applied to Boston University School of Theology (BUST), where I found the same welcoming accommodations. With the help of a wonderful CART reporter and supportive professors, I received my Master of Divinity degree (M.Div.). I was commissioned as a provisional elder in 2008 and ordained in 2010.

While I was in seminary, I read a book that changed my life: *The Disabled God*, by Nancy Eiesland. In her book, Dr. Eiesland describes disability in a way I had never before considered. The problem with disability, she writes, does not rest in the body of the person with a disabling condition. Instead, the problem with disability rests in the structures and attitudes of our society, which is unable or unwilling to provide the necessary accommodations for people living with physical or mental challenges so that they can enjoy the fullness of life that God desires for everyone.

From my reading of *The Disabled God*, I suddenly realized that I was fighting the wrong battle. It wasn't my hearing that needed to be "fixed;" rather, it was those barriers that are found in society – as well as in many individuals – that needed to be challenged and dismantled.

Not Cured, but Healed

My call to ministry immediately took on new meaning. My experience and struggle with disability gave me a wonderful vantage point from which to become an advocate for people in their respective disability issues, and to proclaim – and model – the kind of liberation and fullness of life that Jesus proclaimed. I have learned that although my hearing loss may never be cured, I have experienced healing and wholeness through accepting not just my disability, but also the help I need to remain connected to other people. I believe that such connections can be helpful for anyone coping with one or more disabilities. When we accept the incurable reality of a disabling condition, and make appropriate adjustments in attitudes and actions, then a truly whole life can be lived.

With this new view of myself, I started to study disability theology in earnest. At the time of this writing I am in a Doctoral program at BUST, and my dissertation topic will focus on how the experience of disability can and should affect our understanding of what it means to be the church.

In school, I have access to many kinds of accommodations for my hearing loss, and I experience the liberation and joy of being included and respected by the faculty, staff, and fellow students. In the church, however, it's a different story. The church has inadequate funds to provide the kinds of accommodations that I need, so pastoral ministry will always be a challenge for me.

I have come to understand that the problem with disability does not rest solely in my hearing loss, nor does it rest solely in the inability of society or the church to accommodate and include me. There is a fine balance, I believe, between recognizing the limitations set up by society and those limitations caused by my disability. Now that I have stopped the denial of hearing loss and the pretense of hearing well, I embrace my disability as an essential part of my being. I can face the fact that there are some things I will never be able to do, or to do well. Without the help of accommodations such as CART (real-time captioning in which spoken words are projected a screen), I will always be challenged by situations such as large crowds, talking on the phone, and participating in group discussions.

I am, however, fortunate to have always had strong support from my bishops, District Superintendents, and Board of Ordained Ministry. I like to believe that I have their support because I have learned to stop denying, to stop pretending, and to stop being defensive about my disability. All of that I can do, because I now understand that I am healed, although not cured. In addition, I am able to be open and honest about my needs, and most important, about my limitations. I am, however, aware that some people with disabilities are denied the kind of support and encouragement that I have enjoyed; let it also be said that such individuals too often face discrimination and marginalization, even within the church.

My ministry now includes advocacy for people living with disabilities. I want to help everyone to learn that disability is nothing of which to be ashamed. It is not an act of divine punishment, or a "cross to bear." It is not a sign of weakness, or unworthiness. I want all of us to realize that when Jesus described his mission as proclaiming "release of the captives," he was talking about anyone who is held as a prisoner by the attitudinal and physical barriers that exist in our society; those barriers heinously marginalize people because of who they are. I want the church to realize that it is called by its nature of being Christ's living body on earth to be on the side of people who are marginalized, and to work proactively to name, challenge, and tear down all of those societal and churchly barriers. I want the church to recognize that people with disabilities have gifts and graces for all kinds of ministries, be they the laity or clergy persons.

Moreover, I want people with disabilities to learn to be honest with themselves and with others. I want them to be forthright about their needs, and about their limitations. But what is more important for everyone is that I want the church to provide safe physical, emotional, and spiritual spaces in which people with disabilities can speak freely and honestly about their concerns, needs, and gifts. The church absolutely must foster an atmosphere of acceptance and mutual trust in which the specific situations of people with disabilities can be discussed in truthfulness and in love, without fear or embarrassment. Finally, I want all of us to have honest conversations in which we identify and distinguish the difference between the authentic obstacles caused by disabling conditions and the artificial and harmful obstacles generated by offensive theology or attitudes. When genuine barriers to ministry or full inclusion are identified—regardless of whether they are physical, psychological, or theological obstacles—we need to work together to find ways to remove them, or at the very least, enable people with disabilities to maneuver safely around them.

When Jesus stood up in the synagogue and unrolled the scroll, he announced how things are in the Kingdom of God: the poor receive good news, the captives are released, those who are blind see, and those who are oppressed go free (Luke 4:18.) Jesus was not talking about some eschatological hope of miraculous healing and release; instead, he was declaring the reality of life for those who choose to follow his way of earthly life. In the Kingdom, the deaf hear and the blind see not because they are "fixed," but because people are doing everything possible to include them in the human community. The church is called to proclaim and reveal this inclusive, not exclusive Kingdom in the way it relates and responds to the needs of people with disabilities and to the divine call to be one human family together with all people. Only then shall it be that everyone – despite not being cured – is healed.

Mitchell Galloway

Walking by Faith
By Mitchell M. Galloway M.Div.

It was a brilliant April morning in 1965 when I entered the ornate rotunda of Johns Hopkins Hospital in Baltimore Maryland. I paused in the middle of the grand domed lobby to look at the ten and a half foot tall, six-ton replica of Bertel Thorvaldsen's statue of Jesus intricately carved in Carrara marble. Ever since it was erected in 1896, "Christos Consolator" has been a source of inspiration, hope and consolation for countless patients, doctors, students and visitors of all faiths from around the world. At thirteen years of age my attention was drawn to the awesome size of the statue. I gave little notice to the words inscribed on the pedestal beneath the scarred feet: "Come unto me all ye that are weary and heavy laden, and I will give you rest."

In a few weeks I would pass by that statue again, only this time my eyes would be swollen shut and I would be wearing a green surgical cap that covered the incision made from the removal of a malignant brain tumor. Just a few days earlier the neurosurgeon took my hand and said, "Son, unless it is by a miracle, you'll never see again." Thus began my entrance into a new way of life.

Learning to Live with Complete Blindness

Growing up in South Central Pennsylvania, I enjoyed the love, support and encouragement of family, friends, and members of the Fifth Evangelical United Brethren Church. This loving encouragement enabled me to come to an understanding of my new way of life as being a person with a handicapping condition; but, let it be understood that I was not handicapped, meaning that I could live fully, undeterred by blindness. It was with this attitude that I returned to participating in Sunday school, youth fellowship, and the Boy Scouts of America. The assistance of my family and the support of our local school administration allowed me to accept the challenge of returning to public school long before main-streaming of bodily-challenged children became popular.

In 1967 this new philosophy of life enabled me to join my peers around a blazing campfire listening to a splashing mountain stream and enjoying the fragrance of towering pines along the Appalachian Trail. It was there that our summer church camp director invited us to give our lives to the Lord. As we filled the warm summer night air with the words of "Spirit of the Living God, fall afresh on me" I accepted that invitation and decided that I would pursue a calling to be a minister.

Upon returning home I announced my decision only to have it met with many discouraging words. "Blind people can't be ministers", many said. They supported their argument with such practical questions as, "how are you going to read the Bible," or "how are you going to do a funeral or a baptism?" Since I was still struggling to learn how to read Braille documents and books with my fingertips, and I didn't have the skills to live independently as a totally blind person, their arguments seemed reasonable. Consequently, I resigned myself to seeking a career as a rehabilitation teacher for blind people. It was with this goal in mind that I became a sociology student at Lebanon Valley College in Pennsyl-vania.

When my college days were coming to an end in 1974, I found my mailbox being filled with rejection letters from agencies that didn't need another rehabilitation teacher. My normally positive attitude was being greatly challenged until Easter morning when my pastor's wife suggested that I consider serving as the program director at our Conference's inner city camp. Knowing that part of the director's responsibility was driving the camp bus, I shrugged off her suggestion. But, I then thought if someone else would drive the bus, I could direct the camp. So, I submit-ted my application form, and I was hired.

The Call that Refused to Depart

Throughout the summer of 1974 I once again sensed that God's was calling me into the ministry. Friends, counselors, and acquaintances began asking, "Have you ever considered being a minister?" As the summer camping season came to an end, I was invited to serve as the director of youth and children's ministry in a local church. My work at the summer camp was enough to convince the staff parish relations committee that I was capable of handling the responsibilities of the job.

Part of my tasks included returning to the aforementioned camp as the program director in the summer of 1975. Throughout that summer, the prompting of the Holy Spirit, along with affirmations from family and friends, convinced me to pursue the call to ordained ministry; however, I responded to this call with some reluctance. Before I invested the time and financial resources in a seminary education, I felt I needed more experience in fulfilling the various tasks of full-time ministry. When the opportunity to serve as an assistant to the pastor in my home church became available, I accepted it. This position provided the opportunity for preaching, visitation, and administration. While serving in my home church, my abilities became known throughout our District and Annual Conference. Finally, in 1977, seven days after our wedding day, my bride and I headed for Dayton, Ohio to attend the United Theological Seminary.

Traveling 450 miles away from home, I found myself facing a new challenge; namely, I needed to prove not to myself, but to people I did not know that I was able to fulfill the responsibilities of ministry. Again, experience and familiarity served me well. Skills in referrals and counseling were gained through my twelve-month employment at the Dayton Ombudsman's office. Attendance at the Englewood United Methodist Church paved the way for me to accept the offer to serve that congregation as a student assistant minister. Throughout my seminary years, members of the Board of Ordained Ministry visited me from my Annual Conference. Their affirmation and encouragement supported my belief that I could and would receive an appointment to a local church following my seminary graduation. That belief was realized in 1980 when I was introduced as the pastor at St. Johns United Methodist Church in Chambersburg, Pennsylvania. It didn't take that congregation long to see that the skills I had acquired since my graduation from college had prepared me to serve as their pastor.

Since that initial pastoral appointment in 1980, I have served five very different churches in four pastoral appointments. Over the years there have been challenges and frustrations that made my work more difficult. In those early years of ministry, my biggest challenge was having access to printed material. This barrier began to fall in the mid 80's with the advent of computers equipped with accessibility technology. The demand for desktop publishing made possible the optical character recognition software that audibilize what is on the computer monitor that further reduced the inconvenience of actually reading printed material. The later development of digital media and the Internet communication have greatly increased accessibility to printed material such as references, commentaries, and denominational materials.

Practicing a ministry of presence with people is sometimes challenging when transportation is not available. Throughout my respective parishes', however, I have been blessed with a wife and members of each congregation who have the God-given gift of hospitality. These are the persons who don't mind accompanying me to emergency rooms, intensive care units, or sitting with me by the bedside of a dying parishioner. They are the people who truly understand the concept of the ministry of all believers. Additionally, cellular phones, e-mail services, and social networking now make it possible for me to be more in touch with parishioners even when I cannot be physically present with them.

An interesting challenge that I am becoming more aware of is communicating as a pastor who is blind in a world that is becoming more and more graphically-oriented; i.e., the world is no more graphic than it always has been, but humankind is using graphics more often for communication purposes. When I entered the ministry, the written and oral word was still the primary means of communication. In my thirteen years as a sighted person, church publications largely consisted of rows of print, occasionally illustrated with clipart drawings. In today's graphics-conscious populace I find that effective publications require the knowledge and use of a variety of fonts, consideration of spacing, and placement of photos that have been digitally scanned and reproduced in brilliant colors. Even oral presentations cannot escape the need for graphics. Today's communicators must have the creative skills to produce Power Point presentations with a limited number of words and a graphical background. In this age of visual media many of my colleagues illustrate their sermons with movie clips and visual images. Added to this challenge is the increasing use of video games and interactive material in

Christian education curriculum. The access technology I use to navigate through the Internet highway struggles to interpret graphical web elements such as flash movies, pages written in Java script and ticker tape boxes on the screen.

Healing Attitudinal Blindness

It has been my experience that congregations, much like individuals, go through a process of emotional and intellectual changes that culminates in the acceptance of a person with a disability. This process begins with awareness, moves to adjustment, and finally to acceptance. While these stages are not mutually exclusive, they each seem to have a particular emphasis; namely, "How is he/she going to …?" is the predominant question in the awareness stage. During this stage, congregants are interested in the tools and techniques that I use to perform the responsibilities of ministry. To satisfy the practical questions raised during this stage, I find that it is necessary for me to be open to sharing my lifestyle in recognition of the importance of educating the congregation about my blindness. As I help people to understand my abilities, my disability becomes less important and allows for movement into the adjustment stage.

The emphasis in this new stage shifts from asking the practical questions of "how" to the more theological questions of "why." As persons move into this stage they begin asking why a loving God would allow disabilities and/or suffering in the world. As they try to make sense of this reality they voice such thoughts as "this is the cross God has given you to bear," "this is God's plan for your life," and "God has a special purpose for you." Some people express the belief that there is a remedy for my blindness if "you had a little more faith", or by trying to answer the question the disciples asked as they stood before the blind man, "who sinned?" These classic responses to the "why" question are, in my opinion, inadequate for helping people move to the acceptance stage where they realize and appreciate the value of all of God's human creations with or without disabilities. This transformation is accomplished by helping persons or congregations to move from asking "why" to the more life-changing question of "what?" This, I believe is what Jesus accomplished in the thinking of the disciples when he informed them that the blind man's life, not his blindness, was intended to manifest the glory of God (John 9:1-12).

When the "how" and "why" questions are replaced with the more life directing question of "what," acceptance has become possible. For me, evidence of acceptance is realized when parishioners stop referring to me as their "blind pastor", but simply as their "pastor". It happens when they cease apologizing for saying such things as "look at this," "I'll see you later," or, when they enter my office at night and inform me that I forgot to turn on the lights. At this point I know that we can now focus together on using our unique abilities and disabilities in serving our Lord.

Serving the Lord without sight has resulted in a few embarrassing and humorous moments. More than once I've stepped out from behind the pulpit and later learned that I had inadvertently turn to the right or left and was speaking to a wall. There is one couple that will remember that at their wedding service I forgot to tell their guests to be seated when the bride arrived at the altar. The polite congregation remained standing through the 30-minute service. Likewise, I'm sure, that the gentleman who knelt at the altar rail at an Ash Wednesday service will not forget how I made the sign of the cross on the top of his baldhead. Then there was the evening when I rushed to the hospital after receiving the news that Mrs. Jones had died, and that her family was gathered around her bedside. Tears were flowing when I entered the room so I quietly whispered hello, took Mrs. Jone's hand and began to pray. It was when I was thanking God for her entry into life eternal that I felt my hand being squeezed. I realized then that the beeping to my left was the oxygen machine that was keeping her alive. That was a good lesson in checking the accuracy of information before making embarrassing assumptions.

I made a few hearts skip a beat or two when I served my first communion in a new parish. I was not aware that my predecessor served communion from behind the communion table. The candles were then placed at the front of the table. I realized that they had been moved when I bowed my head and felt the warmth of the flame on my upper lip and heard audible gasps from the congregation. I'm sure that I have caused a few smiles when I occasionally appear at church dressed in striped pants, a plaid shirt consisting of colors that don't match, and a boldly colored tie.

The joy, however, of serving the Lord, and the privilege of walking with others in their faith journey, far exceed the incidents of challenge, frustration and embarrassment.

Among the many words of wisdom written by Helen Keller, the deaf-blind American author and educator, are these: "It is for us to pray not for tasks equal to our powers, but for powers equal to our tasks, to go forward with a great desire forever beating at the door of our hearts as we travel toward our distant goal." The Holy Spirit working through people, experiences, and opportunities that God has blessed me with have been the source of the power that sustained my ultimate desire to make known the glory of a loving God; a God who intends for both the able bodied and disabled   people to have a life of hope, and a future which has been made possible through Jesus Christ.

Evelyn McDonald

What? And She's Disabled, Too?
By the Rev. Dr. Evelyn R McDonald, D.Min.

We Plan, God Laughs

There were many things I dreamt of doing in life; being an ordained minister was never one of them! My call to ministry took a long and convoluted path and if anyone had ever said this is what you are going to become, I would have asked them from what planet they had just arrived, because that was never going to happen on this earth. Over time I understood the saying; "We plan. God laughs," for I had many great ideas about what I would become in my life.

A career as an ordained ministry is my fourth one, so I am truly a late comer to this field. One of the reasons I never contemplated this path was that church became a place where I did not feel welcomed. As a small child of 18 months, I contracted polio in what was to be the last polio epidemic in the United States. The virus devastated my body; I was in an iron lung, not expected to live. In fact there was a day that my Dad—or 'Pop" as I called him—was to report to a National Guard camp when the doctors told him not to go because I would not be alive the next day. Unbeknownst to my parents, a story about me had been put out over the Associated Press (AP) wire into the news media teletype machines. (Of course, we can smile and say that in those days there were no computers.) I was said to be the smallest person ever to be inside an iron lung. God moved, and people around the world were praying for me; to everyone's surprise, on the following day I was still alive. Next the doctors said I would never walk again, and would always be an invalid.

Untrue! I walk with a long leg brace, swim, hike, ride a bicycle, and roller skate—there is very little that I cannot do, or have not attempted to do.

Whenever I wanted to do something, the only phrase I heard was, "Honey, we do not know if you can do this, but let's give it a try. Those words have been crucial for me in becoming who I am today; they gave me the courage to push forward when others said it was impossible, and they have allowed me to step into arenas that I would have never dreamt of engaging; that includes pastoral ministry. That one sentence of support told me that I could take risks or fail, but I was not alone because my parents were there to encourage me. While my physical abilities do cause some limitations, I am not limited by them.

A Hostile God and Church

From the story of my survival there came a deep belief in the power of prayer. As a young child, I felt that Jesus was my friend and protector, but I did not, nor did I want to understand God; God was scary, God was the one who allowed me to have polio. This negating belief came about when I was seven, sitting on a bench in the ornately beautiful train station in Omaha, Nebraska. Mom and I were going to Fort Benning, Georgia to spend Christmas with Pop. She went to get me an ice cream cone. While she was gone, an older woman came over to sit beside me. I remember her eyes; they were hazel and filled with pity. She took my hands and said, 'Oh, I am so sorry this has happened to you; either you or your parents have sinned, and if you will just pray hard enough for forgiveness, God will heal you."

It was several years before I told this disturbing story to my parents; because I knew they had not sinned; therefore, it must have been I who sinned. I am not exaggerating when I say that every night I begged God to let me wake up in the morning healed, but every morning I was just the same. I felt that God thought I was a horrible child, and to punish me had left me crippled. My church did not help to change that belief when I was not allowed to participate in the church camp with all of my friends. Why? The answer is that the camp directors were afraid to have someone there with a handicap. "It," they said, "had never before been done." They also said, "what if you got hurt?" It was from these two hurtful confrontations that a sense of exclusion and my not being good enough for both God and the church began to grow inside me. Eventually, I left organized religion, and vowed never to return.

Discovering and Employing Compassion

There always lay within me the compassionate desire to help others; I truly wanted to be of service. My first career was nursing which I entered because everyone said that I could not do it! Over the years I obtained the Bachelor of Science and Master of Science degrees in Nursing, worked in a major trauma center, taught neurosurgical nursing, directed intensive care and coronary care units, and was the director of education at Hillhaven Hospice of which, at that time, there were only three in the United States. I was successful in my career but my life was empty; little did I realize that God was attempting to tap me on the shoulder, and head me in another direction. Even if I did realize that, I would not have listened because I had my own ideas and goals; hence, it was clear to me that I was to be the youngest female hospital administrator in the country. We plan. God laughs.

Turns and Discoveries

While directing the Intensive Care and Coronary Care Units, I became very ill, and had to leave the nursing profession. That departure was the beginning of the second leg of my journey where I teamed up with three other individuals, and created The New Road Map Foundation. Our purpose was to be educational and charitable. The name implied that we had old road maps for living in today's world, and needed new ones. The four of us led seminars on defining how much is enough so that anyone could get out of debt, and begin living her or his best life. In addition, I did seminars on healing, and that led to my being the lead investigator for a major medical research project that was evaluating long-term versus short-term survivors among individuals with amyotrophic lateral sclerosis (also known as the Lou Gehrig's disease).

During that phase of my life I was living in Seattle, Washington, enjoying life, and feeling full of purpose and meaning in my career. There was no desire, not one single ounce, to do anything different than what I was doing. As I traveled around the city, periodically I would turn onto a street that had a church on it—named the University Temple United

Methodist church—with a sign board outside that read, "Early Christian Worship, breakfast 8:30, service 9:00 a.m." Without exception, every time I read that sign I felt a quiet urge to go try it out, stronger though was my mind which said, "you are not going into a church." My first reaction was to stop going down that street; so I did not have to encounter that disquieting whisper.

One day, as luck (truly God) would have it, there was no choice but to go down that street, and park next to the church in order to attend a meeting on the University of Washington campus. Those haunting words—Try It Out—literally screamed within me. My response was, "All right, all right—if that is you God, I will do it once, now leave me alone!"

It still took some time, but at last I kept my word and walked into that church and into the midst of strangers. Something happened, and I felt like I had come home. For the first time, I experienced being truly welcomed by a group of people who were not just meeting one another early in the morning, but were also committed to learning to live as did the Early Christians; that is, as a caring and sharing community. This experience rattled me to my core, but I kept going back, feeling like I was being drawn into something while I was still attempting to plant my feet securely, and stop this senseless momentum toward the church. The force of love embracing me, however, was too great, and within a few months I became a member. Family and friends were in stunned disbelief, some even felt betrayed by my action, but for me a new pathway opened in my heart. That move into the church was the beginning of my call to ordained ministry.

The Call

Over the succeeding two years, the Holy Spirit went to work within me, healing doubts and the sense of my not being good enough for God or the church. Slowly but surely, the notion of going to seminary emerged from my heart. As I talked with others for them it was a "no brainer," or "of course," each one said; even those persons who were, at one time, against my going back to the church were supportive. At one point, two experiences happened. The first one was a dream. I found myself inside a large old structure and I was going down the steps. On finally reaching the basement, I walked down a dark hallway with rooms on each side. Stepping into a room, I realized that it was a hospital emergency department, and I watched the team working on someone; going into the next room that was an intensive care unit, I saw a man on a ventilator, and then I was standing beside the bed of someone dying. In front of me was a staircase. I ascended, and found myself standing in front of an altar, with the stained glass window from the church of my childhood; it portrayed Jesus standing at the door and knocking. In reflecting on this dream, I felt that all the pieces of my life would be brought together in a professional ministry. Still reluctant though, I kept this dream to myself.

One communion Sunday, I went forward to receive the bread. Pastor Sharon placed it in my hand and repeated the same words as always, "Evy, this is the body of Christ broken for you." In the next moment I felt a wave of energy move from the tip of my head to the bottom of my feet. It was if every cell in my body vibrated with the words, "this is where I want you to be." Tears flowed out of me, I could hardly move and yet, I was still reluctant to say, "yes," to this call.

In a planned trip to Omaha, Nebraska, I decided to meet with Viola, an elderly woman who had the clearest connection to God than what I had ever experienced in anyone else. We went to lunch where she asked, "So, why do you think you have a call to ministry?" I was in the middle of relating the story when she stood up, slapped her hand on the table and said, "Well, girl, are you going to follow God or not?" "Yes," I answered. "Well, then do it," she replied. With that remark, she got up and left, looked back at me and said, "We're done. You know what you have to do."

Doing What I Had to Do

Somehow I found the courage to take the first steps in following God's call. Throughout my life, I collided with discrimination in school, from others who felt they knew what I could or could not do, and from the general prejudice that if you were physically disabled you were, also, mentally challenged. Even though I excelled academically, that did not squelch those first reactions. As I began to bring the message of God's hope of healing to others, I was stunned by some disturbing reactions. A church in Washington State asked me to supply their pulpit one Sunday.

It never occurred to me to tell them that I wore a leg brace. When I was met at the door, the woman was visibly shaken as she started to extend her hand, withdrew it, looked me up and down, said "come in," and then disappeared. Her reaction was not uncommon for people who had no experience of someone with a disability filling the role of minister; furthermore on top of that, I was a woman, thereby creating two distinctly first-time experiences for some churches. Most often, after delivering the message, there was a different attitude toward me because of God working through me to touch the hearts of those hearing the words. I became someone that they wanted to come back to their respective churches, instead of someone they hesitated to accept as a minister.

As I made applications to attend seminary, I reluctantly filled one out for Union Theological Seminary in New York City; that I did, but only because my senior pastor had graduated from it, and was encouraging me to apply. I never wanted to visit New York, let alone go to school and end up living there!! We plan. God laughs. As hard as I tried not to go to New York, it was clear that God wanted me there, and that was it. I made the trek from my beloved community in Seattle, Washington across the country to a place where I did not even know someone who knew someone whom I knew. Much to my surprise, as I stepped into my new room, I once again had the feeling of coming home. For me, that emotional surge was God's way of letting me know this was the right place.

Even here however, I ran into preconceived ideas about my abilities. When asked to read the Scripture for the opening convocation service, I accepted the request, even though I sensed it was given because of my belonging to a minority group. After this beautiful service one of the professors came up to me and said, "I did not know someone like you would be able to read so well." I was startled, even though I now know that the professor's words were meant as a compliment, and that he did not hear what those words could sound like to me. Once again there came the experience that to be accepted, to be seen as equal to other students, I could not just be an average scholar, I would have to do superior work in my studies. That did happen as I was graduated with honors.

During my time at Union Seminary, I was a student associate at a church that was composed mainly of Caribbean Black. As the only Caucasian on staff or as part of the congregation, I puzzled over how

116

warmly I was accepted. In my final week there, the director of music, the pastor and I went to lunch where I asked them about my experience. The director of music quickly replied, "Evy, don't you get it. We know that you know what prejudice is like." My eyes were opened in a new way, and I saw the presence of another gift derived from my disability, in that I can cross boundaries and build bridges where others cannot do so. Consequently, I thought for sure that a New York City church was where I would be appointed to serve as its pastor. We plan. God laughs.

Sent to the Country

My first parish appointment was to two churches; one was in a small village, and the other in the country. In both communities I was the first woman pastor to serve their respective United Methodist churches, and the first one to be living with a disability. My initial experience was mixed as people were initially challenged by this change in tradition. Even in the communities there was little acceptance of a woman in the pulpit. One time a parishioner introduced me to a friend as "Rev. McDonald," and even though I was wearing a ministerial outfit, the person looked at me, and asked, "What is it like to be a pastor's wife?" I replied, "I do not know; I am the pastor."

It is difficult to tease out which was the greater obstacle; that is, was it the fact that I was a woman in the pulpit, or that I had a disability. At one of the first community clergy gatherings that I attended, and after I responded to a question, another pastor spoke up and said, "We do not need to listen to her since she does not carry any authority." At another time, a member of one of the churches I served informed me of her reaction to my appointment: "when they told us we were getting a woman I thought, well, it had to happen sometime. Then they said you were just out of seminary, and I wondered why the Bishop would do that to us, and THEN they said you were disabled, and I thought what did we do to deserve the bottom of the barrel?" She went on to ask for forgiveness for those thoughts, because she realized they were so wrong. A gentleman said, "When they told us we were getting a female pastor, and that she was disabled, too, I wanted to leave, but my wife made me stay. Boy, I am glad that I listened to her."

Three months after my pastoral appointment, the September 11, 2001 (9-11) tragedy happened, and everyone's world was shaken. Some in my community lost family and friends; others worked in the attacked "Twin Towers," but for one reason or another they did not take the train to work on that horrific day. Immediately, my training as a trauma nurse kicked in and I took charge; I called all the other pastors to meet with me to create a worship service for that night, designed to go beyond our theological and denominational differences. The service took place in the larger of the two churches that I served. It was attended by over 500 people, and a profound sense of community emerged from the sharing of our grief and fear. Out of this horrendous experience seeds were planted that would grow into me being fully embraced as a pastor and as a member of two communities.

One of my major discoveries during those years was that to be a pastor with disabilities doing ministry is to be a cross-cultural appoint-ment, akin to being a "minority ethnic pastor" in an all-white church. This particular truth needs to be embraced and shared by every disabled pastor with every new congregation to which he or she is appointed. We are a minority group with a different culture than what is found within the able-bodied community. As a person with physical challenges, there were adaptations that needed to be made for me to administer effectively the sacraments. Other considerations were required, such as the height of the pulpit, and in the parsonage the placement of the washer and dryer, making sure the bathroom was safe for me, plus other relevant concerns. Mine is not an easy journey as a minister, but it is one that has been filled with miracles, along with a binding commitment to discover with my congregations how God is calling us to be in ministry with each other and in our respective communities.

Michael McKinney

Dancing With the Shadows:
Serving God in the Dim Light of Mental Illness
By: The Rev. Michael W. McKinney, Sr., BSBA

More Common Than You Would Think

Every day one out of every four Americans deals with a "faceless" illness. Their symptoms are, at their worst, life threatening and, at their best, life altering. Sometimes these illnesses are controllable, and can be kept hidden, because of the stigma associated with respective diseases. Consequently, those who suffer are forced to hide their symptoms, or blame them on something else more socially acceptable.

Most disabilities are clearly evident, and therefore are used—whether consciously or subconsciously—in defining the person. When you see someone with a white cane you assume that person is blind. When you see someone in a wheelchair, he or she is assumed to have a problem with mobility. Some people with developmental disabilities exhibit certain characteristics that are clearly evident to those around them.

Identifying the illness, however, is not an issue for the previously cited group of "one out of every four Americans". On the surface the majority of these people couldn't be identified as having any illness at all. Yet everything they do, everywhere they go, all of their day-to-day activities are impacted by their illness, and it can set the course for their day, week, year or even their lifetime.

Not Always Obvious

I am one of the four who have a "faceless" illness. I have Bipolar Disorder (BPI) and, like a friend, we usually get along, but sometimes we bicker, and don't get along very well. We fight and shove each other around, but in the end we make up, and return to our usual friendship.

Over the past three or four years, however, my BPI friend has started to win more and more of our battles. And when it gets control of my life, things can get a little out of hand. Now when I say get out of hand, I don't necessarily mean in a bad way. I just mean that BPI causes my life to run a little out of kilter, like a wheel that is slightly out of balance; a little wobbly, but still able to roll from one place to another. In other words, you might get where you are going, but the trip won't be what you are used to experiencing.

In 2008 I started forgetting things more than is normally expected. I tried every memory aid available, but aids won't work when you can't find them, forget to use them, or even how to use them. I also had occasion when words in my mind wouldn't come out of my mouth. If I waited a few seconds, or used other words, I could still get my point across. That memory problem created awkward situations, not to mention that it was a little embarrassing, and led to very frustrating consequences.

Everyone Is Vulnerable...

Whenever the brain, the organ that controls absolutely everything in the human body, is affected, either by an illness or an injury, the result can be abnormal behavior in a variety of disturbing ways. Unfortunately many of us have been indoctrinated to believe that any problem with the brain causes antisocial or maniacal behavior. Of course, that isn't the case at all; however, most people can't help but believe that a person suffering from a mental illness can't be trusted; therefore he or she must be monitored.

I spent the first 25 of my vocational years in manufacturing management. Since the objective for all manufacturing businesses was to get the produced parts out the door to make a profit, nothing else really mattered as long as that goal was met. I was working as a Human Resources Manager in a large silicone-rubber processing facility when I was diagnosed as having the bipolar disorder. Although I didn't publicly announce the diagnosis, I didn't keep it a secret, and it never had any impact on my job.

Bipolar Disorder affects every person in a different way. For me, it was mostly over-commitment, over planning and over-spending. I would make elaborate plans, but never carry them out. I would commit to doing things that I had no idea how to do, or to so many things that it wasn't possible to finish any of them completely or correctly. I would spend thousands of dollars on items that I thought I absolutely had to have, pay them off over time, while, at the same time, swearing that I would never do it again. Then I would do it again … and again … and again.

… Even Those Called By God

In 1996 I felt God's call into the ministry, and started out as a part-time Youth Leader at Rome City United Methodist church, a small church in the Indiana Conference that I had attended as a child. After three years in that part time ministry I was called to be the part time pastor of an American Baptist church. I served there until I was appointed to be the full-time Local Pastor at the previously named United Methodist church.

I have had many jobs over the years, but it wasn't that I had developed some grand plan that would ease me easily into retirement. I didn't discover until years later that this pattern of changing jobs was a symptom brought about by my mental illness. I was always able to get a good job, one that paid well, and came with authority and responsibility.

I was consistently overconfident in my abilities so that eventually I would be moved into a job that I was unable to do. Except for one incident, I could easily move up within a company until my incompetence became glaringly apparent. Interestingly, I had no idea at the time that I was carrying out a job-changing pattern, common to the bipolar disorder.

Every job has a honeymoon period; that period is when you are learning how to do the work, and mistakes can be blamed on lack of experience. I found that typically this honeymoon period lasted about two years. I call this my "two-year warning". If was as if I thought if I "sang and danced" well enough, then no one would notice that the room I was standing in was on fire. I failed nearly everywhere I worked, but I was never fired.

Serving as a full-time church pastor was an entirely new experience for me. My days consisted of meetings, dinners, hospital calls, nursing home and home visits. Throughout the year there were also the occasional emergencies, some typical and some rather bizarre. There were funerals, which I feel are the most important service that a minister can provide.

Evenings were also spoken for much of the time. In addition to the aforementioned duties, as a pastor you have to prepare for just about any situation, because when you are called upon in the middle of the night, thinking on your feet is often a challenge. Fortunately, after a few years, the experience I gained enabled me to manage difficult situations consistently.

My ministry was no different in gaining competency through experience. I think, quite typically, I had in my mind what I was to do, how I should act, and what the congregation expected of me. I was a strongly committed Christian, and was confident that God had given me that task. I wasn't aware that I was at the start of my "two-year warning", so I charged ahead.

Incognito

For me, the honeymoon period was a perfect time to get established, and begin to understand the people and the inner-workings of the church. It also gave me time to acclimate my disorder to my new environment. This is something everyone does when entering a new situation; however, for me it required that I establish what could be acceptable excuses for my various symptoms.

For instance, when I forgot a board meeting, I would say that I had an emergency visit. When I suddenly couldn't express myself during a sermon, I either said I had forgotten what I was going to say, or simply laughed it off and continued. When I was manic, people simply thought I was just weird.

Think about that last statement. In order to keep my diagnosis of mental illness hidden from my congregation, I had to accept the fact that they thought I was weird, or sometimes stupid. This was being dishonest, but given the situation, justifiable. While others brought their diagnosis of cancer, heart disease or physical disabilities to the congregation for prayer and support, I had to let people think that I was weird, stupid, or incompetent so they wouldn't learn of the real reason.

When a pastor's abilities can be questioned, they will be. When a weakness is exposed, some parishioners will try to hurt the pastor at that point of his or her vulnerability. If a pastor is known to suffer from mental illness, the congregation is likely to respond in a variety of ways. Regardless of the specific response, in the current environment within the United Methodist Church (UMC), the people will lose faith in the pastor's leadership, and his or her ministry will no longer be effective.

In my opinion—developed through my "coming out" in a number of different settings—the pastor will find that, out of the entire congregation:

- 10% will be honestly understanding, caring and supportive
- 20% will say they are understanding, caring and supportive, but are not
- 50% will stay at a distance, and question the pastor's advice
- 20% will lose all trust in the pastor's ability to function effectively

The sad consequence is that the ministry at the appointed church has come to an end. Due to no fault of the pastor, but entirely due to the stigma associated with mental illness, several people will no longer see him or her as dependable, reliable, honest, confidential or trustworthy. A number of these people wrongly think that a mentally ill pastor is dangerous.

Even when the ministry is successful, it won't matter once the congregation learns that its minister suffers from a mental illness. All of the inspirational sermons, heartfelt prayers and countless visits to hospitals and nursing homes will no longer matter. What I discovered is that the difference I have made in the lives of so many people made no difference in the church's assessment of me and my ministry.

My dilemma was the guilt that I imposed on me for not "coming out" with my illness. I felt like a coward. I knew that a person with mental illness could be successful, but I was too afraid to prove it. I could have been a positive example of a mentally ill person's functioning well in society and the church, but I never did reveal my faceless illness.

I feel that when God calls us to the ministry we are expected to have good judgment, while always being aware of the needs of the people, and how those needs can best be met. I felt that in the UMC I would be more effective by ministering to the people without revealing information that, at the time, had no effect on my performance.

This Illness Has a Face – Yours!

The problem I <u>have</u> faced throughout my ministry wasn't how the people treated me, but keeping my illness a secret. When I needed support, it wasn't there. When I needed prayer, I couldn't ask for it. When I was in the hospital, no one could know that fact. Actually, I needed to inform someone of my situation, but outside of my immediate family, there was no one to whom I could divulge my condition. That predicament was of my own making, but it left me all alone.

When I considered the large number of pastors within my United Methodist Conference, the aforementioned "1 out of 4" statistic told me that I couldn't be the only pastor that had mental-health issues. I began searching the internet for useful information, and found nothing relevant to my circumstance. I did find some articles on the church and mental illness as a social issue, and how to counsel those with this disorder; however, there was nothing at all about ministers who had to deal with the actuality of their own mental illness, both in and out of the pulpit. If you are a mentally ill pastor, you're pretty much on your own when it comes to finding help from colleagues or the general church. It turns out, however, that there are many pastors who face this same dilemma as did I.

At an Annual Conference session a few years ago, we were told that, according to the prescription drug company that our insurance provider used, around 60 percent of the pastors in the conference had been prescribed for antidepressants during the previous year. This means that after deducting an estimated number for those experiencing seasonal or situational depression, and those who are getting prescriptions for other family members, there are over 200 pastors in my conference who are experiencing mental illness symptoms that require psychiatric medication.

After over 10 years in my UMC conference, I am unaware of a single pastor in addition to me who falls into this category. The reason is simple: such pastors are afraid to reveal their mental illness, lest they lose the confidence of their parishioners. The UMC carries out its ministry and mission at the conference and district levels; but, with this faceless illness never being discussed, only supported, the conference is likely to be uninformed about the bipolar or other forms of mental illness. If the illness had been addressed by my Annual Conference in the past, there are no resultant guidelines currently in place to benefit those who want to get out from under the mental illness stigma.

Wearing My Own Face ... Finally

I applied for Incapacity Leave in August of 2010, and the Annual Conference has been right by my side throughout the entire process. The main problem exists at the local-church level , and is relational in nature; that is, the stigma is deeply ingrained in people's psyche, especially when the person with the illness is one to whom others look for leadership and guidance.

In this inhospitable environment, the pastor isn't able to participate openly in the same ministry he or she has created that calls for openness, caring, and dependence on each other. There is nowhere that this person can go to get the support that he or she works so hard to give to others; nevertheless, that exclusion doesn't have to be the case.

The church leadership, both at the conference and district level, needs to create an environment in which pastors who suffer from mental illness, in any form and level of severity, feel confident that they will get the same support offered for any other illness. My feeling is that the caring and support is presently available, but the affected pastors aren't aware that such care exists. Treating pastors affected by this illness with the respect it deserves will naturally make its way into the congregational level. Eliminating the ugly stigma associated with mental illness requires removing the unfounded fears and anxieties affecting too many people, and replacing those negative feelings with the true love of Jesus Christ.

Addressing this problem will further validate the United Methodist social principles, and go a long way toward removing the mental illness stigma that keeps many mentally ill persons from getting the care they deserve as children of God. Undertaking this challenge, and facing this problem proactively, will put the UMC in a leadership role, and will certainly result in other churches choosing to address mental illness compassionately.

During the last few years of my ministry my mental health began to decline. Also at this time the membership of the church that I was serving decreased, either due to the current UMC trend, or my loss of control as a pastor. One thing for certain was that a small, but powerful faction of the church noticed the issues I was facing took' advantage of the situation, and used it to undercut my ministry.

Whenever I stumbled due to my illness, those in that group would reprehensibly undermine what had taken years to build. We went toe-to-toe over a number of issues, but eventually I couldn't out-push their shove, and I was moved to another church. I never made it to the new pastoral appointment, because I was placed on Incapacity Leave. I loved ministering to God's people, but my declining mental health made it impossible to continue.

Mine is not an isolated incident by any means. It is understandable to relocate a pastor who is not competent, caring or knowledgeable of scripture. But using a person's disability against him or her, supposedly to further Christ's gospel, goes against all that Jesus stood for in his ministry and mission.

When the church follows the established United Methodist Social Principles for the "Rights of Persons with Disabilities", it will inevitably work toward removing the stigma of mental illness. The United Methodist Church has made great strides toward opening the pulpit to all who feel led by God into ministry. By making adjustments for the accessibility to the pulpit, more people are able to answer God's call.

Encouraging acceptability, understanding, and providing open dialogue will put away the stigma of mental illness, and rightly help to put a face on this faceless illness that is too often hidden from sight. When this compassionate move is applied, then_the church pulpit everywhere will be one step closer to being open to all whom God has called to ministry in the United Methodist Church.

Nancy Webb

By the Grace of God Alone
By Nancy Jarrell Webb, M. Div.

"My grace is sufficient for you, for power is made perfect in weakness." So, I will boast all the more gladly of my weaknesses, so that the power of Christ may dwell in me. Therefore I am content with weaknesses,…for the sake of Christ; for whenever I am weak, then I am strong" (2 Corinthians 12: 9-10).

Slowly Losing Sight

A vivid image is emblazoned in my mind. It's Sally with her big black umbrella saying "Look!" on page 2 of my first grade reader. Back in 1953, Sally, along with family members Dick, Jane, Puff, and Spot, became close friends of mine as I sat in the reading circle with the other girls and boys at Columbia School in Anderson, Indiana. I loved learning in school with the other children; however, as I progressed to the 2nd grade, I needed to move my desk closer to the blackboard to be able to read what the teacher had printed there for us to do. Although I had never been an athletic whiz, I began to notice by then that I was almost always the last one to be chosen for any of our playground teams. That was a hurtful discovery.

After that realization, there began a series of trips, first to my local ophthalmologist, and then to the big city of Indianapolis to a series of eye specialists. I can still feel the dread in the pit of my young stomach as the wand was moved over a piece of dark felt with the oft-repeated question, "Do you see it now? Do you see it now? Do you see it now?"

In the second grade I wore glasses, but by the third grade those glasses did very little good. By the time I was in the fifth grade, and definitely by the sixth grade, my mother was reading some of my lessons aloud to me. My eye problem, which had been diagnosed as macular degeneration by the Indianapolis specialist, was definitely getting worse. The font size and darkness of Sally's "Look!" had been much larger and darker than the print I now found in my junior high school books. By then, and throughout all four years of high school, my mother, Frances Jarrell Noland Webb, was reading all my lessons aloud to me. Before his untimely death, my father was drawing out the figures for my geometry class with large black markers, as we bent over the kitchen table with the pull-down light just above my work so I could see them. By the grace of God, alone, and with the love and care of my parents for their only child, I graduated as one of three valedictorians in my class at Anderson High School, class of 1965.

Hearing the Call

From birth on, I was nurtured in the life of the First Methodist Church in Anderson. I sang in all the choirs, from angels up through juniors to youth. Even though I could not see to read the music, I seemed to learn it easily, even as a gift from God. Each summer during high school, I attended the Epworth Forest Choir School to sing in the women's choir. The music drew me closer to God and reinforced my growing sense that I was being called to a full-time Christian vocation. It was at Epworth Forest, in the summer of my ninth grade year, that I felt God stirring within me and answered the call.

Back in 1962, in the North Indiana Conference, there were no clergywomen to serve as a role model for me. I had experienced a clear call that God wanted me to serve, but my imagination could not yet conceive any role for myself except being a missionary or a director of Christian education.

Subsequently, I chose the latter and applied to Illinois Wesleyan University in the fall of 1965. When the women of the church said to my mother, by that time a widow, that surely Nancy would apply to Anderson College in our home town and live at home, Mother wisely replied, "She will go to any college she wants to attend where she can get some finan-

130

cial aid." My loving parent knew that I needed to become independent at the same time that I was obtaining higher learning. A wise woman of faith my mother was!

After graduating in 1969 with a Bachelor of Arts degree in Christian Education, I returned to my hometown and taught religious education to fourth graders in the public schools in a program sponsored by the Anderson Council of Churches where, with a signed permission by their parents, children could walk to a church nearby for one hour per week of religious instruction. Even though this was useful and often satisfying, it was clear to me that this was not enough for my growing aspirations and needs. That call to local church ministry would not let me rest.

During the summer following that initial year in the ecumenical program for children, I felt called to visit two seminaries, namely one in Texas, Perkins School of Theology, and one in Washington, D.C., Wesley Theological Seminary. Wesley Seminary and the allure of our nation's capital won out, so that in the fall of 1970 I entered the school of my choosing and never looked back.

It expanded my horizons considerably. In addition to spending copious amounts of time getting good grades, I found that there was a whole wide world out there beyond the textbook about which I should care. I even might be called to explore Christian ethics and social justice along with Christian education and worship. There were three bold sisters in my class who'd entered with the intention of earning a master of divinity degree. Earning such a degree had never occurred to me. They were talking about things like inclusive language which had also never entered my mind. I knew that the word "mankind" included everyone so, "What was the big deal?" Needless to say, that is not where I am in my feminist journey at this point in my life.

After receiving my Master of Religious Education degree, I applied for the job of Director of Christian Education at Towson United Methodist Church in Towson, Maryland. It was a good experience for me, but my bolder soul sisters were being ordained and answering the call to parish ministry. In fact, one of the members of the congregation to which I was assigned, at age 54, had bravely determined to begin seminary. Her decision threw me into a crisis; through prayers and many sleepless nights, I reexamined my call and decided, with more experience and knowledge that I now had, the ordained ministry *was* my true calling. I resigned my Christian Education position at the end of July 1976 and returned to Wesley Seminary.

At Last a Minister, by the Grace of God

By the grace of God alone, I had always had reader services, both in person and some who read onto cassette tapes or over the telephone; I was fortunate enough to have this practice continue in seminary. More readers contributed to this process when I returned to complete the Master of Divinity (M.Div.) degree in 1977.

Then came the rub. According to the *Book of Discipline* at that time, I would have been eligible to attend the Board of Ordained Ministry examination retreat in the spring that I was to receive my M. Div. degree, a crucial step toward ordination. The bishop, however, was concerned that I would, if ordained, be eligible for guaranteed appointment until retirement, and possibly then become a burden to the system. Since I didn't drive, he believed that pastoral ministry could not be possible for me. Because of a directive from the bishop to the district superintendent, my first meeting with the district committee included only the chairperson and the district superintendent; no committee members were present. I was told that, even though I was completing my M. Div. degree that spring, and--according to the *Book of Discipline*—I was eligible to become an ordained deacon that year, I should "try being a lay pastor for a couple of years and see how it goes."

I returned to seminary with a strong sense of injustice having been inflicted on me. I spoke to a professor who was a member of the Board of Ordained Ministry who spoke to its chairperson who spoke to the bishop and reminded him that, as bishop, his duty was to appoint, not to examine candidates for ordination. The district superintendent then called a full meeting of the District Committee on Ordained Ministry, at which all members were present. By the grace of God alone, I was passed through the district committee on to the conference examination retreat and ordained deacon in June, 1977.

My first pastoral appointment was as "minister at large" to 22 mostly small three point charges in Jefferson County, West

Virginia. I served as associate pastor to nine pastors of the station, two point and three point charges. Throughout my ministry I have been blessed to have volunteer readers from the congregations who read to me the materials to prepare for sermons and liturgy as well as junk mail. They help with computer projects and occasionally give me rides when my mobility and taxi access services are not sufficient. With transportation being provided by people from my appointed congregations, I was able to preach in all 22 parishes as requested and did other kinds of pastoral ministry: hospital calls, weddings, funerals, as needed by the other pastors.

At the time of this writing, I'm in my 34th year of ordained ministry, having served as pastor in charge of two point and station churches and as associate pastor on the staff of a church in Washington, D. C. and at Grace United Methodist Church in Baltimore.

All this is by the grace of God alone for "Whenever I am weak, then I am strong" (2 Corinthians 12: 10).

Tom Hudspeth

God Doesn't Call Half of You...God Calls ALL of You

By The Rev. Thomas H. Hudspeth, D.Min.

It was Tuesday after Memorial Day, 1990 and the last day for the Texas Annual Conference held in Houston, Texas. "TOM, IT'S NICE TO MEET YOU!" My about-to-be senior pastor spoke loudly and exaggeratedly to me to the point of catching the glances of those passing by. That last day of annual conference was our first meeting with each other. I was to be the associate pastor of the church that he served, and it was my first ever pastoral appointment. Tapping finger tips to finger tips, the senior pastor continued in a raised voice, "AH, TOM...TELL ME ABOUT YOURSELF!" More words poured out but I had stopped listening to him. I sensed that he was uneasy with me, and from the exorbitantly elevated decibels emanating from his voice, I quickly surmised that someone had warned him that I was a hard of hearing person.

Sitting in oversized chairs in a quiet alcove of a downtown Houston hotel, I shifted forward, suppressing irritation with his patronizing voice. "It's okay", I replied in an inflected tone of reassurance, "I can hear you fine. You can speak normally to me." I went on to explain that in reading lips, it is important that people speak normally and that I see their face. When people exaggerate their mouth movements it makes it even more difficult to understand their words. Adding in jest, I was not trained to read lips that move all over a person's face.

"Introducing My Deaf Ears"

I suspect that what my shouting senior pastor saw of me was my deaf ears. I was born hard of hearing. My mother's concerns made the first diagnosis that led to wearing my initial hearing aids at 18 months of age. For my left ear, the audiology chart shows a wide gulf between what little I hear and that line of sound where conversations are discerned.

To be precise, my left ear has a 90 decibel loss, a severe to profound absence of hearing, far beyond the capacity of any hearing aid to lift to the conversational range of 20 decibels. In my right ear, I have a 40 decibel loss, a more manageable decibel gap for a hearing aid to bridge and to discern words. Years of speech therapy would give my mouth and tongue the muscle memory to produce "s", "th", and "z" – those super high frequency sounds that elude the range of even the most powerful hearing aids to grasp with clarity.

Mainstreamed as I was in hearing schools, I experienced the odd looks, the taunting finger, and the teasing labels from my hearing classmates. To hide my behind-the-ear hearing aid, I wore my hair longer than did most boys of my age. When I was in the third or fourth grade, I was with my parents as we stood at the colonnaded entrance to the Brooklyn Museum when a load of Deaf children left their yellow bus to file up the wide steps to the museum. I instinctively hid behind my father's back, so as not to be seen "as one of them" as they passed by in their clumsy-looking hearing aids and signing hands. Most often in those earlier days, it was adults who fed my self-esteem, as they would remark with a declaration of surprise, "Tom, you speak so well! I didn't know you were deaf!!" So it was that I began to sense that there was value in being a hearing person, but never as a deaf person.

Yet in that Houston encounter, and on the eve of going to my first pastoral appointment in the United Methodist Church, I received a reaction that had cut across the grain of all of my growing up years in the church. As a son of a United Methodist minister who later became a pastoral counselor, and in the course of writing this chapter I scrolled through the stories and memories of my father's local church appointments, and our family memberships in those churches. Here is what I recalled:

I was baptized at 3 months of age at the Hoyt Methodist Church in Kansas; at age 6, watching my father start St. Andrew Methodist Church in Florissant, Missouri; at age 10, singing *"We Are Climbing Jacob's Ladder"* at Park Slope United Methodist Church in Brooklyn, New York; attending Sunday School at Lebanon UMC, New Jersey; confirming my faith in Christ at Riverside Drive UMC, Macon, Georgia; completing an Eagle Scout project at University UMC, Peoria, Illinois; and lastly at St. Luke UMC, Kilgore, Texas, declaring my candidacy to ordained ministry.

"Not What I Could Not Do, But What I Could Do"

In reviewing all of those memories, I must say that I could not recall a more visceral nervous reaction to my deafness than that exuded by this senior pastor. Until that day in May of 1990, never had anyone in the church spoken to me in a tone and body language that exhibited such discomfort over my presence. For the first time, a representative of the church in which I had matured, demonstrated uneasiness with the deaf part of me. In that Houston hotel - two blocks from the church where I had been ordained a deacon the previous year, I felt the first inkling that my deafness might be a hindrance, or even a preemption of my ministry.

I suppose that from the perspective of my soon-to-be senior pastor, and his being a nearly 40-year veteran in the ministry, I was a disconcerting unknown to him. After all, I had to complete one more year before graduating from seminary, and there I was, a 28 year old man with no pastoral experience, and with (gasp!) a hearing loss. Seeing the teeth behind his lips, I was struck by how worn they appeared, perhaps from years of gritting through pastoral conflicts and divisions within the congregation. My guts flashed a protesting thought; namely, *"I'll prove myself to him… I'll show him…he won't see [only] my deafness."* So began my first pastoral appointment with a suspicion of what I could not do, rather than what I could do.

For the next three years that were served under that senior pastor I worked hard to prove my abilities. In my first month, I saw a woman take her last breath, and prayed with the grieving husband and daughter. I worked with parents and ministers of other churches in that small county seat East Texas town, crossing barriers of racial prejudice and denominationalism. I drove the youth on a retreat to San Marcos, Texas, learning

137

that more effective ministry seemed to happen through play and down time along within prepared devotionals. I ministered to an emotionally tormented homeless man, whose brother's name I later rubbed from the engraved black granite Vietnam Memorial wall in Washington, D.C.

Working for three years under this intellectually grizzled senior pastor, whose faulty preconceptions of me were akin to a thrown gauntlet, did paradoxically usher in a wealth of pastoral confidence in me. When the man asked me to preach on the last Sunday before his retirement, I felt not only honored, but also that I had passed his test. There was, however, still another test greater than that of passing as a hearing pastor in a hearing church; namely, the test of fulfilling God's call as a hard of hearing person.

"God, Give Me Something That I Can Be Good At"

Four years before that Houston interview, I had prayed, "Oh, God give me something I can be good at." That plea came while I was recovering from flunking out of law school. When the answer became "ordained ministry"—divined in part through a Presbyterian minister in New Zealand and a letter from my father—I enrolled in the fall of 1987 at the Perkins School of Theology, located in Dallas, Texas. While approaching the end of my second year of seminary, my prayer then became, "God, what kind of minister do you want me to be?" The answer came through the hands of Calvin, a Deaf man in Oklahoma who had looked at my hearing aid and signed "You belong with us."

Oh, let me *walk backwards*. In American Sign Language (ASL), the previous sentence is a common conversational sign in Deaf-talk when a person suddenly finds him or herself ahead of the story that's being signed, and will then pause to sign "*walk backwards*," and then adds contextual information to fill in the gaps created in the rush to tell the story. Thusly, allow me to turn back here to include the left out information.

While in seminary, I did feel that I was in the right place, more so than I had anywhere else. I felt that I was at last lining up with God's call to ministry– or, at least, almost doing so. At Perkins seminary students were required to take an internship in their third year. I had a disquieting thought that I needed to take a non-traditional internship. Being traditional would mean going to a large church, and serving as an associate pastor. There was an available internship in Oil Trough, Arkansas so named by early 19th century pioneers who rendered bear fat into oil that was collected in a trough. The thought of going there certainly felt non-traditional, but my spirit was still searching for a fit, a niche that could answer the question of what kind of minister was God calling me to be.

In February of 1989, I had discovered that a seminarian was already interning under Rev. Andy Hall for the Oklahoma Conference Ministry with the Deaf. The internship was split between serving as a youth director at Rev. Hall's pastoral appointment at St. John's United Methodist Church in Oklahoma City, and ministering among small groups for Deaf people that were set up around the state. Intrigued, I accepted an invitation to attend a state-wide April rally for the Deaf at St. John's UMC. On that weekend after Easter, I drove north on I-35 for three and half hours from Dallas to Oklahoma City. This was to be a look-and-see event for me, to discern whether being with Deaf people would somehow draw me nearer to the answer to my "it's halfway-to-ordination-and-I'm-getting-anxious" question: "God what kind of minister do you want me to be?"

Arriving at the red-bricked church with windows barred for security purposes, I parked my car, and then walked into the fellowship hall. Knowing neither the American Sign Language, nor how to interact with Deaf people, I felt somewhat intimidated by the situation. Rev. Hall, along with a sign language interpreter, introduced me to a few Deaf people. It was then that I learned that when meeting Deaf people it's important to introduce yourself as either hearing or Deaf. In my situation, I am neither hearing nor Deaf, but hard of hearing. Through an interpreter, I explained that I wore a hearing aid and that I had learned to read lips and how to speak. A large, bearded man in overalls then looked at me and signed something to me. Looking to Andy Hall for a translation, he chuckled, "He said you belong to us." When I asked why, the answer was "because you have a hearing aid."

I was stunned. In less than 15 minutes of stepping into a Deaf-world event, I was told "you belong." At age 27, and having spent years of striving to feel normal in a hearing world through speech therapy, wearing awkward looking hearing aids, and hiding my hearing loss, I'm told by a Deaf stranger, "you belong."

"Claiming the Deaf Part of Me"

During the concluding worship service, I sat in the back pew of St. John's rounded arched sanctuary. Several empty pews lay between me and the full front pews. I gazed at the backs of mostly gray and white heads. Although I was hard of hearing, yet considered Deaf by the Deaf man, I still wondered about the different paths that those Deaf people and I had traveled in terms of education and experiences.

When the Deaf people stood and signed a song in silence and unison, my eyes were drawn to one man's face. Able to see just the profile of his turned face, my eyes traced his lined cheek, and steady eye gaze. The fingers of his right hand touched the upturned palm of his left hand, and raising his right hand up and away – tracing half of an arch - wiggling his fingers. My mind drifted back to Central Institute for the Deaf, reviving dormant memories of children signing in the hallways. Empathy—along with a haunting sense of guilt—dwelled within me, as I thought of these older Deaf adults as being part of a community that I had shunned throughout my life. Once again, I caught the half-arched, one hand-wiggling-fingers sign. I did not know the meaning of the sign as it was being repeated with steady, graceful deliberateness. Tears began to flow from my eyes. What I would learn later, the sign that affected me so, was "Glory."

On the southbound return to Dallas that Sunday afternoon, tears flowed again as I said "Yes, God, yes, I'll go". I was, however, answering a new question. For God had replaced my question of "What kind of minister do you want me to be?" with "Tom, will you serve my Deaf people, and learn their language?" A few months later, I would be returning northward to embark upon an internship that changed my life, giving me a language of signs, and a community for whom God has great love, as declared in Leviticus, "Curse not the deaf" (19:14a). The Deaf community of Oklahoma gave me my sign name as the sign "T" over the heart, patiently taught me their signs, and suffer my clumsy attempts to express the good news of Christ in their ASL language. Near the end of my internship, I received a cedar wood "Jesus" plaque from Calvin, the man who told me that I belonged with the Deaf people.

The Church is Not Just an Ear

It took three more church appointments, including a stationing with the Methodist Church of New Zealand, before God would provide a way for me to establish a Deaf ministry in a welcoming United Methodist Church. There are fewer Deaf United Methodist churches today than there were in my internship days. Within five years after my internship in Oklahoma, its annual conference stopped funding the Deaf ministry.

Nevertheless, the need for a ministry that is with, for and of the Deaf is still locally and globally present. Figures cited by other denominations and the subcommittee on Deaf ministries of the National Council of Churches have consistently estimated a range from 92 to 98 percent of the Deaf are un-churched world-wide. Why there is such a high rate can be attributed to the Deaf community's unfortunate perception that church is solely for hearing people. Nearly every deaf person I've met has a story of a hearing church person misguidedly trying to cure him or her. Such experiences create distrust and the erroneous belief among Deaf people that God has made them defective individuals who are nothing more than a mere object for hearing people's pity. Yet, within the Deaf community in the United States there is a competing vision and self-perception that is theologically oriented; it is expressed in these words: "I hope that you all will cherish and defend this beautiful language [of signs] as the noblest gift that God has given us [Deaf people]."[10]

In 2011, I marked ten years of Deaf ministry at Lovers Lane UMC in Dallas, Texas. Thinking back on that April weekend of 1989, I have come to realize that when God called me to ordained ministry, God didn't just want my hearing side. God wanted the deaf part of me too. Since that grace-filled moment with Calvin, God has sent me to preach, teach and baptize Deaf people in Ecuador, Mexico, Honduras, Kenya, Korea and parts of the USA. In learning American Sign Language, my preaching to hearing people was enhanced as I learned to express concepts visually

---

[10] George Veditz, "*On the Preservation of Sign Language*", 1911.

rather than in abstract words. Through God's world-wide Deaf community and language, I celebrate all of God's gifts in my ministry that benefit not just Deaf people, but all of God's people in Christ's Holy Church.

A Post Script: Accepting Disabilities Can Bring Blessings

In July 2011, I was introduced to Rev. Russell Ewell, from Florissant, Missouri, who is blind. He shared a story from another town in Missouri where a church lay leader told a father and husband of a disabled daughter and disabled wife that they were not welcome to church because "they would scare the children." The problem was that this father and husband was also the pastor of that church!

I asked Russell, "You're from Florissant?" Receiving a "yes," I continued, "You should tell that church leader that if not for my deafness, my parents would not have moved to St. Louis where I could attend Central Institute for the Deaf. Given the choice of serving an existing church or starting a new church, my father chose the latter option, and started St. Andrew Methodist Church in Florissant." Nowadays, St. Andrew has a reputation as a vibrant, multi-racial church. Thinking aloud with Russell, I asked, "If God used a four year-old deaf child in planting St. Andrew, might there be more vibrant United Methodist Churches if they would respond with favor, rather than in fear when meeting children or adults with disabilities of various kinds?"

Helen Betenbaugh

My Journey to Holy Orders
By The Rev. Dr. Helen R. Betenbaugh

The Call, Onset of Disability, and Changing Call

As I recall, I was no older than 6 or 7 when I became aware that Church for me was Home. It was always a place set apart—in a special way, a holy way—that I couldn't begin to understand or describe at that tender age. I wouldn't call it a vocation that led me in those earlier days to be quite certain that when I grew up I wanted to preside at the "regi-cashiter" at the A&P during the week, and at our church's pipe organ on Sundays. Growing up in Burlington, North Carolina until my Father was transferred back to New Jersey when I was in junior high school, I was an energetic and committed youngster in the First Presbyterian Church: choir, youth group, Presbyterian youth leader, and more. A wise churchman in town had provided funds for an annual hymn playing contest for young piano students, and so I learned to play hymns almost from the start of my lessons. (Let it be known that the great accomplishment I celebrated was not so much winning a medal and cash each year for excellence, but mastering the waltz-like "fancy" left-hand part to "Follow the Gleam." I shudder now over the memory.)

My high school orchestra teacher happened to be the organist of our New Jersey church, so that in my junior year I fulfilled my heart's desire to start studying organ. He soon had me playing preludes and postludes, substituting for him, and then in the spring of my senior year, serving a small Lutheran parish in a nearby town when its organist took maternity leave.

Having long since forsaken the opportunity to "play" the wonderful check-out instrument at the local A&P, I earned a Bachelor of Music degree at Westminster Choir College in Princeton, New Jersey, where I sustained a spinal fracture from a fall on ice after returning from a concert we had performed at Carnegie Hall with the New York Philharmonic. Princeton, home of many of the country's great geniuses, was nevertheless where the hospital staff was depleted due to hangovers from a Christmas party the night before, simultaneously made worse by the results of an ice storm which shut down the entire region. Thus, it was a student who took x-rays that showed no bone at all! Sometime later those x-rays were cited in the *Journal* of the American Medical Association to demonstrate malpractice. After the student's x-rays were taken, the hospital's Chief of Staff told me they showed no fracture (how could they, with no bone visible!?) and sent me on my way to begin a life of disability and excruciating pain.

In my Junior and Senior years at the Choir College, my field work was as Director of Music and Organist for a Revolutionary War-era church about 50 miles from campus. Later I earned a Master of Music degree from the Peabody Conservatory in Baltimore, Maryland while serving as co-Minister of Music with my then-husband for a suburban church; beginning my studies after a year in which I also taught various church music courses as a sabbatical replacement at the Philadelphia College of Bible. When my husband and I respectively finished our Master of Music degrees, we moved to a large Methodist Church in El Dorado, Arkansas. After a number of years there, I somehow began to study seminary catalogs, and was surprised to find myself more and more excited about the course offerings; however, for a decade or more, my response was "Not now. You have a graduate degree and your children must get their educations first. But study, prepare, get ready...." Subsequently, I read the works of Scott Peck and Parker Palmer, whose *The Promise of Paradox* affirmed, explained and blessed a life that seemed to unfold in a steady stream of paradoxes. I also became a devoted student of Julian of Norwich, the first woman to be published in the English language. Throughout her book, *Revelations of Divine Love*, she wrote, "All shall be well. All shall be well. All manner of thing shall be well."[1] Twenty years of reflecting on her experience of near-fatal illness and disability led her to conclude that "Love was our Lord's meaning."

In 1975 the family and I moved to an even larger parish in Lincoln, Nebraska, where the effects of the misdiagnosed and mistreated spinal fracture that had sent me to doctors all over the south grew steadily worse. Finally, in January 1977, after a day of climbing up and down many flights of stairs for group and solo rehearsals, a wedding, and my final practice session for the next morning's services, I found that I could not get out of the choir loft without help. It was 10:30 on a Saturday night. Fortunately, a choir member who had chaired the church's search committee that called my husband and me to its music ministry lived two doors away and had keys to the church. That night was the last time I ever drove a car without hand controls, and it was to be the last time for 6 and a half years that I drove at all.

Suffice it to say that doctors of all kinds, along with physical therapists, consumed a significant portion of my days for the next several years. Included during those years were a spinal fusion in Lincoln, a trip to the Mayo Clinic, and an experimental procedure at the University of Minnesota Hospital. All of the medical specialists concurred that "something else was going on" besides the damage from the 1961 injury. It would be 1996 before the catch-all "non-specific motor neuron disease" was finally named definitively as post-polio syndrome and fibromyalgia.

During all of that time, the issue of my potential vocation as a clergyperson kept percolating deeply within me, but was often ignored even though women had just begun to be ordained in the Episcopal Church. Contrary to the national shift was the fact that I lived in a diocese where the bishop would not ordain women. Consequently, I explored the permanent diaconate with my parish priest, but at that point in my life moving out-of-state to a diocese with an unprejudiced bishop was not an

---

[1] Julian used the singular "thing" in this phrase throughout the book.

option. I also held firmly to my insistence that the time for a career change could not be right until my girls had achieved their respective college degrees. Furthermore, I resisted because of my profound belief in the validity of my call and others' to lay ministry—whether professional or volunteer—not being able to find language to describe my new feelings of changing vocation without sounding hierarchical. My feeling that I needed to go "deeper" or "farther" by pursuing the priesthood felt at that point like a betrayal of both my entire lay ministry and my colleagues. Furthermore, I had experienced far too much of the rich, the big donors, gaining power and control in various parishes large enough to hire a team of church musicians. That meant that these folk —behind closed doors, or over dinner and drinks with the senior pastor at the local country club—made most of the significant decisions about everything from the church's buildings to its budget, outreach and various ministries. I couldn't believe that God wanted me to be "one of them!"

The biggest stumbling block, however, was my own feelings about my disability. God deserves our best, biblically our "first fruits." The body I could present to a bishop and a Commission on Ministry was anything but ideal. Like Jacob, I wrestled with that issue for a long time. Finally, I know not how, there came the realization that I lived an Easter faith in a Good Friday body. Little did I know that Martin Marty, a renowned Lutheran church historian and author, would one day summarize my story using that quote, and that it would be preached all over the country by folks who used his newsletter for sermon ideas.

Five years after the spinal fusion and my needing a wheelchair for mobility, we moved to southeast Texas to a parish which called my husband as its first ever full-time minister of music. I took a job as Administrative Assistant to the Dean of the College of Business at a university in the area, and soon found the Pilot Club and Sears naming me Handicapped Professional Woman of the Year, with the city's mayor designating the occasion as Helen Betenbaugh Day. That was a welcome antidote to the pain of the ending of our 22-year marriage so that my ex-husband could marry a woman in the choir. What astounded me, what I never would have believed, is that my daughters' education was not the reason why I was so certain that my call was to prepare for ordination, but "not yet." Instead, I recognized that the delay was very clearly about not going forward while I was still in that marriage.

146

The divorce freed me from hours of *pro bono* duties in my husband's parish so that I could take a part-time paying position at a nearby Episcopal Church. I was finally worshiping "at home," and at the same time earning a modest second income to help meet the needs of two teenagers. Freed at last and without hesitation, I made my call to the priesthood known to the Rector (senior pastor) during our initial interview, and so we began meeting regularly in discernment in addition to staff meetings. Finally, there came the morning when, before the worship service began, I said to him, "That itch is just too big to scratch anymore." With tears in his eyes, he nodded with understanding.

Immediately I signed up to take Graduate Record Exams (GREs) for seminary applications while the rector contacted the Diocese to get the requisite paperwork for me. Even though he was effusive in his support of my call to ordained ministry, he was cautioned, "Don't put that in the pipeline. We don't like having things put in that can't come out the other end." He passed that awful message on to me right away, saying that I should know what I was up against, but that he was certain that when it was a person instead of an anonymous issue in front of them, all would be well. To go forward in the ordination process, one must secure the recommendation of one's priest and of the parish's Vestry (Administrative Board). It turned out that I was the first person to come forth for Holy Orders in the 132-year history of that parish, and there were several on the Vestry who were adamant opponents of women's ordination. The Holy Spirit was at work, because one of the most vocal of the naysayers ended up being the one who made the eventual motion that they vote to send me forward.

Confronted by Bigotry

I set off for my first interview with the suffragan (assistant) bishop to whom I had submitted not just the required forms and references, but speeches, published articles, and more. Although he was the one who had made the "pipeline" comment, it became clear that he was won over. He sent me on to what they called pre-interviewers; namely, two clergy members of the Commission on Ministry. Each would interview me one-on-one at length in order to make their own evaluations and reports to the full Commission. As it turned out, both of them were enthusiastic about my call to ministry, with one of them telling me that he had never before read such a letter of support from that Suffragan, and the other suggesting that I would be happiest at the seminary he'd attended. My GRE scores came back so high that they left me astounded. I had taken the exams in the morning after being up all night typing case studies for business students to earn the money for my elder daughter to fly to Dallas for her violin lessons. Furthermore, I had not been a student for 20 years. All seemed to be proceeding with ease and speed.

What came next was my meeting with the full Commission on Ministry. One woman in particular asked more questions than I thought appropriate about my medical condition, the wheelchair, and more, often interrupting others to keep the focus on my disability. Another commission member insisted on focusing on my divorce. I grew more and more frustrated that we were discussing everything except my priestly vocation. Since I did not have a spouse with me, the Chairperson invited my Rector to sit in on the meeting if he wished. After several hours, we were dismissed and headed on the 75 miles toward home and food. He was delighted with my performance. "All you need to be a bishop," he said, "is a purple shirt and a golf cart. You've already got the cart."

I, however, was very uneasy about the interview. With all of the furor over sexuality in our Church and in most denominations, there had not been a single question about it. "They didn't want to know who I am," I told my rector. Perhaps worse, I was certain they never saw me as a sexual being, as a whole person. I was certain the answer to my application to become a Postulant for Holy Orders would be "No."

Only time would tell, and so the rector and I held our opposite views of the day and waited. His call came to my office about a month later. His mail had come; mine would be waiting at home. I was right: "No" was the answer. No explanation was offered. My "true calling," we heard later, was the music ministry in which I had been engaged for 27 years and for which I was nationally known. My Rector seemed even more upset than I, perhaps because I, although devastated by the decision, had expected it. His advice was that we do absolutely nothing for at least 48 hours to let the shock sink in. He then made a number of "under the stole" phone calls to clergy members of the Commission. All of them told him the same thing. Instead of voting on my application, the group had called in the bishop. Apparently, like Caesar at the Coliseum condemning Christians to the lions, he had literally turned thumbs-down after I was

148

described, saying "She's unemployable. Where would I send that? Who would want that?" Although a number of the members still voted for me, most followed the bishop's wishes. Had I "passed" that day, my folder would next have gone to the bishop's desk. That bishop, I was later told by a different bishop suffragan, wanted to be shielded from having made the decision because he was paranoid about lawsuits.

I made appointments to talk one-on-one again with the Houston priests who had been my pre- interviewers. I also sought the respective counsels of the Dean of the Cathedral, the Director of Chaplains at the Episcopal Hospital at the famed Texas Medical Center, and others among the senior priests in the Diocese. All of their answers can be summed up in three directives: (1) You're clearly called, so you need to get on with it; (2) There's no appeal process here, there's no such thing as a loyal opposition, so start looking elsewhere; and, (3) Don't waste time so that your age also becomes an issue.

Prejudice against Women and Disability

My Lincoln, Nebraska priest and I had corresponded ever since the move to Texas. He asked if I would permit him to present my file to the Vestry there, asking them to vote on the basis of their experience of me gained before we had moved to Texas. My paperwork could then be submitted to the Nebraska bishop in hopes that he would make me a Postulant. After seminary, he could ordain me for service in another diocese or could transfer me to the bishop of the diocese in which I resided, ready for ordination. The Lincoln vestry voted unanimously in support of my going forward. On Good Friday I got a call from the priest that the bishop's response was another negative one. Although he was retiring, if he made me a Postulant,[2] he would feel that he was handing a *fait accompli* over to whomever would be elected to succeed him. He

---

[2] Postulancy is the first step in the ordination process and permits one to attend seminary. Near the conclusion of one's studies, one is made a Candidate and is thusly permitted to take the written General Ordination Exams and appear for final interviews before the Commission on Ministry and the Standing Committee.

intended to pray fervently, he said, that the next bishop would likewise not ordain women.

In the interim, I had contacted our seminaries around the country, most of whom were curt in telling me that they accepted no one for the Master of Divinity (M.Div.) degree who was not a postulant. Furthermore, their facilities were not at all accessible. I was, however, granted an interview (or so he told me) by the dean of the seminary in Austin, Texas. He said that I would be considered with other applicants who, through no fault of their own, had been deemed "not called to Holy Orders" by their respective dioceses. In those days that statement predominantly meant that the rejected aspirants were females in dioceses whose bishops were opposed to women's ordination. My priest dampened my enthusiasm considerably when he told me to be only very guardedly optimistic because the dean was, in perhaps the most picturesque description I've have ever heard, "Slicker than warm snot on a freshly polished brass rail."

When I arrived on campus for the interview, the dean and every member of the admissions committee were off-site for a meeting with the trustees, despite the fact that he had told me that my interview would be more intense and more far-reaching than normal so that they could ascertain whether or not they might be successful in helping me find a supportive bishop for ordination while I was a student. A highly embarrassed secretary scrambled to find three faculty members to put together to conduct an interview. It ended with one of the members pounding his fist on the table in front of him, saying "This woman is clearly called. The problem is ours, not hers. We need to do what is needed to give her access and get the hell out of her way." I left feeling slightly more optimistic.

I waited and waited, and then waited some more. Two months later I received a letter from the dean saying that the committee had "declined to act." I should, he said, pursue postulancy in another diocese and re-apply once I had attained that level in the process. Was that the true answer? No. In fact, the committee had voted unanimously and enthusiastically for my admission, and at least one of its members had looked for me throughout the opening days of the fall semester. Austin is in the Diocese of Texas, under the authority of the same bishop who had already turned his thumbs down on me in front of the Commission on

Ministry. The seminary, therefore, and its dean, himself a priest, were both on his "turf."

All along I had insisted that I would attend a denominational seminary despite the presence of Brite Divinity School at Texas Christian University in Fort Worth and Perkins School of Theology at Southern Methodist University (SMU) in Dallas. I'd been to Perkins/SMU for church music conferences over the years, and had worked with students who either headed there for seminary or for a graduate degree in church music. My rector was equally insistent that I belonged in either of those two schools because of their academic standings. Grudgingly, I sent off postcards requesting the schools' catalogs and admissions materials.

In the meantime, I was due to take my new van to Houston for its 3-month checkup. The van itself was the gift of anonymous donors, all arranged by the priest for whom I was working as organist-choirmaster. The Texas Rehabilitation Commission paid for the conversion of the van, adding a lift, hand controls, and reduced-effort steering and braking, which they will do once in the lifetime of a disabled person for a vehicle the person owns. I made arrangements to have the checkup on the same day as the Presiding Bishop (the PB), The Rt. Rev. Edmond Browning, would be preaching for the evening service at the annual convention of the diocese. As my older daughter and I left the enormous George Y. Brown Convention Center arena where the service was held, there stood the PB himself with only a handful of people around him. By the time we drew near, just two fur-coated dowagers remained. I started to go on by them. "Mom!" exclaimed my daughter. "Aren't you going to speak to him?" It was more of a demand than a question. I heard it as a challenge. I waited as the PB ended those conversations and then looked toward me. I greeted him, shook his hand, and said that I hoped to be ordained some-day. "Have you," he said, "spoken to my brother over there?" Wow! I had no intention of being a "tattletale" or being confrontational. Either I muttered my reply, or else he couldn't believe his ears, because he said "What!?" and then leaned down to hear me clearly as I repeated my statement: "I went through the process here and he said I was unemploy-able," all the while nodding my head across the long hallway to where the local bishop was standing with his wife and some friends, waiting for the PB.

"You listen to me," the PB said, taking my right hand between both of his. "My son was turned down for Holy Orders. He's now in his senior year in seminary, and I will ordain him in June. You keep on keeping on." I told him that I was astounded that the son of the PB would ever be turned down. "That's why I told you," he said.

During a whirlwind week including a job interview at a major national bank, admissions interviews at both Brite and Perkins, and hunting for a rental home, I took a significant step forward. Visiting a liturgy class at the Perkins School of Theology (the topic was funerals, no less!), and participating in an exciting worship service made my choice of that seminary a simple one. All went smoothly until near the end of the first semester at Perkins when I decided it was time to pay a visit to the local bishop. I was certain that by then he had heard that there was an Episcopal student running around campus in a wheelchair saying that she was preparing for ordination. I wanted to assure him that I was not trying to be defiant or to cause him any problems. I was simply following a powerful call to ministry in faithful response to God. When I had been a resident in the diocese for the required period of time and had the approval of both my new rector and the vestry, I would come forth in the designated steps in the ordination process.

More slick talk ensued. Even though he hated to criticize a brother bishop, he said that he felt his colleague in the Diocese of Texas had been "short-sighted." He assured me that neither my disability nor my divorce would ever be an issue in the Diocese of Dallas. Further, he recommended that I see one of the clergy at the parish where I now had my membership and have him or her submit documentation for the adjudication of my divorce. Adjudication is a process by which a counseling priest who is familiar with at least the major details of the marital history states that the applicant was not involved in an affair, and not the person who otherwise "broke faith" with the marriage vows. "That way," he said, "your divorce can never be an issue when you go through process here."

With that done and safely on file, I continued with my full-time course load, a 32-hour per week job, more than 30 hours of commuting, a home, laundry, and two teenagers. Thus, I was stunned when a few months later I received a letter from the Bishop telling me to proceed posthaste in seeking ordination in another denomination. I was shocked, sick all over again, heartbroken, and for the 99th time, I wondered aloud what Book it was that these men who were *pastor pastorum* were reading, and how it was that I, reading the same Book, heard totally different things in it. Although Episcopal protocol required that my Rector receive a copy of such a letter, he was dismayed and angered not only over what my letter said, but also over his not receiving notice of any sort. Perhaps the greatest comfort I received from the supportive clergy of my almost-new parish was from the woman who had been the third female ordained priest in the Diocese of Dallas and had preached on the Sunday of my first visit to that congregation. She started to walk away after comforting me, only to turn back and look me square in the eyes. "Just you remember," she said, "the fat lady hasn't sung yet."

Letters, meetings, phone calls, all sorts of things continued over the next months as my rector insisted that the bishop must forget that he'd ever sent me the "go elsewhere letter." Once again there came the word "unemployable." It seems that this time my "true vocation" was conveniently defined as Director of Christian Education. The pattern became clear: whatever the ministry in which I was currently engaged would be proclaimed as my "real calling."

Did the "Lady" Ever Sing?

At the end of September 1990 the National Cathedral in Washington, D.C. was to be consecrated. After spending 3 months in the Cathedral's music department on a mini-sabbatical in the-mid 1970s, I had vowed that if the Consecration ever took place in my lifetime before I was *non compos mentis*, I would somehow be there. It was a glorious three days of concerts and services. On Saturday, after the setting of the final finial atop the last tower in an outdoor service which included President George H.W. Bush and First Lady Barbara, I once again found myself in close proximity to the Presiding Bishop. Again he was nearby with only a few folks left speaking with him. I waited, and then started to re-introduce myself. There was no need to do so, as he remembered me.

"Well?" he asked.
"I'm at Perkins, my studies are incredible, and I'm Director of Christian Education at The Church of the Transfiguration in Dallas," I replied.
"And ordination?" he added.

153

"Still 'No,'" I replied.

The bishop in Dallas also said I was unemployable."

The presiding bishop sputtered, thought for a few seconds, and then reached for pen and paper only to realize that he was vested in layers of liturgical garb. Frustrated, he asked if I would write to him to remind him to take on the task of finding a bishop and diocese for me.

Would I?!?!?!

So it was that we began a correspondence whereby he would tell me to which bishops he'd written, followed by their replies. Sometimes he included their letters to him; other times he simply repeated whatever excuse they had given him, ranging from geography not conducive to a wheelchair to a long line of aspirants already waiting for postulancy.

The subsequent illness of the Dallas bishop put the matter locally on hold for months. That was followed by his brief return to work, and then came the announcement that he was taking early medical retirement. The entire ordination process was shut down for everyone. It took a couple of years to carry out the search for candidates, the interviews, and the election of a new bishop. With no bishop in office, the moratorium on ordination process continued. Finally, when the newly elected bishop from California was in Dallas to look for housing, he happened to visit a mid-week noon Holy Communion service for us Episcopalians who worked downtown. I decided to be bold and introduce myself to him as he moved among the twenty or so of us worshipers prior to the service. I shook his hand, announced that I was an aspirant for Holy Orders, and also a student at Perkins. He could see my gray hair and my wheelchair, so I figured that my divorce was the only negative issue not immediately obvious. He greeted me, made a point of coming to me during the passing of the peace, and then came to me again after the service to clarify who I was. Thanksgiving Square is a wonderful downtown Dallas facility, a small park-like area that's conducive to finding peace, calm, centering, and identity during a hectic work week. The chapel is on top of a tower-like structure in the center of the park, and a ramp snakes around the tower in spiral fashion with high concrete walls on either side; at least the walls seemed high to me, riding as I was in a wheelchair. As I left that service, I had the most profound sense that those walls represented the biblical waters that Moses had parted in the deliverance of the enslaved Israelites, and that this bishop-elect whom I had just met would part the waters that barred me from access to ordination.

I met with the Presiding bishop one last time. It was in the lobby of the Meyerson Symphony Center, about an hour prior to the service in which he would consecrate our new bishop. He asked about progress and all I could report was that I was about to graduate from seminary with honors. Frustrated, he said, "I can't think of anything more I can do. Do you know of anything?" I'm not sure which one of us was more startled by what came out of my mouth in reply, but my next words were, "As you ordain him, whisper in his ear, 'Ordain Helen.'"

For a moment he was taken aback, needing to process such a bold statement. And then he said he would do just that, talking with him quietly if it were calm enough backstage, or finding a later time and place if necessary. Some weeks later, after a national gathering of all the bishops, I received a note from the PB telling me that he had spoken with the new bishop and was keeping me in his prayers.

After his consecration, our new bishop felt that the process in the diocese was so abusive that it needed to be totally restructured, and so it remained closed. Finally, in the summer of 1994, I made an appointment to see him to seek his support and possible financial assistance so that I could begin studying for the Doctor of Ministry degree. It was clear from the first words out of my mouth that I was not there to pester him about the delayed ordination process, but there on an entirely different matter. He was very supportive, and did pledge assistance with my tuition each semester. And then he said, "Now I want to talk to you about process. It is finished, the notebooks are being printed right now, and as soon as they are finished they will be sent to each parish. You should receive a letter in the next few weeks. The deadline for submission of the required paperwork is mid-September." Four-and-a-half years after it was closed, the ordination process was being reopened. Just like that, almost 15 years of discernment, prayer and frustration, tears and jubilation, were ending. Or so I hoped it would be, "From my lips to God's ear."

Ten of us whose folders had languished in the offices of the diocese during all that time were offered the chance to enter the process before it was opened to the whole diocese. In late October seven of us spent hours in intense interviews on our academic abilities, our vision of ministry, family histories and life stories, our spirituality and spiritual disciplines. I was interviewed by a priest and a lay person at each step. Several in both orders, I knew, were vehemently opposed to the ordination of women. What, I wondered, could come of this when all seven of us were women?

My follow-up interview with the bishop was to be on October 28th 1994, a Friday. My rector and the priest who had reminded me again and again that "The fat lady hasn't sung yet" accompanied me. We hoped that I would not be sent away for a year of Anglican studies, and that my time of supervised ministry in the parish could be shortened. There was already a record of my two years under the supervision of a priest and an active lay committee that met regularly, critiquing everything from my Christian Education work to my preaching.

Far more than that happened. After a few minutes of pleasantries during which the pounding of my heart could surely be heard across the room, the bishop suddenly announced that I was a Postulant. Done. Period. No qualifications. All three of us were stunned. All I could think of was getting out of there and asking both of the accompanying priests what had happened. It turned out that they were just as anxious to ask me the same question! One last hurdle remained; namely, the national written General Ordination Examinations. They were infamous, and I had dreaded them long before I made my vocation known to my Nebraska parish priest. They covered everything from Bible to pastoral care, liturgy to church history, and more. Further, the tests were not divided into days by subject area. Instead, most of the questions directed the respondent to include 2-4 specific areas in each essay. The deadline for registrations for the 1994-95 exams, held right at the turn of the New Year, was the next day. The overnight packet and the registration check for my exams sat on the bishop's desk, ready to go, if I wanted to take them immediately. I gulped. I looked at my colleagues for the answer. Silence greeted me. I gulped again. "I'll be bold and take them right away," I said, to the bishop's great pleasure. Despite my fears, it turned out that I did so well that I soon became part of the national team of folks who read, discussed, and graded the exams for all Dioceses. The bishop gave me one final gift: "You should know that the Commission voted 100 per cent in favor of your postulancy," he said. "There was not a single negative comment." He certainly didn't owe me that information, but it settled on my soul like a balm after all of the years of wounds for being female and disabled.

156

Stunned, excited and elated, the three of us headed for a celebratory lunch. The letter which I received from the bishop a few days later confirmed that on the Eve of All Saints Day, commonly known as Halloween, 1994, I became a postulant for holy orders in the Diocese of Dallas.

And so it was that on the 29th of June 1996 I was ordained transitional deacon with two other women, and was ordained Priest on the 17th of June 1997. Flush right in tiny print at the bottom of the final page of the ordination bulletin were the Latin words *Obesa cantavit*. The fat lady has sung.

Eric Pridmore

Seeing the Light: My Journey of Ministry with Disability
By J. Eric Pridmore, Ph.D.

Retinitis Pigmentosa Diagnosis

In 1985, I was diagnosed with retinitis pigmentosa (RP), an un-common eye disease affecting about 1 in 4000 people in the United States. Although I was only fourteen years old, and too young to fully grasp the life-changing significance of this diagnosis, I was inescapably devastated by the news. Retinitis pigmentosa is a genetic eye disease that causes degeneration of the retina, starting from its periphery and eventually engulfing the entire retina. The retinal degeneration is usually quite slow, occurring over years from adolescence into adulthood; nevertheless, the disease is progressive and almost always leads to significant blindness in adulthood. I could not know at such a young age how profoundly this disease would affect my life. Neither could I imagine how God could and would use me as a person with a disability to shine the light of God into the dark places of this world.

Born in 1971, I grew up in Columbus, Mississippi. As a young child in kindergarten, my teacher began noticing that I had difficulty following objects along with not placing my hand directly on a specific object. My parents had also seen these tendencies; as a consequence, they began taking me to a local eye doctor. At the age of four, I was diagnosed as simply having a "lazy eye" in my right eye, and then I was fitted for eye glasses. The glasses helped a bit, but my difficulty in seeing continued. Although I could see to read and could see the chalk board in class, I often ran into various things and could see almost nothing at night. More problematic than the physical implications of my eye problems were the socializing effects. As I grew older, especially as I entered my middle school years, I began to experience a great deal of teasing from my classmates. Of course, children are often quick to pick up on the slightest differences in other children. In my case, the difference was not slight, and that prompted other kids to tease and bully me relentlessly. Despite these continued difficulties with my eyesight, my doctor never changed his initial diagnosis.

Even though I had no way of articulating the fact that the doctor's diagnosis was inaccurate—plus not having the ability to describe my visual acuity adequately—I was fully aware at age fourteen that I needed more help. After some discussion with my parents, we eventually found an eye doctor at a university research hospital who possessed some expertise in diseases of the eye. After a battery of tests and extensive examination of my eyes, I was given the RP diagnosis. Along with that decision there came the news that as an adult I would almost assuredly go blind.

Consequently, I had no capacity for processing such devastating news. As a result, I entered into a prolonged period of denial. Part of my denial was a concerted effort to "pass" as a sighted person. I resisted any suggestion that there was a problem, and even refused to talk about the physical and emotional reality of my disability. In fact, I insisted to my parents that I needed a driver's license. At that time, Mississippi licensed drivers began at the age of fifteen. My parents reluctantly gave into my insistence. When I could not pass the vision test at the license testing center, my parents took me back to my local eye doctor who— inexplicably—signed off on my visual acuity for driving a motorized vehicle. Subsequently, I passed both the written and driving portions of the test, and received my driver's license just one year after I had been pronounced as legally blind. My parents even bought me my own car; however, this freedom to drive did not end well. Within six months of getting my license, I had two minor car accidents, both of which were primarily a consequence of my lack of peripheral vision – a hallmark of RP. After the second accident, it was clear to me that I could not and should not be driving. The ability to drive my own car was, in my own mind at least, my only means of pushing back against the growing reality of my disability. This was yet another devastating blow to my already difficult circumstance. If there has ever been one moment in life when I wanted to cease to exist, this was that moment. Already filled with all the usual teenage angst, the reality that I could not drive was almost too much to bear.

In the Warmth of a Church Family, there Came the Call

Fortunately for me, my family was very involved in a local United Methodist congregation. Outside my own home, the church was one of the only social settings where I felt at home. Virtually, I had no friends in middle school or high school; however, my church youth group, comprised of about ten members, was a place where I found acceptance and inclusion. These youth became my friends at a time when I urgently needed them. I found acceptance and inclusion in a way that I had never before experienced; consequently, the church as a whole became a home for me – a place of safety and peace in the midst of numerous physical, emotional, and social struggles. The youth and adults of my congregation were as Christ to me, giving me acceptance, inclusion, peace, and hope. The church was a true means of grace for me, helping to save my life at a time of deep despair and loneliness.

Around this same period of time, when I was between fifteen and sixteen years old, I began to sense God's call to ministry. Like most people confronted with the possibility of being a church pastor, I initially resisted that idea. Even though the church was a vital part of my life, I was sure I could not adequately serve as a pastor given my emerging disability; however, the sense of God's call upon my life persisted. Through opportunities for leadership within my youth group, along with conversations with my pastor, I eventually accepted the call to ministry. I preached my first sermon as part of a Youth Sunday service when I was just sixteen years old. Although I was quite unsure how ministry would play out for me, given my impaired eyesight, I was willing to follow what I believed to be God's leading. Again, I found affirmation and support among the youth and adults in my congregation. Their support and encouragement made a critical difference in my approach to a consideration of ministry as my calling.

After graduating from high school in 1989, I went on to higher education in Wood Jr. College, a small liberal arts community college of the United Methodist Church. I found the faculty, staff, and students to be accepting and inclusive. Despite my continuing denial of the disabil-

161

ity—and still attempting to pass as a sighted person—I was slowly being forced to come to terms with reality. Remarkably, after having had virtually no friends or acquaintances in my high school days, I was elected student body president of Wood Jr. College in my sophomore year. Additionally, since the college was a church-related institution, I was given numerous opportunities for leadership in congregational settings. The college chaplain always provided a driver for me—who usually was another college student—as I led worship services, and taught classes in local congregations. Were it not for the support and accommodation of the chaplain, I would not have been able to engage in such ministries.

The Force of Reality

After graduating from Wood Jr. College, I enrolled at Mississippi State University. Knowing that I was headed to seminary, I chose sociology as my major, in hopes that this would provide a good background for engaging a theological education along with as the praxis of pastoral ministry. With the larger campus, more students, and increased academic load, I was finally forced to ask for help. Nevertheless, I was still none happy with the idea of vocational rehabilitation. Needless to say, denial and passing were still my primary means of coping with my visual impairment. In the summer of 1991, I spent two weeks at the state rehabilitation center for blind people. I should have stayed longer, but I absolutely refused to do so. I was convinced that I did not need any rehabilitative services whatsoever. The only reason I agreed to go at all was to satisfy my disability services counselor at Mississippi State University. All the while, my vision was slowly worsening, and—reflecting back on my negating attitude—I could have truly benefitted from mobility training with a cane; but, at that time, I refused to cooperate with the program leaders. Despite my belief that God was leading me into pastoral ministry, I could not entrust God with the fear and frustration that I had for my disappearing eyesight. I was overwhelmed with shame, and did everything I could to hide that reality from God and others. I acknowledged my visual impairment only when I was forced to do so, and covered up the remaining facts. I thought I was doing a good job at passing for a sighted person, but—of course—my efforts only made my situation more frustrating in the worsening course of my vision. Sadly, I was missing the opportunity to know the true depth of God's love and wholeness that were also exemplified by God's people.   Continuing to pursue my call to ministry, in 1993 I entered Candler School of Theology at Emory University in Georgia. God was not through working on me just yet. In my first semester, I read an article in the campus newspaper that profiled a doctoral student in the sociology of religion at Emory. The article was about Nancy Eiesland and the publication of her master's thesis, entitled "The Disabled God." The article also described Nancy's personal story of physical impairment. It was clear to me, even in this brief article, that Nancy was a person of intellect, strength, and faith whom I needed to know. I sought out Nancy in the Graduate Division of Religion at Emory, and we began to talk; she shared with me her own story, and that prompted me to do the same for the first time with anyone. Nancy was the first person I had ever encountered who was able to integrate the physiological, theological, emotional, and social components of disability. Through my interaction with her in person, as well as through her writing, I began to put the pieces of my own disability puzzle together. I started questioning my harmful attitudes and fears regarding my visual impairment. My years in seminary were for me an incredible time of growth.

With my background in sociology, I was intrigued by Nancy's sociological approach to the intersecting fields of religion and disability studies. The academic approach to religion and disability became a significant approach to coping with my own experience, as well as its being a meaningful avenue for helping others to cope with their disabilities. As my vision continued to worsen, the feelings of shame, guilt, and fear slowly began to diminish. Nancy was a true inspiration and a valuable mentor for me. After being accepted into the Master of Divinity Honors program at Candler, I began researching and writing my master's thesis on religion and disability. With Nancy as my thesis advisor, I wrote the resulting treatise on the Christian Reformed Church's voluntary compliance with the Americans with Disabilities Act (ADA). For the most part, religious entities are exempt from the provisions of the ADA; nevertheless, the Christian Reformed Church, a small denomination located primarily in the American Midwest, was a shining example for all Christian denominations by voting to comply voluntarily with the Act as an act of discipleship and service.

The Insolence of Attitudinal Barriers

The academic study of religion and disability was a means of God's grace for me in understanding and dealing with my disability; however, it also brought to light the reality of how religion in general, and Christianity in particular, have throughout history contributed to the oppression and marginalization of people with disabilities. As I continued to pursue my call to ministry, I became painfully aware of the all too prevalent attitudinal barriers to my journey into ministry in the United Methodist Church. Despite the fact that I had always found the church to be a place of acceptance and inclusion, that positive experience was no guarantee of support for my chosen future as a blind pastor. On entering the ordination process, that unfortunate and unjustified reality came to bear. Inexplicably, both my psychological and medical examinations indicated that pastoral ministry would be a difficult vocational choice for me. In my interview for ordination as Deacon (now called "Probationary Elder"), the committee was deeply troubled by my academic interests, and suggested that teaching might be what I really wanted to pursue. When I insisted that pastoral ministry was my calling and desire, the committee told me to go back and reflect on this for another year. I finally mustered the courage to suggest that perhaps their problem had more to do with their discomfort regarding my disability than having anything to do with my academic pursuits. They rejected this assertion, and suggested that I come back in a year if I really wanted to be ordained. For me, that was a heartbreaking moment. I had never before felt such rejection from my own church; however, this barrier was also a good dose of the reality that I would be facing in my journey to ordination.

In 1996, I went back before the Board of Ordained Ministry in the Mississippi Annual Conference. I submitted the same paperwork and the same responses to the theological questions. I also made it clear to them that I would be pursuing a Doctor of Philosophy degree (Ph.D.). This time the Board relented, and I was ordained as a deacon (now known as "Probationary Elder").

Nancy encouraged me to continue my research in religion and disability studies by pursuing a Ph.D. at Drew University. She was instrumental in my acceptance into the Graduate Division of Religion at Drew. In 1996, I was graduated from Candler and began my doctoral work in the sociology of religion at Drew; although I continued to feel God's call to pastoral ministry, I also knew I needed all the academic training and credentials I could gather in order to make sure I could make a living for myself if the Church refused to ordain me as a full Elder. I also had something to prove to myself that even as a blind person I could accomplish the lofty goal of attaining my Ph.D. degree; moreover, I felt there was a real need for further research in the area of religion and disability. My hope was that my study, presentations, and writing in this area would help others as I had been helped.

While in seminary at Candler, I met my future wife, Lisa Hautzenrader. She was also pursuing the call to pastoral ministry. She was fully supportive of both my calling and the academic pursuits. We were married in August 1995, and together we moved to New Jersey in 1996 so that I could work on my doctoral degree. After completing my course work, Lisa and I moved off campus, and both of us served churches in the Greater New Jersey Annual Conference.

An unexpected consequence of my enrollment at Drew was that I found myself living less than ten miles away from The Seeing Eye, one of the premier dog guide schools for persons who are blind or visually impaired. At first, that guide dog school seemed to be only an interesting fact; however, as I found myself increasingly depending upon a white cane for mobility, I gave more thought to the possibility of a Seeing Eye guide dog to lead me around physical barriers. I had never been much of a dog lover, but I did not like using a white cane and felt very uncomfortable when using the cane. In fact, I felt more disabled by the cane than aided by it. At the end of my first year of graduate school, I was enrolled in training at The Seeing Eye for a dog guide.

Gene, Lisa, and I Together in Ministry

Getting a guide dog was one of the best and most healing things I had ever done with regard to my journey through disability. My first dog, a Golden Retriever named Gene, brought me a sense of independence and confidence I had never before felt. I absolutely fell in love with the dog, and remarkably he became a significant part of my pastoral ministry. In 2004, I was ordained a full Elder in the Mississippi Annual Conference. As part of my ordination, Gene was commissioned as one of God's very

165

own servants. This was a powerful moment for me, because I at last felt that the Church had fully accepted me as a person with a disability. Gene died in 2006, and I received another dog, a black lab named Orson. Although having a guide dog makes it impossible for me to pass as a sighted person, I feel completely comfortable in my own skin. I feared that my congregations would resist having a dog in worship services and in clinical settings; but, that has not been the case. In fact, my guide dogs seem to be a valuable asset for my ministry, opening up doors of conversation and dialogue. As I write this chapter, I am getting ready to go back to The Seeing Eye for my third dog guide. My present congregation seems full of excitement and anticipation regarding this new dog.

My interview for elder's orders with the Board of Ordained Ministry was remarkably smooth and positive. The board members were very affirming of both my call to ministry and my abilities for pastoral care. Perhaps this affirmation was a result of my own growth and feelings of independence and confidence within the inescapable blindness. Perhaps the committee felt better about my ministry as a result of my being married to another United Methodist pastor. Perhaps it was my dog. Perhaps it was all of those three possibilities. Whatever the case, the committee was quite affirming of my call and ability. There is no doubt, however, that my ministry is made enormously easier by being part of a clergy couple appointed as co-pastors. Being co-pastors solves numerous issues that would otherwise be tremendous barriers to my ministry; for example, the need for transportation and a reader of inaccessible-to-me written materials. Ministry would be much harder without a spouse to assist me with a variety of issues. Having said that, let it be known that my annual conference has been very accommodating, and more than willing to appoint my wife and me to congregations where we could serve as co-pastors, thereby allowing each of us to fulfill our separate calls to ministry.

Finally, after starting my doctoral studies in 1996, I finished the Ph.D. program in May of 2010. Much of my research was in the fields of the sociology of religion and disability. My dissertation was an exploratory study of the United Methodist Church's response to the disability rights movement in both society in general and the denomination in particular. I looked specifically at the General Conference actions from 1968 to 2004. I also conducted interviews with United Methodist pastors with disabilities, and I did a small survey among both disabled and non-disabled clergypersons and laypersons. What I discovered was not terribly surprising. While the church has made great strides in the inclusion and acceptance of women and racial and ethnic minorities, very little has been done to include people with disabilities. In spite of the ADA, and other federal and state legislation designed to include persons with disabilities into all aspects of our shared public life, the United Methodist Church has given only a cursory attention to the capabilities, needs, and human rights of children and adults with disabilities. My dissertation argues that more could and should be done to be inclusive and accessible for all people. Religious beliefs and institutions have too often equated disability with sin and shame. Many of us who cope with disabilities have often felt the powerfully damaging force of negative thinking in the church. Innumerable persons with disabilities have been harmed by poor theology and hurtful churchly practices. The United Methodist Church, therefore, must do more to become inclusive and entirely accessible to those with disabilities and their families who have been excluded and hurt by the world and the church. Hopefully, my dissertation and my research will continue the push for disability rights within our United Methodist Church.

Again, at the time of this writing, I am in my 14th year of full-time pastoral ministry in the UMC. While I am finally comfortable with whom I am, and my status as a person with a disability, I do sometimes struggle with the age-old demons of inadequacy, shame, and fear. We live in a world that idealizes the false worshipping of self-sufficiency, power over others, and one's physical appearance. The people of God sometimes fall prey to these false gods. As a pastor with a disability, I have felt both the love and the hurt of life in and amongst God's people called Methodists. While my ordination as Elder was a tremendously positive experience, I continue to be confronted by exclusion in many small—yet large—ways. Conference and district meetings seldom offer any written materials in advance, or in a format that is accessible to persons who are visually impaired. But my call from God for pastoral ministry continues to burn within me, and I firmly believe Methodism has valuable gifts to offer a hurting and searching world. So, I will continue the ministerial journey, pressing on toward perfection in love, and pressing on toward an accessible and inclusive denomination where all of God's people are welcomed and accepted just as they are. I will continue to live in solidarity with others who are disabled, fighting the good fight for social justice through disability rights in our denomination.

Ruthann Simpson

A Call to Transparency and the Gift of God's Grace
By The Rev. Ruthann Simpson, M.Div.

Three Heard, Two Listened

In June of 1990, a call went out to the local United Methodist churches in the Conference for anyone interested in singing in a mass choir during the annual conference's ordination service. As laypersons, my friend and I decided to join the choir. It was a fairly uneventful evening. We sang, the to-be-ordinands were ordained, the bishop preached, and gave an altar call for others to become ministers. There was nothing unusual about the event, but it was a unique experience for me. I had never before seen an ordination service. I remember thinking that must be the coolest thing to have an actual job working for Jesus. I'm not sure about what other thoughts I had, but they were certainly not about answering a call to ministry or anything like that. I was sure that everyone thought it was the most fulfilling job in the world. Why wouldn't they?

On the way home in the car, my friend asked me "why didn't you go up when they invited those interested in the ordained ministry to come up? I was waiting for you to get up out of your seat and go." "Why would I?" I replied. Her answer was simple: "Because you were supposed to." Suddenly I knew what it meant when Mary, the mother of Jesus, "pondered these things in her heart" (Luke 1:29). It was close to two weeks later that I finally went to my pastor and told him about the ridiculous conversation that my friend Betty and I were having. His reply about knocked me over. When I got to the part where Betty said she was waiting for me to answer the bishop's call, he said "so was I." The joke from then on was, "The Holy Spirit spoke to three people at annual conference but only two listened!"

Having spent my high school years in a Baptist church, I knew this call to ministry was not supposed to happen. Men, not women were to be church pastors; nevertheless, I continued to investigate the possibility of becoming a minister. I read and read several books– especially Tom Oden's book on pastoral theology—and I was convinced that God was calling me into the church's ordained ministry. This was not the first time that I had experienced a divine call. The initial one came when I was 16, but I just took a rather long detour around that moment. This time I knew that it was pastoral ministry to which I was summoned, rather than the mission field to which I would have gone, had I answered that call many years ago. Friends in the church continued to support me, and some gave me that essential push by saying, "you know what you need to do, now do it!" By September I was in a seminary.

Doing What I Needed to Do

In July of 1992, I began a new adventure when I was sent by my Annual Conference to the Local Pastor's School at Drew University, and was then appointed to my first church. Things seemed to go well. I was enjoying my studies, and working in the church at the same time. The following year at the Annual Conference session, I was ordained as a Deacon. I continued to serve in pastoral appointment as a student. It was anything but easy; nevertheless I was challenged and felt that pastoral ministry was truly my calling.

By 1994, during my last semester of seminary, my world changed again. It was rather amusing in some ways. I had just taken a psychology class in seminary where we talked about different mental illnesses that we might encounter in the congregation. I can remember—long before I really understood what mental illness was—our class talking about how difficult manic/depression must be. Less than a year later, I stood on that precipice called the bipolar disorder.

The Bipolar Precipice

I had struggled with "moodiness" even as a child, but never to the point of it causing problems for me. Later, after some difficult life experiences, I had what I thought were a few bouts of depression. But this time it was different. Hyperactivity, to the point of not being able to sit calmly in class, running up and down stairs at school to get rid of excessive energy, racing thoughts, poor concentration and an extremely high opinion of me combined to cause me to seek help once more. That was when I was diagnosed as having the bipolar disorder. As I struggled to finish seminary, I requested a temporary leave of absence from my pastoral position so that I could concentrate full time on my studies. The Conference Board of Ordained Ministry (BOOM) was very gracious, and gave me time off with pay so I could complete seminary with the rest of my class. I didn't realize at that time just how gracious, fantastic and unusual was the Board of Ordained Ministry's' action.

In due course, I resumed my pastoral appointment, thinking that all would be well; however, in the fall of 1994, I once again had difficulties. By the end of November in that challenging year, I was convinced that I should go to the hospital in order to get my "meds" regulated. Little did I know how much of a turning point this would be in my life and ministry. I was officially "crazy." I spent a couple of weeks in the hospital, certain that I would be "fixed," and then everything would be fine. Once again, when I returned home and back to the church, reality set in. Many in the church were suspicious of their pastor, and that was a concern for me; but, an even bigger concern for me was that I was NOT fixed as I had expected.

The following year I was appointed to a church in another district. I was told it was "so that no one would know what had happened." It was to be a secret. That, however, meant that I was several hours away from doctors, therapists, friends and family. My support system was gone overnight, and paradoxically, due to the nature of our ministry and the size of our conference – the cat was out of the bag, and some people at the new appointment were aware of my situation before I had arrived.

Accepting and Controlling the Disorder

For the next 6 years I struggled to prove to the Board of Ordained Ministry and to myself that I could serve in the capacity of pastor and as an Elder in the UMC. There were times when I could barely convince myself that God had called me to be a pastor, and other times when friends and colleagues assured me that I was in the right place.

Each year during the conference's Board of Ordained Ministry's interviews with me, my illness/disability became, as I nicknamed it, the "elephant" in the room. No one would talk about it, but I knew that my history of the bipolar disorder was coloring both their questions and their ultimate decision.

During my seven years as a Deacon, I continued to pray for healing. Everyone I knew was praying for me. We were asking for a miracle to make this mental illness go away. There were many times during the succeeding years when I was ready to give up the ministry, but somehow, I couldn't imagine doing anything else. At times I felt over-whelmed with the work, the people and the demands on my time. There were occasions when I didn't think I could get through another meeting. Sermons could be extremely difficult to write, and almost impossible to preach. I found myself crying out to God at every turn. My sense of self-worth was disappearing, my fears were compounding, and the Board of Ordained Ministry time line was closing in as the limit of seven years allowed in the journey from being an ordained deacon to being an or-dained elder was coming to a close. Would I become an Elder, or would I be discontinued as a minister in the conference? It was a soul wrenching question.

One year, I found myself speaking to the BOOM registrar on the phone. I somehow got around to the issue of my effectiveness, and I said I was pretty sure things were straightened out, because I was properly medicated, and my illness would not be an issue. His reply was: "We'll be the judge of that."

God, however, continued to be faithful. I survived the meetings and managed to do ministry in spite of the difficulties hindering me. As I look back on those days, I realize how much they were my essential

172

training grounds. Learning to be dependent on God for my every step was essential, not only because of my illness but also because it was His desire

On a happier note, it was also during those anxious years that I met the man who became my husband. In spite of all the difficulties, along with my frustration over being moved away from my support system, God was providing a new one for me. It was a system that I would have no matter where I was appointed. How like God, to fix something that made it better than what it had previously been; however, having a spouse did not solve the problems of receiving adequate medical care, and the issue required more solutions.

In the course of 15 years of ministry I served in four districts, and 5 pastoral appointments. I was unable to find helpful doctors that were in some areas to which I was appointed. Sometimes, the available situation called for sitting in an open clinic, so that everyone passing by knew you were seeing a psychiatrist. In other times, the problem just meant poor communication that led to poor medication. As a result, I sought care outside my areas of appointment. In one situation I was traveling for 3 hours each way to see my therapist and my doctor.

Although I continue to pray for a miracle of release from this illness, I have discovered many other miracles along the way. Miracles do not come solely in the form of physical healing, or getting rid of the problem. A miracle is finding God's grace in the midst of life's itself. It is watching Him show up at those times when you think you can't go on any farther. A miracle is seeing the faithfulness of God everywhere we look. For almost 20 years God has sustained me in every way. He has sent me to places and used me in areas I never thought possible, and he has given me a husband and a daughter along the way. I celebrate all that God has done, not only those deeds that he has enabled me to accomplish in spite of my illness, but also those actions that He has allowed me to fulfill because of that illness.

During the Board of Ordained Ministry interview in the year of 2000, I brought up the "elephant." I told the board members that I realized this was causing them a great difficulty in their decision-making, and I wanted to talk about it. Questions were asked. I responded to the best of my ability. Could I guarantee them I would never be sick again?

No, could any of them say they would never have a heart attack, and therefore be out of the pulpit? Finally, I was approved for ordination as an Elder.

In 2007, I was preparing and praying for a new pastoral appointment. My then current parish work was not going all that well, and I decided that despite there being a ministerial file with my name on it, the bishop and the district superintendents who made up the bishop's cabinet didn't know me very well. They knew I had the bipolar disorder, but I wasn't sure they knew what that condition meant. They also were unaware that I felt God leading me to be more transparent about my illness. I contacted my district superintendent, and told her I needed to speak with her. I wanted to share with her all that was going on in my life. I poured my heart out to her. I placed my body, mind, soul and spirit in her hands as I told her about my needs, along with my continuing desires to be in ministry despite the illness.

I also told my superintendent that I wanted her to represent me before the cabinet and the bishop. I felt that if I was open with them, they would attain knowledge to add to their wisdom, discernment and prayer. To her credit my DS listened to me for two hours, taking notes and asking questions. When I was finished, she asked "and I can share all of this with the cabinet?" I said yes.

Currently, I am serving a pastoral appointment in an area where not only can I receive adequate care, but also I am able to help others find care as well. I have finally found myself in a pastoral charge where, although I do not share everything with everyone, I do divulge additional facts to some of my congregants. This has led to a new act of ministry for me. I have found that more people than we ever realize are struggling with mental illnesses. I have learned that we are still trying to hide mental illnesses as much as possible, not just from our respective annual conferences, but also from each other. So many people along the way are struggling to some degree with what I have gone through. I believe that God is calling me to be more and more transparent in order to reach these hurting people. I can honestly say that I believe that my current pastoral appointment is the best one that I've have ever had. It fits me. Whether you—as a reader of this chapter—are a lay person or a clergyperson you know what I mean.

174

I know that it is scary to acknowledge a disability in the presence of others who might judge you. I know that it is scary to admit it to colleagues who may someday be your district superintendent. I know that it is scary to think "I may not have a job if I tell anyone". But, for me, there is also the concern that by hiding my illness—my disability—I am thereby hiding the person God created and called into ministry. I realize that there is a chance that telling the truth could jeopardize my job, my income, my housing, my insurance, and any number of other things. Even as I write these words I wonder if I trust God enough to take that risk.

Jonathan Campbell

A Journey to Wholeness
By The Rev. Jonathan Campbell, M.Div., Th.M.

Growing up a PGK

"Preach it, Papa!" I look back and realize that a typical child of three or four does not make a statement like that very often, if at all. Being a PGK (preacher's grandkid) meant that church life was in my blood. I loved Sunday mornings. I loved the music, I loved my grandfather's fiery sermons, and I loved all the heartfelt "AMENS!" I found out recently that, as a very young child, I would sneak up to the pulpit after service and give my own rendition of Papa's sermons. What I vividly remember is standing in the back row wildly gesturing and actively mouthing the sermon my grandfather was delivering to his congregation. Early in my life I felt church was a safe place for me. The church was where I could play hide and seek and basketball. More than anything else, it was the place to be with my grandfather, Papa, who seemed larger-than-life to me. My grandfather was able to draw large crowds with the way he had of telling the scriptural stories and presenting the Gospel. He had a voice that was forceful and seemed to grab and hold the attention and interest of listeners. People were drawn to that tall, lanky minister, and as his only grandson he and I developed a very special relationship for more than 12 years.

I did not think about growing up to be a pastor. God never sent me a special sign. The church was important to me, at that time in my life, because I was happy when I was there. I could feel the love of God when I was at the church. That feeling is still beautiful even after all of the distance of time and space between my childhood and my present life as a pastor of First and Trinity United Methodist Churches in Stony Point, New York. My grandfather recognized the gifts in me and God's hand working in my life. He always encouraged me to believe in myself and what God had planned for my life. He taught me to believe my disabilities were going to be used by God to serve a greater purpose. Throughout the journey of my faith and life, the idea that God had a call on my life proved to be more powerful than the hate and fear I encountered as I grew older.

In many ways my life could be described as a long succession of experiments. I say that because I often served as a test case, a trial run. I was one of the first special needs children in Wichita, Kansas to be mainstreamed in the public school system; however, I was not welcomed with open arms. I was shielded from a lot of this opposition by my parents. Unfortunately, the Anger and prejudice directed at me have a way of slipping through protective barriers. There were parents of my grade school classmates who believed that their children were at risk being in the same class as a child with cerebral palsy. Their children picked up on their fear and anger, and shunned me, called me names, and at times physically hurt me. I know this may sound strange, but it took me a while to connect their attitude toward me to my disability.

It was an event outside of school that made me believe that "something was wrong with me." When I was two years old, my parents placed me in a pre-school for children with disabilities. My classmates had a variety of physical and intellectual disabilities, but that did not hinder our relationships with one another. Until my seminary enrollment, those four years marked the end of any quality time spent with other individuals with physical disabilities. I now realize how much I missed when I left that special pre-school program. Disability viewed as being "normal" is a wonderful experience in a world that so often makes individuals with disabilities feel like freaks.

My earliest friend was a boy named Craig.[11] Craig was an intelligent and funny kid who wanted to be an architect when he grew up. He,

---

[11] For protective reasons, "Craig" is not my friend's actual name.

with the help of his brother, built amazingly beautiful and creative structures out of Legos, a popular brand of toy building blocks. The reality that he had cerebral palsy, which profoundly limited his ability to move his arms and legs, did not make that dream seem impossible to either of us. The idea that being disabled might make our "dreams" impossible would soon become the way I thought about my future. One night, when I was about eight, my parents rushed to Craig's home. Craig's mother had called because he had been badly abused by his father. In this instance, Craig was at home recovering from a major corrective hip and leg surgery. His father was tired of all of "it." In a state of frustration and anger, he picked up his eight year old son and threw him against a wall. It may have been the alcohol, the medical bills, or the stress of raising a child with a severe disability. He just wanted it to be over. I still remember Craig crying in pain, and it made me wonder, why his father would hurt him? That night I began to believe that a disability was something "bad." A disability became something to "hate and fear" and I, unfortunately, began to believe it to the core of my being.

It is amazing how events have a ripple effect in our lives. After those hurtful events, I started to feel as if no place—not even a church—was safe. Perhaps I finally removed the proverbial "rose colored glasses" and started to grow up; in any case, I began to realize that people treated me differently, and expected less of me than they expected of others of my age. Teachers would ignore me; the other children would tease me or completely ignore me.

The Cruelty of a Bad Theology

The hurt of exclusion continued, when as a young adult I learned that many in my grandfather's church believed God was punishing my parents by cursing me with a disability. My father was divorced when he met my mother and they eventually married each other. My grandfather ultimately approved of the marriage and actually presided over the nuptials; however, many in the congregation disapproved of their union. My grandfather's congregation was comprised of fundamentalist Baptists. They believed divorce was a sin and they believed that the wrath of God was more powerful than God's grace. My parent's marriage was never openly confronted, but ugly gossiping took place behind their backs.

179

These moralistic behaviors and judgmental attitudes resulted in creating what I regard as a cruelly erroneous theological understanding of God and how God chose to punish the "sinners $among us." I have had more than a few "good Christians" inform me that my disability was likely a result of sin. These "good Christians" never defined the relationship between a specific sin and my disability, but the link was forged early and often. For some it may have been as simple as the idea that disabilities were not a part of God's original plan.

Looking back it amazes me how we human beings can be so arrogant as to believe we know the mind of God. My grandfather believed, and preached, that disabilities were a negative consequence of a sinful and fallen world. I don't think my grandfather ever realized how much that heinous theological belief wounded me, or he would have never said it because he loved me too much to hurt me knowingly.

The belief my disability was the result of sin, along with the fundamentalist belief that God sent everyone except "Bible-believing" Christians to Hell, perpetuated my belief in a God of Anger. God was angry, and worse than that, God was specifically angry with me. No one, especially a shy adolescent, needs to believe that doctrine. Growing up is hard enough. Young people can feel like an alien in their own body even on a good day. When you grow up hearing that your disability is the result of sin you begin to believe that you are the problem, and that you are evil and sinful.

As you can imagine, self esteem was not my strong suit in those earlier days. That misguided type of theology robs you of so much. It steals hope and life from you, but worst of all, it steals the love of Jesus from you. Jesus was the lamb sacrificed to an angry God, so goes that bad theology. Jesus, so I felt, was a healer who clearly didn't have the desire to heal me. During those painful times, I never learned about the three dimensional Jesus; namely, the Jesus who joked or struggled with the discriminating realities of his life against harsh religious and political leaders who dominated the marginalized people of his time. The focus of my Christian education was not about the Jesus who loved the poor, the oppressed, and even the disabled people. It was not about how he wanted "all of us" to have a place at the table. It was later in my life journey that I got to know and understand who Jesus really was; meanwhile, in my growing up years Jesus was a simple shadow of his gracious reality and was of no help to this hurt and angry young man.

The God of Hope and New Beginnings

I don't know when I started to pull away from life, or when I took down my welcome sign, and boarded up the windows of myself. I stopped trying to make new friends, and I kept my head down. I became bitter about all of the jokes, laughs, stares, and abuse poured on me. I hated myself. I hated most, if not all, of the able-bodied world, and I hated God. I felt like God had burdened me with so many problems and no real solutions. God had given me a great desire to learn, but first, I had to overcome a severe learning disability. I have great difficulty encoding and decoding words, which seriously hampers my ability to read and write. If I had been born in a previous generation, I would have been labeled as being "phonics-deaf". I wish I could have seen all of the blessings life can provide, but at that time I could not. I had hardened my own heart. I did not look and see the amazing parents who believed that I was more than a collection of problems, I had been blessed with a creative mind, and I had been given the opportunity to have a good education when so many people with disabling conditions are never given that chance. At that time, however, I was incapable of counting my blessings.

It is amazing how the negative voices seem to be the ones that linger. They are the erroneous sounds that crowd in and fill up our heads to tell us wrongly who we are. I still remember the middle school students that demanded to be tested for advance placement classes when a "retard" like me could qualify, or the teacher who refused to have me in his class because "kids with learning disabilities were just lazy and he didn't go to college to teach special ed. kids!"

Fortunately, the negative voices from the church became easier to avoid. When I was ten my family moved out of Wichita and away from my grandfather's church. Over the following years my family became less and less involved with churches. The next eight years saw us moving to three different states. Each move seemed to push us farther away from the church. I have to say that I was not sad to see God go. By this time I believed with all my heart that God was willfully punishing me. I often had dreams about cutting off my left arm and leg so I could be free of my disabled limbs. I prayed to God on a regular basis to forgive my sins so I could be healed. I believed that my disability was an anchor around my neck and I was emotionally and spiritually drowning. All the moves led me to hide away even more in my own world. It was a world often devoid of hope, but God is a God of resurrection, and God was at work bringing new life and healing to these dry bones.

Changes in me began slowly with teachers and my family who encouraged me to find my true voice. Additionally, there were people who saw the gifts that I had otherwise buried to be ignored. I thank God for all of the people who stayed with me through my bitterness, and believed that I could find my way out of the darkness. In high school and college I was engrossed with politics and became passionate about justice and civil rights movements. A political science professor encouraged me to do a term paper on the Americans with Disabilities Act (ADA). I realized the need for continued achievement and felt a calling to better the lives of people coping with disabilities. I began to understand the importance and singular effectiveness of individuals to speak out about the needs and subsequent mistreatment of people living with disabilities. God, I maintain, was working on my hardened heart.

About that time, I took a World Religions course, and the professor encouraged me to read the writings of Martin Luther King, Jr., and Mahatma Gandhi in light of how their respective faiths shaped their work for justice. In reading their words, I realized that their religious traditions and compassion for oppressed people had given them a core structure from which they built great political movements. The readings, once again, exposed me to to a truer Jesus. The Mahatma and Dr. King wrote about a Jesus who challenged the status quo and the power structures, showing us that his main ministry had not been to get souls into heaven, but to help the manifestation of the all-inclusive Kingdom of God here on earth. I liked this still relevant radical trouble maker of two-millennia ago, and I wanted to learn more. While reading Dr. King's "Strength to Love", a collection of four powerful sermons, I heard a still small voice saying, "Go and learn about me." At that time, my sister was dating a graduate from Princeton Theological Seminary (PTS). Despite the fact that I was less than a year removed from planning to go to law school and helping lead a political revolution, through my sister's prodding I applied at the last minute, and was accepted into Princeton's Master of Divinity (M.Div.) program.

No Need to be Healed to be of Sacred Worth

I went to PTS not having a clue to what I was there to do. Everyone seemed to be so well versed in the Christian faith, and unarguably sure that God had called him or her to ministry. I would like to say that my questions and passion for justice to be inclusive, not exclusive were welcomed with open arms, but that is not how my story of being with the church ever seems to begin. Within my first week I had one student tell me that I was blaspheming God by having pictures of Gandhi and the Dali Lama on my wall. Several students told me Jesus did not care about political problems. By the first month I was assigned by my Old Testament professors to read passages from Leviticus that stated Aaron's sons with disabilities could not be priests. Their disabilities defiled the Holy of Holies. By the end of that first month I was ready to pack my bags and leave God behind. God blessed me with a roommate, friends, and teachers that encouraged me to continue to search for where God's leading was directing me in my life.

One friend encouraged me to share my journey of faith. He knew I liked poetry so he encouraged me to write a poem about disability. I accepted the suggestion, and throughout the poem, I wrote about people often asking me what it is like to have a disability. My cerebral palsy was a result of my birth, so that I have never known a different way of life; consequently, my response is usually in the form of a question asking "Can you tell me what it is like to breathe?" My point is that my disability is as normal and natural to me as breathing is for all of us. I then go on to tell about how—as a child—I prayed to be healed, and now—as an adult--I feel God responded to that prayer with a powerful statement that there is nothing wrong with me. I did not need physical healing to be of sacred worth.

That poem changed my life. The biggest change came in the fact it touched the heart of Jessica Kinde who later became my wife. Jessica wanted to meet me and refused to let me hide behind the wall I had built to protect me from the outside world. She worked to get to know me. Then she worked even harder to get me to open up to her and everyone else. She challenged me to let the world in and build relationships with a variety of people. Through the grace of God transforming me through Jessica, I found more than love; that is, through her love I started to believe in and understand that God had a purpose for my life. The power of love is amazing. Often other people are God's great gifts to us. I am grateful beyond measure for the blessing Jessica is to me.

I have been enriched by building relationships with innumerable people, unique in many ways. I have learned, through that process, how bad and misleading is the church's theology regarding disabilities. One of the best examples of this misled theology occurred when I was talking to a classmate about the challenges of ministry and, at one point, he looked at me and told me how "blessed" I was. He went on to tell me that I was blessed because I had an open mark of my sinfulness on my body. "Jonathan," he said, "everyday you are reminded of your need for God's grace." I was speechless. Unfortunately, I found many of these highly educated and future pastors had a terrible theology concerning people with a disability. They may have used more eloquent verbiage than did the members of my grandfather's church, but they had the same belief that disability and sin are definitely linked. In those painful moments I began to realize that someone needed to do the theological work to clear away the debris that hides the grace of God from so many people. I, however, found it difficult to believe that I had the ability to do that heavy lifting. How, I asked, could my story and my life make a difference for others? It is amazing how tightly we hold on to the pain and the lies even in the face of Christ working in our lives.

Later in my journey to ministry, I had an experience that would help me believe that God could, and would, use me. I was given the opportunity to work as a student chaplain at a school and hospital for people with developmental disabilities. I was thrilled with the prospect of this opportunity. I hoped this experience would help me understand how God worked in their lives, and how they understood and lived out their faith. As is a reality for so many people who live in medical facilities and institutions, their lives are defined and shaped by the high rates of staff turnover; the result is that people come and go so quickly, and—to avoid the pain of the loss—they shut people out of their daily lives.

Often I was shut out, but There were some individuals who were willing to give me an opportunity to get to know them. Bob[12] was one such individual. He was extremely intelligent, and dreamed of being a preacher some day. He asked to meet with me. After several really interesting conversations about the scriptures, Bob asked me to heal him. He was a wheelchair user who, due to Cerebral Palsy, had limited movement of his arms and legs. He feared his disability would keep him from living out God's call.

My first instinct was to run away, but God kept me there. I did not want to be part of a healing service; I had spent my adult life trying to convince myself that I did not need to be healed. What could I say? God gave me the words. I told Bob I would pray with him, but first I needed to tell him about how God healed me. Out of my mouth came my story of pain and fear. I told Bob how I hated myself and the world, and how God had worked in my life to help me understand that I did not need to be physically cured to be a whole person.

God was healing me of the real problems in my life, the problems of hate, anger, and fear. I told him about how I hoped God would use me to spread God's grace so more people could be healed from feeling like they have no value and no worth. I then prayed for healing and wholeness in Bob's life.

As I left that meeting, I finally understood that the church needs pastors, theological schools need professors, and the church needs laity to believe and proclaim a Gospel that is big enough for everyone. We need a theology that rightly understands healing and salvation encompass all aspects of our lives. I wish I could tell you that I no longer struggle with anger, fear, or doubt since that would be a lie. The truth, however, is that I have found a God who is bigger than the anger, fear, and doubt and loves this person with disabilities. Now, that is a story worth telling!

---

[12] To protect this person, I have changed his name.

Anonymous

Spat Out

Editor's note: the author of this chapter requested anonymity.

A friend once told me that when God wants you to move on from somewhere, God spits you out. Spat out is certainly how I've felt since I've been unwillingly placed on incapacity leave by my annual conference of the United Methodist Church. I was in midlife when I answered God's call to ordained ministry. I chose to follow the Course of Study route, because of the distance between where I lived and the nearest seminary's location; furthermore, utilizing the course of study permitted me to take advantage of on-the job training, putting what I learned into practice immediately. I started my studies walking. I graduated in a wheelchair. I had been diagnosed with several autoimmune diseases, and for fifteen years I thought that with five knee surgeries behind me, the illnesses had run their course. I fought against using a wheelchair, but realized I was reducing my energy and killing myself with a walker. The eventual purchase of a power chair proved to be a blessing in that the chair quickly became my wings.

The church I served at that time welcomed me with open arms and a new pulpit custom-built to accommodate my wheelchair. The members also constructed a ramp into the parsonage, and had the county put in a curb cut in front of the church. I naively thought all churches were as equally accessible; they were not.

I was approved by the Conference Board of Ordained Ministry (BOOM) for commissioning as a probationary elder before I was placed on incapacity leave; at the same time, I was informed that I could not have any contacts with my congregation, even though a new pastor was not being sent to the church. I had a parishioner who was dying, but I was told I could not attend her funeral. I felt fortunate that we had held a Lay Speakers Class earlier, and had two strong lay speakers who could hold the church together until a new pastor might be appointed.

Although I am not able to serve a church full-time, I am a capable minister with a strong desire to serve God. I joined the choir at my new church, but a few members let me know that wheelchairs were not welcome; after all, they said, it is the Chancel Choir, and since my wheelchair cannot enter the chancel, I do not belong in the choir. I stuck it out for about eighteen months, but finally I could no longer tolerate the inhospitable looks, sighs and kicks on the back of my chair, so I left, spat out.

I was asked by the Sunday School Director to teach a middle school class, and I gladly accepted the request, only to be told by the Assistant Pastor that those children were scheduled to take a confirmation class, were expected in church every Sunday, and there would be no Sunday School class for the youth. Spat out again.

A United Methodist Women officer called and asked me if I would teach a year-long study group. I readily agreed. The following Sunday another officer told me they had decided to go another way. Spat out once more.

I had offered many times to serve as a pulpit supply preacher. Originally, I came out of that church, and was the local pulpit supply preacher for this and several other local churches for many years. But I am never asked to be a substitute preacher; instead, a retired lay pastor with no formal training is the occasional substitute preacher. At the time of this writing, in the previous five years all I have done in a worship service is read scripture twice and assist with communion once. Spat out.

I was able to work with the Vacation Bible School (VBS) for several years, and that was a joy. I have taken the science table, which no one seems to want, conducting simple experiments and relating them to God's Word and God's presence in our lives. I have also headed the VBS mission project that has always been very successful, but VBS always ends, and there you are, thinking, "Okay, Lord, what next?"

Being on incapacity leave is a lonely experience. There are only three United Methodist Churches somewhat near where I live; the nearest one is 15 miles away. The second is my former parish, 40 miles from home. Since I cannot drive out of town by myself, I'm pretty well stuck in my current locale. I have considered jumping denominations for worship services, but I'm uncertain about what repercussions that would bear. Besides, my husband is quite happy at our local church.

There is no collegiality among the pastors. The District Office is more than five hours away. When I asked if I could share a ride with someone to district events, the answer was invariably "No." Because I'm in a wheelchair and have a special van, I always offer my van, my gas. I just need a driver. I'll even pay for a separate room! Spat out again.

Eventually, I wrote a letter to my District Superintendent expressing my loneliness and spiritual pain. It arrived at the District Office a few weeks before our local church's annual charge conference at which the Superintendent would preside. I hoped he might mention the letter when he was amongst us; he did not. I hoped he might call me; he did not. What he did do was to send me an e-mail directing me to a Yahoo e-mail group for the Conference pastors. How is that supposed to help? How can I share my pain in an open forum, some of which has to do with those people? I needed pastoral care, but I was   spat out again.

My question now is this: "Where does God want me to go?" I have developed my own little ministries. I do belong to the church's electronic "Prayer Vine." We get prayer requests via e-mail, and no one can stop me from praying! I began my ministry years ago in the Hispanic community and the people know that they can still come to my house or call me for help. I counsel them, pray with them, and help them with immigration issues, Healthy Families, and Social Security matters. I work with kids, encouraging them to stay in school and consider and plan for college. I send greeting cards each week to everyone I know who is ill, grieving, or needs a lift. I belong to an online group called Love Drop that helps a struggling individual or family each month. I am part of another organization called "It Starts With Us" that performs random acts of kindness each week.

I have two service dogs (one is in training), who keep me from overexerting myself and out of the sun. The dogs join me in visiting the residents in assisted living and nursing homes each week. There is one person at each location who objects to the dogs' presence, but everyone else loves them, and they brighten many lives. I also enjoy those planned visits, and I believe I get more out of the occasion than do the residents.

I am a member of the Rotary Fellowship of Quilters and Fiber Artists, and the International Fellowship of Rotary Musicians. At a recent International Convention held in New Orleans, I was pleased to work in the Quilt Booth and see that a small group of people scattered around the world had raised more than $8,000 to fight polio. I also crocheted baby booties which we donated to "Soles for Orphan Souls." I joined the musician's fellowship after I heard the International Choir sing at the Interfaith Worship Service. Wheelchairs are no impediment to the Rotary Club, and its members were glad to have me in their midst. I just wish the church was equally hospitable to me.

I comfort myself by reminding me that when I started on the pathway to ordained ministry in the United Methodist Church, I committed myself to the Covenant Prayer in the Wesleyan Tradition in our *United Methodist Hymnal*, wherein I vowed to be put to use or put aside according to God's will. If the church has no use for me, there are other places that do and accept me "just as I am." I close with John Wesley's 18th century call for our humane actions in gratitude for God's freely given grace: "Do all the good you can, By all the means you can, In all the times you can, In every place you can, To all the people you can, As long as you ever can."

Brian Burch

Truths to Tell: What Can I Do?
By Brian Burch, M.Div. D.Min.

Moments to Tell

Lance enters the church sanctuary. Immediately you begin to make observations about him. First, his smile—it was one that would brighten the room. Attached to the smile was a gangly body accompanied by a strange gait and distorted speech. In the moments before Lance's birth, the umbilical cord wrapped itself around his neck, and cut off the oxygen supply for a few precious minutes. An accident of a minute or two should not define a whole person's life. Should not a person be measured by that individual's accomplishments? As a young adult, Lance earned a Master of Education degree and teaches at a middle school. Additionally, he is the coach for several athletic teams. Your first impression, however, would be to label him as handicapped and wonder, "What can he do?"

John sits in a wheelchair in church. His father gives him his daily bath. He uses a closed-circuit television (CCTV) to do his homework. More than one church member has raised an eyebrow when observing one of John's six siblings experience the joy of pushing him in his wheelchair down the church hallways. The kids had learned that if you hit the corners right, you can get the wheelchair up on two wheels. Recently, the church members raised the money for a powered wheelchair, because they hoped John would wheel himself over to them to give them one of his famous hugs. Of course, a few persons donated money for the sole purpose of making the halls safer. John is an active participant in the church—always present for youth retreats and the church choir tours. To make this possible, the congregation has chosen to provide some changes for John's sake. When he started sixth grade in school, with the rest of his classmates he expressed interest in joining the church youth group. The youth faced the decision on whether or not to move out of their attic hideaway, and spread out into the church's old Fellowship Hall. The young people gladly made the move for John's benefit. So, if you see John rolling up to you one Sunday morning, get ready, he will not run over you, but he does want to give you an amazing hug and tell you "hi." As you watch him roll away, you might be asking in your mind, "What can he do?"

It is the first Sunday morning in the year 2011. I am sitting in my wheelchair. I give thanks for the handicap ramp at the entrance to the church. It is good that the sidewalk was scraped, because the morning snow was deeper than the footrests on the wheelchair. The handicap ramp at the church is nice; however, the one-inch bump where the 1950's addition joined the original 1916 building makes for a nice hurdle. My knuckles are almost skinned as I pass carefully through the 27-inch entrance into the sanctuary. I am glad I used the restroom at home; the one in this building is not accessible for a wheelchair. The only accessible restroom on the church property would involve another trip through the snow to the educational building. I ponder going to my office; however, I decide that it is not a needed stop this Sunday morning—which is a good thing, because the wheelchair won't fit through the door anyway. I roll to the front of the sanctuary, and after the morning hymns are sung I prepare to spin my wheelchair around and begin to preach. This congregation loves me, and I am convinced that if I fussed about the inaccessible areas in our church buildings, accompanied with enough love, they would make all the obstacles disappear. They want to do what is right. They also know that my time in a wheelchair is only temporary. My shattered ankle is going to heal, and in another few months, I will be walking my normal two miles a day. Yet, as I sit there waiting for the choir to finish singing the anthem I wonder, "What can I do?"

Grace Applied and Grace Received

While the needed wheelchair, walker, portable toilet and shower chair are temporary, being physically disabled is not temporary for me. At birth, I was born blind. My first eye surgery was when I was one-day old, and my most recent operation was in November of 2010. One eye is now plastic. I can see out of the other, but certainly not the way most folks do. My wife envisions it as looking through a paper towel tube with Saran Wrap covering the end of the tube. When I play golf, any shot that gets off the ground means I have no idea where the ball landed. When our church takes prayer requests during the worship service, the parishioners have learned not to bother with raising their hands, because I cannot see them. I order food at fast-food restaurants based on my memory of what they offer or what is advertized on the front windows in huge print. Ever since that life-redirecting evening of the Walk to Emmaus—a weekend spirituality event—when God called me to "feed his flock," the question always quietly asked of me by church leaders is, "What can you do?"

Replying to the query, I allow others to show love. For instance, years ago the church league basketball group welcomed our church team into their rotation. With twenty-three guys on the bench, we looked intimidating; however, in order to win you need some talent. Our team was a little short on that count therefore we rarely won a game. I regularly dressed out with the team for moral support. A couple of times our team captain would tell me to go out and play a few minutes. It wasn't that I was going to change the outcome of the game; that was for sure! In the closing minutes of one of those games, however, I found myself holding the ball. I was in shock, what should I do? Where was one of the right-colored jerseys? Suddenly, the players on the bench started yelling, "Preacher, take the shot." Following their directions, I did take a shot. The ball did not even come close to the basket. The other team got the rebounding ball, and my one second of glory was over. Contrary to my supposition, the opposing team handed the ball back to me and said, "Shoot it again." Ten rebounds later, the ball finally went through the hoop. "What can I do?" Well playing basketball professionally is not a wise choice for me. But it did allow those guys on the court to practice grace and love. Maybe I was there for them. A few years later, that same spirit of compassion was shown by another congregation. The members surprised me with the gift of a several thousand dollar high-powered portable magnifier. Another congregation built a pulpit that holds a closed-circuit television system (CCTV) so that I could easily read the Bible, the hymnal and the bulletin.

Another area of grace deals with transportation. You do not want me driving a car. Thus to get around, I walk, use public transportation, or beg for a ride. I made a discovery years ago that many church members can drive. So, I ask for some company when visiting in homes and hospitals. To my constant surprise, my drivers love this plan. They get to know other members of the church. Often when I sense it is time to leave, they want to continue the visiting. On more than one occasion the volunteer driver enjoyed their act of service so much, that they started making visits on their own as a form of lay ministry. Yes, every time I ask for a ride, I feel I am imposing on others. Christ continues to remind me that he is bringing good out of my need for assistance.

On longer trips, such as meetings held at the conference office, I seek the underemployed persons, and offer them a chance to assist me. In exchange, I try to pay for their gas, food, and time spent in transporting me. I am blessed by these individuals, and my prayer is that I can be a blessing to them in return. I desire is that instead of being one of Job's non-understanding friends, I might remind them that true hope is in Christ.

Yes, I still wonder when walking with my white cane or using a high-powered magnifying device, "What can I do for Christ?" Perhaps what I can do is no more than have the pleasure of allowing the Holy Spirit to work through me in my life and around me in some talented laity. From 2000 to 2004, I was involved with a group leading a contemporary worship service. Our average attendance decreased from 30 to 20 in the first three months which is not the way to grow a vital church. Then the service took off and stabilized at 125 worshipers in attendance. Since 2004 I have been blessed to be a part of a rural congregation filled with talented leadership that has seen attendance grow from 100 to 135 and their offering has increased by 77 per cent. What can Christ do through me? The answer is, "Anything!" By the grace of Christ, I have the joy of serving as a pastor in the United Methodist Church. And yes, by the grace of Christ, I have some visual limitations.

That Insistent Thorn in the Flesh

2 Corinthians 12:7-10 tells of St. Paul and his well-known "thorn in the flesh." Reading the list of what Christians over the years have

thought this thorn could be is like reading a medical dictionary. Rather than trying to identify the "thorn," the spiritual lesson for us is to learn how Paul responded to it. His response was to pray three times for the thorn to be removed, but without success. Thus, for those of you who have a disabling condition, I suggest that you pray for healing in the belief it is possible. While you pray, listen to how the Lord responds to you. Perhaps like Paul, you will hear, "My grace is sufficient for you, for my power is made perfect in weakness" (2 Corinthians 12:8, NIV[13]). Paul was willing to boast of his weaknesses, and then be content with whatever the circumstances might be (Philippians 4:11, NIV).

Paul's model of boasting in weakness and being content with the circumstance is not always the route chosen by those with disabilities. Former President Franklin D. Roosevelt—in addition to leading our country through the Great Depression and World War II—had a private battle with polio. Too often forgotten by many, were the lengths he went through to keep the public from knowing the extent of his paralysis. For instance, he allowed only one picture ever to be taken of him sitting in a wheelchair. Being contented in our weakness develops from the Lord's promise of sufficient grace. Prayer, contentment, and accepting God's grace are three answers put forth in Scripture for those who are in the midst of suffering. Admittedly, those are hard lessons to learn.

Joni Earickson Tada is the author of forty-eight books, and is known for her art, musical abilities, and being a motivational speaker. In 1967, Joni's spinal column was fractured in an accident. For the next three years, Joni was full of anger and bitterness towards God. During that time, she felt that the wheelchair symbolized her confinement and alienation from the world. The turning point came when she realized God loved her, and had not left her. She let go of the anger and realized that the wheelchair symbolized her independence. She trusted a God who had also suffered. What can she do? The answer is that she sings, teaches, paints, and inspires others.

While I was in seminary, I prayed more than three times for this thorn of blindness to be removed from me. One morning after listening to a guest pastor share with those of us in the chapel service how God

---

[13] NIV is the acronym for the New International Version of the Bible.

healed his blindness, I felt called to the altar. As the guest pastor came to lay hands on me, I began to pray; in doing so, the story of the healing of a blind man in John 9:3 came to mind. I don't recall what the pastor prayed that day, but I hope I'll never forget the conversation I had with Jesus. I declared by faith that I knew Jesus could restore both my eyes to full sight, and if so I would be glad to give him the glory. On the other hand, if it would bring more glory to the Kingdom of God for me to be completely blind, then I would accept that, and pray that I would find ways to be used for Christ's sake. I closed the prayer with a request that if my sight would not change, and it basically hasn't since then, would the Holy Spirit set me free of the rage inside me? On that day, a spiritual healing took place for me in the same way it did for Joni Eareckson Tada; namely, the grace of God was sufficient, and my intense anger departed.

Not All Are Cured

Not everyone in the Biblical record experiences miraculous healing. Trophimus is left by Paul in Miletus to recover instead of continuing the missionary journey (2 Timothy 4:20, NIV). Jesus brought up the lack of universal healing while preaching at the synagogue in Nazareth. He reminded the listeners of what happened during the days of Elisha. "There were many in Israel with leprosy in the time of Elisha the prophet, yet not one of them was cleansed--only Naaman the Syrian (Luke 4:27, NIV)."

Jesus performed miracles, and the Gospels share that every ill person who came to Jesus was freed from sickness. Nevertheless, not everyone in Judea was healed during the years when Jesus walked among them. One example is the lame man who begs for a handout from a gate at the temple. In Acts 3:2-4:22, he approaches Peter and John for money. Instead of meeting his financial need, this forty-year-old lame man who was handicapped from birth left walking and leaping and praising God. What did he do? The controversy and his testimony led a number of people to listen to the disciples, and the early church continued to grow rapidly as another 2,000 people joined those who believed the truth about Jesus.

Low Self-Esteem

A common issue for a number of people with handicaps is that of low self-esteem. It can manifest itself in many ways, such as in public speaking. In Exodus 4:10-14, Moses declared that he was "slow of speech and tongue (Exodus 4:10, NIV)." In response, God reminded Moses "Who gave man his mouth? Who makes him deaf or mute? Who gives him sight or makes him blind" (Exodus 4:11, NIV)? God said that he will teach Moses what to speak and will be with the mouth of Moses. Still trying to find excuses for not obeying the summons to free his people from Egyptian slavery, Moses requested more help. God provided Aaron to be the mouthpiece for Moses. At the same time, God found fault with Moses, not because his limitations were imaginary, but because he was expressing a lack of faith in God. Could it be interpreted from this passage, that if God calls someone into a ministry, He will give that individual the skills necessary to fulfill the calling? God encourages Moses by saying, "I will help you" (Exodus 4:12, NIV). What a promise! I am one who needs to hear that word of encouragement, because I still wonder at times, "What can I do?"

One Biblical character who never overcame his low self-esteem was Mephibosheth. At the age of five, he injured both legs in the panic after the death of his father Jonathan. Years later King David, recalling his friendship with Jonathan, sought out Mephibosheth. In the process of offering him wealth and honor, Mephibosheth wondered why he who is a "dead dog" should receive any such gift (2 Samuel 9:8, NIV). His story serves as a reminder that the mental pain in those facing physical disabilities can run deeply within them.

Practical Lessons Gleaned

When it comes to caring, the people called Methodist readily respond to human concerns. They do not always know exactly what to do, but they want to assist those who are in need. The money may not be in the bank to deal with the structural issues that make church buildings a challenge for those who utilize wheelchairs; however, when love prevails, all is made right, and sometimes the solutions might just be a little creative. You would be surprised to learn how many people drive by the parsonage or the church, with the idea of stopping in and talking with the pastor. The quickest way to tell if your pastor is present is check to see if his or her truck or car is in the parking lot. What if your pastor doesn't drive? One creative solution the United Methodist Men put into place for me is installing a flag pole at the church. When I arrive, I raise my "cross & flame" flag (the United Methodist emblem), and when I leave I take it down. Yes, as a denomination we know how to care for others, and for that important gift I am grateful.

Another lesson I have had to learn is to be careful with what my other senses tell me. Investigating random noises has put in me some foolish places, and one incident was the cause of an overnight hospital stay. (Blind people should not track gurgling water in a patch of poison ivy.) I need to learn from Isaac. Genesis 27:1-27 records that he was visually impaired, and he could not tell the difference between his two sons by sight. He had to trust his other senses—touch, smell, taste and sound. What is intriguing is that not only did his impaired sight fail him, but by the time he blessed Jacob instead of Esau, it is apparent that all five of his senses were fooled.

Yes, I am like those who are disabled in one sense in that the other senses become stronger. I may not see you leave the worship service, but I have heard and responded to whispered conversations shared in the back room of the sanctuary or the choir loft during the sermon. Like Isaac, I do have to be careful how I interpret the data I glean and make sure I am not easily fooled again.

Independent or Dependent

Isaac's son Jacob also dealt with a disability. In the midst of wrestling all night, his hip was wrenched out of socket (Genesis 32:28, NIV). As dawn is breaking on that morning, Jacob is given a new name "Israel" as a celebration of his ability to overcome. The limp would be a lasting reminder of the struggle. However, the "over-comer" is no longer self-sufficient. Persons coping with disabilities have a choice of how to view their situation. They, as I am prone to do, can fight to prove that they are not hampered by any physical challenge; or they can view the challenge as a reminder of their constant dependence upon God. Perhaps they can raise their viewpoint even higher to understand that in our weakness God is made strong. Our culture celebrates the persistent one who overcomes a challenging situation. Does God, I ponder, celebrate the one who is self-sufficient, or the one who trusts in God alone?

In the struggle between seeking independence and being dependent upon God and others, I recall Eli. In 1 Samuel 3:2 we find Eli's vision is impaired, and by the time of the events of 1 Samuel 4:15 he is blind. Part of the reason that Eli was able to continue to function as a priest for Israel was because of Samuel's assistance. Due to his limited vision, Eli needed help, but was not clueless. He was aware of the evil his sons were doing, and he was concerned about the battles with the Philistines. Being dependent on others can be a great joy or a major frustration for the disabled person. However, it can be a tremendous experience for the one providing aid. In those years working alongside Eli, Samuel learned much about leadership that enabled him to be a significant change agent for the Lord. So, when I coerce others to help me, could I be doing more than using them for my needs? Could I also develop them as spiritual leaders for the work of Christ?

Even with the help of Christ and the amazing outpouring of love from my congregation, I still am reminded that I have a few remaining problems because of my blindness. Seven months after I shattered my ankle when sledding in the snow, I no longer needed a wheelchair or walker. I was back in the pulpit at a funeral home. As the soloist came forward to sing, I stepped aside to make room for her. I took one too many steps and fell off the platform. I knew the step was there, but I never saw it. A gasp raced across the room as I grabbed the wall. The flower arrangement beside me swayed, but—Hallelujah!—did not fall. The service continued, and I found myself sitting in humiliation. The shattered ankle tingled, letting me know that it was still not completely healed. In desperation, I pondered: "What can I do?" The truth came back to me. What can I do when I work in unity with God and those who love him? Everything!

Lisa Lavelle McKee

Church or the Circus?
By The Rev. Lisa McKee

Prejudice Leads to Discrimination

Writing about the removal from active ministry portion of my life is hard for me to do, and I wince at the anger and sarcasm revealed in the title for this chapter, even though I will not change it. That's because I love my Church and I love her people who make up the church. I knew that being a pastor would be hard work, but hard work has never been a stranger to me. I had successfully accomplished things beyond people's expectations of me; however, my life as an ordained minister has been more difficult than I ever expected it to be.

At first, all seemed to be going well for me as a minister, because I was able to finish the candidacy process, followed by successful interviews with the Board of Ordained Ministry for my 1996 Deacon's Orders and the 1998 Elder's Orders. Members of the respective oversight committees told me that I did well in the interviews, and that all of my written work was well done. Some of the members even said that I was the best and the most prepared candidate being interviewed at that time.

Unexpectedly, local churches—along with bishops and cabinet members—had a different opinion about my ministerial abilities. Shortly after arriving at my first pastoral appointment, I received a letter from the bishop's office that I'm not sure that I was supposed to see. The letter was addressed not to me, but to the chairperson of the Pastor-Parish Relations Committee, and was thanking the congregation for having the kindness to receive me as their pastor. At first, I thought that it was a nice gesture on the bishop's part; but, I then asked another clergywoman in my parish, "Does everybody in the church get these letters?" Of course, I already knew the answer. The members of my congregation, no matter how ready I was to love and learn from them, had not even met me, yet they immediately doubted my ability to be their pastor. Intentional or not, the bishop, by being nice and making extra overtures to the church members and constituents, had reinforced their fears; furthermore, the bishop had undermined the authority that he had not long before conferred on me as an ordained minister. Rather than trusting God in me and my gifts and graces for ministry, he prejudicially saw nothing but a woman in a wheelchair.

Midway through my three-year tenure in that first pastoral appointment, a man stood up during a worship service, and declared, "God and the annual conference have made a mistake by sending you here." Somehow, I managed to lead the service and deliver my sermon, but it was immediately after the benediction that a vote by the congregation took place to seek a new pastor. When, for the sake of my family and me, I told my district superintendent that it was time for me to move to another pastoral appointment, he delivered an additional blow by saying that there was nowhere for me to go.

The following year, after having been courted by the bishop to take family or incapacity leave that I rejected, I then was appointed to be as part-time associate pastor on a 5-point charge under the authority of a probationary deacon. It was upsetting to be second to a deacon, but even more disturbing was that my salary was supported by equitable compensation, meaning that the 5 congregations we served had little interest and even less investment in my presence. As a matter of fact, they had not been told that I was appointed to that five-church charge.

Since then, I have served two other congregations within the West Virginia Annual Conference, and the stories that accompany each church are similar to my first two pastoral appointments. In each case, bishops and cabinet members have unwittingly undermined my authority and potential ministry by attempting to allay congregation's fears, providing financial support for needed architectural changes, and offering salary support under the assumption that my presence would drive away several members. It seems I am caught in a double bind; I am to lead churches, love them, and invite them to engage and transform their world, but if I attempt to make those changes, standards are lowered for the churches, but are seemingly made higher for me. Instead of recognizing me for the transformations that I had attempted, I was judged by the churches' often erroneous perceptions of my efforts.

Battling a Discriminatory Hierarchy

Following what I call a fake appointment, I was placed on a life-altering incapacity leave. Prior to that hurtful moment, there was a two-year battle with the bishop and cabinet over the matter of incapacity leave. It began with a supervisory committee meeting in which my bishop invited me to consider the incapacity relationship while I was to be "discerning" another kind of ministerial appointment or employment. I initially agreed – thereby wanting to take the high road and be agreeable. When the paper work arrived at my house, I realized what I had unwittingly done, and immediately called my district superintendent to declare that I could not comply with the request from the Bishop and Cabinet; inexplicably, the superintendent has denied the fact that the conversation occurred. Thus began the two-year battle that included administrative charges of my ineffectiveness, and being placed by the Conference Board of Ordained Ministry (BOOM) on Involuntary Leave of Absence. In United Methodist parlance, that means the discharged minister maintains her or his clergy credentials, but is no longer allowed to perform any of the functions of the ministerial office; perhaps what is more important is that the discharged minister has no claim on the financial resources of the General Church or the Annual Conference.

At the advice of my clergy counsel, I appealed the BOOM ruling, and pled to the lesser charge of incapacity leave. In doing so, I was further injured by the church. I felt as if my colleagues had thrown me out with the trash. Being forced into the incapacity leave was the hardest thing for me to accept.

The Dark Side

In order to remain safe in the institution of the church, and secure the livelihood of my family, I went over to the dark side. It would seem plausible to someone who is "normal", someone who is outside disability circles that the unexpected or "abnormal" characteristic in an individual is often not embraced by others in that person's family. While this is true for some people, it is not true for me. As a person with cerebral palsy who had since the age of four been called by God into ministry, I was loved and supported by my family all of my life in every crazy endeavor that I pursued.

Instead of protesting the removal further, I—in a manner of speaking—drank the Kool-Aid; I took the 30 pieces of silver. That is my confession, stated here for the first time. I ask for forgiveness from God, my family, and from all who recognized the lie at work in removing me from active ministry.

That was the moment—the moment of The Lie. I thought the church had done all that it could to, and therefore it could do no more than it had already done to diminish me, to deny my call to ministry, to misunderstand my personality, and to misuse the God-given gifts I possess. But I was wrong. In our open-minded, mission minded, edgy "reach new people" church, my colleagues had succeeded in pushing me away from the table of ordained ministry. For me, the memory of that brutalizing moment is indescribable.

The Brutality of Abandonment

Today my eyes are dry and my voice is controlled, but the stone in my belly is no smaller as it weighs heavily within me due to the disappointments and betrayals inflicted on me. As I once said to a clergy colleague, "Please, let me be naïve just a while longer." My belief in the church as an institution has been severely shaken and— I fear—in other ways that I have yet to discover. Despite all of that, my belief in both the redemptive character of God and God's plan for all of life is more firmly grounded than ever.

My experience is that the imposed "incapacity leave" has at times become both demeaning and brutal. To be told by bishops and district superintendents that there is no place for you in the conference is to be abandoned and forgotten. In effect, you become a non-entity, a non-person. Your best friends and family no longer remember to include you in their activities; neither do they expect you to add anything meaningful to your life held in common with them. The painful reality is that you are adrift on a sea of connection among many, but you are excluded, and there is no corporate lifeboat to rescue you. It really is something of a cross between "The Island of Misfit Toys" and "Survivor." No one wants you, and there is no way off the island.

The truth is that because of the pressure against me, I was not being the leader God called and created me to be. Several church members repeatedly told me that my being sent to them was a mistake. I think the outward, but incorrect appearance of weakness coupled with my direct, out-of- the- box leadership style proved to be too much for them.

In my private life over the years I have dealt with a lost pregnancy, a blood cancer scare, and a gastrointestinal condition called mega colon. The structure of The United Methodist Church provides for various types of ministerial leave, changes of appointment, usage of the slush fund we call equitable compensation, and—depending on the situation—limited workplace accommodations. Little is done across our denomination to embrace diversity in leadership or leadership style. We consistently fail to acknowledge that prejudice is often more alive in our churches than is our worship of God, and is more outreaching than is any of our local or global mission. I fear that prevailing prejudice will be our denomination's death knell. I have begun to see prejudice as a living thing, similar to J. K. Rowling's dementors in the Harry Potter series; namely, prejudice dealt against us sucks the life out of us, leaving us with the feeling that we will never be happy again.[14]

Journeying Toward Recovery

The truth is that I was drowning in disillusionment and choking on what I interpreted as my daily failure. On most days I was gasping for air, barely breaking the surface. My self-esteem became so eroded that I barely recognized me. I struggled to remember whose child I was, and who it was who made me. I had forgotten my center of being, and was screaming for life, other people's understanding of me, and a rescue from the overwhelming morass of self-criticism.

---

[14] The Harry Potter reference comes from Year III, The Prisoner of Azkaban.

Having written the above pleas, I can see red flags going up; that is, I am not generally a person who cries out for rescuers, because I like to be seen as one who rises to the challenge on my own merits. For me, rescue would have meant—at any given time in my process toward ordination—I received a strong and well-placed "no" to my being ordained, rather than being subjected to a patronizing, charitable "yes." Otherwise for me, a post-ordination rescue would have meant that my vocation and gifts were actually valued and supported just as they are.

One day I told someone that I am in recovery; that is, now I am able to remember whose I am, and without hesitation I am claiming what I am called and created to be and do. That is why I continue to declare that I am a servant of Jesus Christ, who calls me to share his love with others. Indefatigably, I am called to preach, teach, lead, challenge and innovate ways of communicating God's abounding grace to everyone with all exceptions put aside. Meanwhile I cherish my vocation and office as an ordained elder in the United Methodist Church that I unquestionably love.

I have been reflecting for a long while on what we call "the Great Commandments" about loving our neighbor as ourselves and loving God, with our whole heart, soul, mind and strength. John Wesley, the 18th century founder of the Methodist movement within the church, declared in one of his sermons titled "a Catholic Spirit" (meaning "universal" in 18th century English) that Jesus' summation of the biblical law and prophets is the only creed that we ever need to profess. Love for God and each other are meant to be the core of our existence with God through Jesus Christ.

The prevailing theme for this period in my life has been about finding my way out of the darkness of despair. I know, for a fact, that I'm not in that darkness alone. How do we, as people and the church, move as needed when we feel there's no hope and no breath left? How can we move when we are fearful of every step and have forgotten where it is that we were intended to go? What probably is most important is to ask how can we claim the strength that is already ours as God's gift.

My reflection on the importance of Jesus' dual-commandment was prompted during my reexamination of two theological terms; namely, "Anamnesis" and "Perichoresis."Anamnesis refers to the theological idea that in the presence and action of Holy Communion, we are actively remembering the history of God being with us from ancient to current times. We are reminded of the Hebraic exodus from Egyptian slavery, God's gift and action through Christ Jesus in his Nativity, on the cross, and our hoped-for future through his resurrection. I am also reminded of the corporeal nature of our human bodies in that there are muscles, bone, nerve and mind in whatever is our bodily capacity. St. Paul's conception of the body implies connection and movement and necessity of every part for optimal functioning as spelled out in 1 Corinthians 12; it is there that he used the human body as a metaphor for the church, declaring the need for a fully connective church body that demeans no one. As members of the church as Christ's current body on earth, we are not presented with an organizational chart or a hierarchy. Instead, we are presented with a God who continues to be with us, feeds us, and empowers us to serve others in ordained and lay ministries. In someone's aphorism, "I am God's and God is mine," we are offered a remedy for our human tendency toward forgetfulness in that we are united to one another as the body of Christ on earth.

Perichoresis is a term that describes the mutuality of the Trinity. Although each person in the Trinity—Father, Son, and Holy Spirit—is a distinctive individual, they are also one as each person shares in the life of the others. Within the Trinity, we are provided with a magnificent model of community. I loved it when my systematic theology professor would say either "the perichoretic dance" or "the filial dance." My mind and heart would race with images of a church filled with endless possibilities. What marvelous fluidity is offered us in that only the combination of power, grace, and Spirit can provide an authentic ministry in the church, community and world! Those dancing images remind me of the power of the Holy Spirit in us. I am hopeful when I realize, that even though our mission of making disciples of Christ is a shared task, we also have the capacity to move separately to take the risk of employing different ways to meet different needs. Furthermore, we have a greater capacity than we could ever have imagined for welcoming all of God's people into our lives and the church. The hospitality of oneness in the Trinity teaches us that as a church we can likewise be hospitable in sharing a common life with one another, as we were created to be and do.

Swimming to Wholeness

I offer a closing thought. A year before writing this chapter, I started going to a swimming pool. I'm not a good swimmer, and I confess that there are days when the water terrifies me. What was started as a strategy to reduce the swelling in my feet and legs has ended up as something completely different. It's funny how God does that! What began as merely "getting by" has blossomed into a commitment to water therapy.

One day in the pool, a switch just flipped on, and I was reconnected to my true self. I began to remember and embrace who I was. I am tempted to say that the water saved my life, but that is not true since there is no magic in the water. Nevertheless, a life-enriching epiphany occurred while I was in the water. My cerebral palsy is not going away, nor will I wish or pray it away. It is part of the unique way I was created for God's purpose. I will continue to exercise in the pool, because God has used it to restore my memory of who I am and whose I am.

Those of us who know the baptismal liturgy well can say that baptism is an outward and visible sign of an inward and spiritual grace. We are also reminded of our history; namely, the waters of creation, flood waters and the covenant with Noah, through our baptisms sharing in Jesus' baptism, death and resurrection, and more. Our history and memory as the body of Christ, we can say, are in the water. The water is never static, and we are called to move and change with it for the betterment of all of our lives.

Gary Dillensnyder

Disability: Ministry as a Wounded Healer
By Gary L. Lake Dillensnyder, OSL+B.A. B.A., M.Div.

The Childhood Dream

My sense of calling to the ministry as an ordained elder is so tightly woven with my lifelong disability that I sense the first would not exist without the second. While it took a longstanding process to come to this awareness, I knew early on that my wanting to serve Christ in the Church would be a challenge to my consideration of who I am as a person. As a child, I was absolutely sure that I was going to be a pastor, but with a limited understanding of what it meant to be called into a pastoral ministry. I simply loved being in worship and Sunday school, and thought our pastor was somebody whom I not only liked, but also he was someone whom I wanted to emulate. Despite my limited knowledge of what our pastor did, I knew that when I grew up I wanted to do whatever he did.

The challenge presented in that dream of an 8-year-old child was with the factual knowledge that I was somehow different in ways that I would not know how to talk about or name until I reached adulthood. At first, looking back at that time, I knew that I was keenly introverted, offering few if any words in a conversation or group setting, and very oriented toward feelings. The affections of heart and soul were certainly in connection with the cognitional ways of my mind, but the depth of the feelings I felt was definitely in disproportion to what could be considered normal for one of my age. I lived and experienced much of life as a person having a natural inclination toward introspection and contemplation. While others seemed to do quite well in the forming relationships with people and communicating their thoughts along with their feelings, I—on the other hand—usually had a sense of not "fitting in." That is, not "fitting in" seemed to be the result of who I was, how I was wired, and how my days were more inclined to the intuitive processes that kept my heart and mind churning in high gear. Those inner stirrings loomed large as sadness and pain. It was as if there existed a nagging wound deep in my heart of hearts that I could not reach, except to feel an emptiness and a longing for an inner peace.

I would not know until decades later that I was in fact moving through the journey of life with what society refers to as a "disability;" namely, a mental illness. Furthermore, not only is that condition defined as a disability, it is also defined as a stigma, and that definition is indicative of how "mental illness" is so often misunderstood. My lifetime companions have been clinical depression and an anxiety disorder. I learned those descriptive terms once I was already into the third decade of my life, and the first decade of serving Christ as a pastor.

While my disease—yes, depression and anxiety are diseases, not unlike other diseases treated with medication—has been an inescapable present part of who I am and have been. I can, however, say that there was and is someone also present in my life; that "someone" was my faith-walk that has always been incarnational, precisely because I have known God through the life and actions of other people. As a child, God was real to me in the love and care of a mother and father who were as devoted to being parents as they were devoted to each other within their marriage covenant in Christ. Likewise, God was found in a brother and sister. Later, I would come to know God as being wonderfully present in teachers, professors, pastors, friends and colleagues. There was, however, another way in which the incarnational nature of my pilgrimage took shape.

The Wounded Healer

While there was a time when I had to step away from college and the rigors of the academic world, and that occasion proved to be a source of helpful insights. Mainly, I was without any system of support at a university that was much too large for me to find ways of establishing friendship. Communities that were to be places of connection were actually abusive in nature, and divisive in agenda. While I felt both alone and lonely, it was clear that others knew first hand an isolation and alienation not unlike my own. I was, however, without the ways and means of connecting with them. With my own life steeped in crisis, I was unable to escape from an overarching sense of despair.

It was in my return to college that I made an important and life-understanding discovery. In retrospect, it one could suspect that I made this discovery by accident. I have come to believe, nonetheless, that few things in life as simply matters of circumstance. I had taken a drive during my lunch break to the local Cokesbury store in Harrisburg, Pennsylvania. It was only a thirty-minute drive from Lebanon Valley College. Searching the shelves for something to read in addition to my assigned texts for the courses I was taking, a book by Fr. Henri J. M. Nouwen caught my eye. It was one of his early works, entitled *The Wounded Healer*.[1]

As I began to read the book, I soon found myself immersed in the stories and ideas that Nouwen was sharing with his readers. I highlighted a particular statement with my yellow marker. It reads: "[The Messiah] is called to be the wounded healer, the one who must look after his own wounds but at the same time be prepared to heal the wounds of others."[2] This God, as known in the Messiah, is not merely human incarnate, but so essentially human as to take upon God-self the depth and breadth of all suffering and loss.

Hence, the Messiah is not only a person in vocation, but also a person in being. There is such a dynamic and intricate connection in life between the ontology of whom and whose we are, and what that identity means in terms of how we are in life and what in life we do.

It was the thoughts of the book that helped me to appreciate the need for the marriage between the personal and professional selves, while at the same time, keeping each in a creative tension with the other. Then the wounds of the servant become not an impediment to ministry but a resource from which one can minister more faithfully and powerfully. Is it any wonder that my faith is such an "incarnational" reality!

Nouwen continues his emphasis on the wounded healer by saying that "Making one's own wounds a source of healing ... [calls for] a constant willingness to see one's own pain and suffering as rising from the depth of the human condition which all [people] share."[3] Thus, the more one is in touch with the depth of his or her own disability, the more one is able to minister to others in their wounded selves. Furthermore, for Nouwen, acceptance of anyone's disability is to known as radical hospitality.

The "Incarnational" Ministry

I remember that in the early days of pursuing my sense of calling to ministry, the District Committee on Ordained Ministry asked me, "Why do you understand your call as being that of an ordained elder?" I did not stop to think about a reply. It was as if the answer was on the tip of my tongue before the questions was asked. I had not yet had a seminary education and formal training in theology; however, there was a theology that I knew and found to be a fire in my bones. Thus, I replied, "I want to have hands laid upon me and to have the opportunity to lay hands upon others in a sacramental way that is found not only in preaching, but also in the sacraments of baptism and the Eucharist."

Assuredly, those were strange words coming from a young adult who had been raised in a congregation that was, for the most part, neither liturgical nor sacramental in its worship patterns. It was early in my journey that a foundation was laid upon which I would build a theology and ministry that served me well. I hope and pray that such a theology has served Christ and the Church equally well.

The Wounded Healer in the Practice of Ministry

In my last semester of seminary, I had experienced the deepest and darkest time in my life thus far. It was a time when I found a psychiatrist who finally gave me a diagnosis with which to work. Until then, I simply knew that there was something different about me, different in a wounded sense of the term. Now I knew that what I was experiencing from early childhood into adulthood was clinical depression, along with an anxiety disorder.

While the work I did with the psychiatrist was helpful, even more helpful was the last semester at the seminary when I took my unit of Clinical Pastoral Education (CPE). I found within the context of the hospital and my colleagues a support group and place of ministry where the "wounded healer" took on more shape and formation for me. It was not that the parish lacked such a context. Rather, the parish did not bring to my ministry the feedback and supervision that had proved to be so helpful.

While my graduation from seminary, and the appointment to my first full-time parish had reached me, a still darker place surrounded me. Even after serving as a student pastor for eight years, parish ministry without the easily accessed support of other students and supervisors soon became overwhelming for me. I was in a setting where I could only serve in the role of an interim minister, following a much beloved and highly missed pastor. The richly gentle and professional touch of my District Superintendents made it possible for me to find my way in that first pastoral appointment. Some highly skilled physicians were also key elements in that troubling time.

Naming and Claiming My Wounded Self

A couple of years earlier, I had received the gift of a diagnosis, medication, and an introduction to ongoing therapy that helped me to find my way. I was concerned, nevertheless, that my ordination would be jeopardized due to my disability. It was at that point that I had a candid discussion with my District Superintendent. That exchange was both an epiphany and a time of setting my course for the future. I had become convinced that one of the most important things in ministry is for the clergy person to be of a high integrity. Without such honesty and trans-parency, a basis on which to build a professional relationship with the people I was called to serve would be lacking. Therefore, it was that I did not hide the fact that I was a "wounded healer". In fact, I knew deep within myself that the only way that I could minister faithfully in the church was to be authentic about the person I was, even though I was one who coped with a disability.

I must say that my openness regarding the depression and anxiety hounding me did not always result in having blessings come my way. In fact, I was often reminded of the stigma that mental illness carries with it.

While some Staff-Parish Relations Committee members were accepting in knowing that I had my own "wounds", other members were not as understanding, despite the years spent in building a relationship. I remember painfully how many times I was asked the same question: "How can a minister, a person of faith, be depressed?" It was not only some people in the congregation who raised question. Intrusively, the same query came repeatedly from pharmacy employees, and even some counselors.

At first, I was annoyed with such inquiries. Later I discovered that the queries could be a boon of opportunity to help others to understand that each pastor is a person, and that each of us—whether clergy or laity—faces challenges in life. Being a pastor did not make me exempt from suffering; rather, suffering is the common human dilemma that all of us share. In our sufferings, there is a common ground where we can meet and join in a shared journey through life.

Our In-common Wounded Nature

For me, that is the crux of authentic hospitality, and my dream is that the church will someday claim more readily her calling to be inclusive toward all people. For as different as we each may be, there is so much that we all have in common—things to learn from each other, things to share with each other, things to do together as disciples of Christ serving others in God's precious world.

If there are only a few things that we hold in common, there always are two common denominators binding us together. The first one is that as finite human beings we know losses, injury, and illness. The second one is that within us—as people created, redeemed and sustained by God—there is a sense of something beyond us, greater than we are, that is not only holy as a transcending reality, but also is intimately imminent as a presence of love. For this reason the community we call the church not only makes sense, but also the explicit call to either an ordained or lay ministry as servant-disciples of Christ means that each servant has a reasonable and logical outcome. We come together as the body of Christ and minister to one another not because we are able, but because in all of our disabilities God is able!

As I look back over my several years of life, I do not think I want to be different from what I have been. The presence of my disability has played a major role in shaping who I am and the way I minister to others. The fact is that without the disability, I would not have had the opportunities to serve others as I have. Still, there are people who push me away or otherwise avoid me because of the nature of my disability. I nonetheless continue to be open to them, all the while knowing that depression and anxiety had not prevented my graduation with honors from high school, college, and seminary. I know that my disability is tightly woven into my sense of call to pastoral ministry, along with my understanding of the church and its mission and ministry in the world. Furthermore, it is due to my acceptance of my disability that I am able to be in connection with others in a place that is of mercy and compassion, of hospitality and inclusion.

Even In Times of Need God Is Present

In 2007, my disability became disabling. I woke up one day and knew that I was empty. A void within me had been growing for the past several years. In the midst of being the "wounded healer," I had forgotten the important lesson Fr. Nouwen noted so well; namely, I had concentrated too much of myself and my resources on healing others without tending as well to my own wounds. I was in the midst of a severe burnout from which I am not yet fully healed. Hence, it is in these current days that my ministry focuses on self-care, and allowing time and energy for the return of the wholeness that I need.

I am hugely thankful for my colleagues who share a calling to ministry despite having a disability in one form or another. Our collegiality is a source of grace and hope that shall lead to wellness and health, even when being well includes having depression and anxiety as my life-companion. I suppose that is why the Apostle Paul's words resonate so deeply within me. Here they are:

> "Therefore, since it is by God's mercy that we are engaged in this ministry, we do not lose heart. We have renounced the shameful things that one hides; we refuse to practice cunning or to falsify God's word; but by the open statement of the truth we commend ourselves to the conscience of everyone in the sight of God. And even if our gospel is veiled, it is veiled

215

to those who are perishing. In their case the god of this world has blinded the minds of the unbelievers, to keep them from seeing the light of the gospel of the glory of Christ, who is the image of God. For we do not proclaim ourselves; we proclaim Jesus Christ as Lord and ourselves as your slaves for Jesus' sake. For it is the God who said, 'Let light shine out of darkness,' who has shone in our hearts to give the light of the knowledge of the glory of God in the face of Jesus Christ.

But we have this treasure in clay jars, so that it may be made clear that this extraordinary power belongs to God and does not come from us. We are afflicted in every way, but not crushed; perplexed, but not driven to despair; persecuted, but not forsaken; struck down, but not destroyed; always carrying in the body the death of Jesus, so that the life of Jesus may also be made visible in our bodies. For while we live, we are always being given up to death for Jesus' sake, so that the life of Jesus may be made visible in our mortal flesh. So death is at work in us, but life in you (2 Corinthians 4:1-12 NRSV)."

Works Cited

1. Henri J. M. Nouwen, *The Wounded Healer: Ministry in Contemporary Society.* Doubleday, New York, NY, 1972.

2. Ibid., page 88.
    The Talmud records a message concerning the coming of the Mashiach [i.e., Messiah]. *The Talmud (Sanhedrin 98a)* relates that one day; "Rabbi Yehoshuah Ben Levi was walking and ran into Eliahu HaNavi, (Eliahu the Prophet). After exchanging greetings, Rabbi Yehoshuah begs to ask Eliahu one question: "Eimatai Ka Ati Mar?" When will the Master (the Mashiach) come?" A logical question, to be sure, as the prophets tell that one day, Eliahu HaNavi will be the predecessor of the Mashiach, heralding his coming and ushering in a new age of redemption. The story continues that Eliahu responds by saying, "Ask him yourself!" To which Rabbi Yehoshuah asks: "but where can I find him?" Eliahu explains, "If you will go to the entrance to the market-place, you will see that all the lepers sit at the entrance to the market, with their bandages removed so that the warmth of the sun can heal their wounds. However," says Eliahu HaNavi, "pay attention and you will notice that there is one beggar who only allows himself to remove one bandage at a time, so as to be ready to move at a moment's notice, in the event that he is called." "This," says, Eliahu HaNavi, "is the Mashiach."

    The point is vividly made: the Messiah is found among the "wounded", in the places where there is suffering, among those who are in need, identifying with those who are together as if a tapestry woven with threads of mercy in human brokenness and compassion in human vulnerability. In addition, the Messiah is always in a state of readiness, willing and able to "make haste to help us" and "make speed to save us".

    To carry this metaphor even further, Walter Wannegrin describes the Messiah as the "Ragman" who not only is present in the places of human need but who exchanges new rags for old, tattered rags. In doing so, the "ragman" takes upon himself the rags of those who cry carrying them in weeping, the rags of those injured carrying them in bleeding, the rags of those who are dismembered carrying them as without limb, the rags of humanity carrying them as one who is fully human while also being fully God. This God is one who is not above getting dirty and soiled in the bane of our existence, but rather embraces the most earthy of life's challenges making them his own, thus transforming curse into blessing (cf., Wannegrin, Walter. *Ragman and Other Cries of Faith*. HarperCollins, New York, NY, 2004, pp. 3-6).

[3.] Ibid., page 88.

David Seymour

Life with Physical Disabilities, the Christian Life, and the Ordained Ministry
By The Rev. David T. Seymour

In 1955, I was born prematurely at six and a half months, causing the condition known as cerebral palsy. The back part of my skull was soft, like a sponge. It wasn't hard enough yet to fully protect me from the pressure formed by normal birth contractions; consequently the oxygen to my brain was cut off, causing some brain cells to die. The area in my brain where the damage occurred had affected my motor skills and physical coordination. My brain is like a telephone switchboard with some of the panels burned out. Although that damage is permanent, it—fortunately—doesn't get any worse, and my abilities to think and reason is not damaged.

Cerebral palsy is sometimes described as a birth defect. I can't argue with that definition, but I prefer to describe it as a one-time birth accident; consequently, using a wheelchair is an essential part of my daily routine.

Up until I was 14 years old, I attended special schools for disabled children. At that time our family lived respectively in Baltimore and Catonsville, Maryland. Schools for children with disabilities were few and far between. I had the same classmates for 9 years, and all of us were bused to three separate schools; all too often, my daily routine was to ride the school bus for 3 hours a day-90 minutes in the morning and 90 minutes in the afternoon. In those days, schooling was composed of the usual curricula; namely, literature, mathematics, history, all combined with physical therapy sessions to strengthen my muscles and upper body strength. My friends were at school, not in the neighborhood, and not at home. I was not mainstreamed into a regular school system until I was in the middle of the ninth grade. By then I had separated from my childhood friends. I spent that half of the ninth grade and the entire tenth grade as the only disabled person in the student body of 1,500 kids in a high school in Annapolis, Maryland. There was no elevator in the school building, but flights of steps were everywhere. The result was that my classmates generously carried me—wheelchair and all—up and down those stairs every day of the school year. It was a tough challenge, but I survived it.

My life in the United Methodist Church followed a similar path. From my perspective, church was a part of my parents' life in a community service and social club sort of way. Looking back, my current theological judgment is that Jesus was presented as a teacher, never as a personal Savior. Our possible sins were never talked about or confessed in any specific or life-changing way.

In Sunday school I memorized lists of books in the Bible in order to win ribbons of various colors, but I cannot say that we were taught what can be found in any of those books. In the Letter to the Romans I didn't know its message until ten years later when I went through the process of being born again. If God was mentioned at all by pastors or Sunday school teachers, He was for me a remote figure. There was no hint of a personal relationship with God. There was no belief in a great personal sacrifice by God in our behalf in order to rescue us from the power of sin or hell. There was no mention or discussion of passages of Scripture such as Psalm 22 or Isaiah 53, with the latter passage written some five centuries prior to Jesus', era, and addressing the Babylonian captivity along with other sufferings of the Hebrews.

Currently, I stand within the framework of a conservative evangelical theology that these Old Testament passages nevertheless describe in vivid detail the atoning sacrifice of Jesus Christ due to our sinfulness. Pastors and teachers of my childhood operated from a liberal theological perspective. My judgment is that the importance of making a personal commitment to follow Jesus Christ was not part of their presentation about the Christian way of life.

What was talked about were the duties and obligations of church membership, but not—so I declare—what it means to follow Christ. For my brother Chris and me that meant years of choir practice in the children's and later the youth choirs. We treated those rehearsals like a homework chore. It was something we did to please and entertain our parents, not God.

What moral values that I did pick up came from being part of my family in which our free time was spent together. My parents have always loved to travel and take camping trips. During my childhood we camped all over the country. I have been to California, Utah, North Dakota, Maine, Arizona, Texas, Virginia, Pennsylvania, Illinois, and New York. My parents have a strong marriage and are devoted to each other. Birthdays, Mother's Day, Father's Day, Thanksgiving, 4th of July are big events in our family life, both then and now; however, as I reflect on it, it was family life that took the place of God. I believe with all my heart that family life is important, but that alone cannot bring forgiveness, holiness, righteousness, salvation, reconciliation, healing and personal peace into your life. Only Jesus Christ can do that.

The Gift of Being Chosen

It was when I turned 19 that God in his mercy began to draw me to Himself. "You did not choose Me, but I chose you and appointed you that you should go and bear fruit, and that your fruit should remain, that whatever you ask the Father in My name He may give you" (John 15:16, New King James Version-NKJV). I wasn't looking for God but, fortunately, God came looking for me.

During my 1974-1975 sophomore year in college I met a young man in our dormitory that lived down the hall from me. We had many quiet conversations during the year. His name was Alan Fredericks, and he had a quiet peace within himself that, at first, I didn't understand, but I was intrigued by it. He was a Christian who lived by what he believed. He had integrity and personal peace with God that I lacked.

It was Alan who first explained to me the meaning of Romans 5:6-11, as follows: "For when we were still without strength, in due time Christ died for the ungodly. For scarcely for a righteous man will one die;

221

yet perhaps for a good man someone would even dare to die. But God demonstrates his own love toward us, in that while we were still sinners, Christ died for us. Much more then, having now been justified by his blood, we shall be saved from wrath through him. For if when we were enemies we were reconciled to God through the death of his Son, much more, having been reconciled, we shall be saved by his life. And not only that, but we also rejoice in God through our Lord Jesus Christ, through whom we have now received the reconciliation."

Certainly not all, but at least some people with disabilities will understand what it is to be broken both physically and spiritually. Physical brokenness has many causes, but it can be said that some biblical passages offers different promises of physical resurrection after death (see Job 19:25-27 and 1 Cor. 15:42-44, 54-57 NKJV). My personal belief is that Christians with disabilities can have a victory over death through faith in Jesus Christ. As I see the matter, our spiritual brokenness and alienation from God are set aside due to Christ dying for the ungodly, who reconciles us back to God by forgiving our sin, and gifting us with eternal life. Therefore, I hold that through faith in Christ we become whole— spiritually and physically- again. That is the good news of the gospel for those who cope with disabilities.

To state my convictions further, it is possible for Christians with disabilities to understand the scope of the victory that Christ achieved for us. I declare again that reconciliation with God in Christ has its physical and spiritual aspects. We can comprehend on a deep personal level how vital it is for us to have peace with God. God is in Christ to accomplish that purpose, and we are called to an ordained or lay ministry of reconciliation with all people.

Earlier in my life God seemed distant and remote. That isn't true anymore. Christ came very close to me. Slowly, over the years, as the weight of sin in my heart increased, I realized that I was a sinner, a sheep that had gone astray. I was also sure that Christ was reaching out to me as the proverbial square peg in the round hole. I was overwhelmed and humbled by Christ's gift of forgiveness, love and acceptance that—I believe—came for me from Jesus' sacrificial death on the cross.

Before that insight reached me I had never been chosen by anyone. The gift of acceptance echoed in my mind and heart. I resonated to the this verse: "'Come now, and let us reason together,' says the Lord, 'though your sins are like scarlet, they shall be white as snow; though they are red like crimson, they shall be as wool'" (Isaiah 1:18 NKJV).

Christ and I engaged in an exchange. I gave him my sin, self-centeredness, pride, emptiness, brokenness and despair. Christ embraced me. He gave me himself. A tremendous weight was lifted off me that I actually felt. I received a deep personal peace in the center of my heart that endures to this day. I became a believer through studying and reflecting on passages in Isaiah and Romans. That is how the gospel of Christ became real to me, and how I became a Christian.

Six months later, I came across the story of Mephibosheth in 2 Samuel 9. King David had been ruling in Israel for 20 years. He wanted to know if there were any members of King Saul's family still living, and to whom he could imitate God's kindness. There was one survivor name Mephibosheth who was "crippled in both feet" (9:3 NKJV). The descendant was brought before King David without being told what to expect. The fellow's royal blood flowed in his veins, and as King Saul's grandson, he had a claim to the throne of Israel. Mephibosheth faced the possibility of being executed by David as a rival to the throne. He considered himself "a dead dog."

Dogs were not pets in biblical times. They were wild, vicious and like wolves, they hunted in packs, sometimes   roaming the garbage dumps for food. To be called "a dog" in biblical times was considered a major insult. When Mephibosheth called himself "a dead dog" it meant that he despised himself, supposing that he had no future. King David, however, embraced Mephibosheth, and adopted him into his family; the good news was that Mephibosheth had a future after all.

For me, this is a story of God's grace for the Hebrews, told in their Scriptures. But, I also see in the tale what Jesus did for me. For the first time, I saw myself in a Bible story, identifying me with Mephibosheth. I had supposed that my sins made me a "dead dog" before God. I remember being brought before Jesus as if he were a king, and feeling that I had no future. I was wrong about that. Jesus embraced and adopted me into the family of God. I was reconciled to God through Christ. I didn't deserve it, but the kindness of God changed my life.

Life in the Ordained Ministry

During my 1977 senior year in college I received the call from God to enter the ordained ministry. For me, honoring that call has been an uphill struggle that continues to this day. Generally speaking, it is likely that the campus of many theological seminaries are not accommodating for a person who uses a wheelchair. At Wesley Theological Seminary in Washington, D.C., where I enrolled, its buildings were constructed in the 1950s— a time when creating physical access to persons with disabilities was unheard of in both the human mind and the typical building codes. The only elevator on the campus was housed in the library. Some of my fellow seminarians graciously carried me up and down flights of steps so that I could attain a seminary degree; that lifting was hard on all of us.

Physical barriers in seminaries remain a current problem. Congregations will never accept individuals with disabilities as pastors as long as seminaries themselves are filled with physical barriers that face such students. We need to remodel our seminary, educational and church buildings, making them fully accessible for individuals with any kind of disability.

All of my fellow students were appointed as student pastors at the end of their first year. In contrast, I never received any church appointment or salary during my entire time at the seminary from which I graduated in 1985. My only church appointment came three years later in 1988.

It was on June 3, 1990 that I was ordained as an elder of the United Methodist Church in the Peninsula conference of the United Methodist Church. Leading up to that ordination, I was appointed on July 1, 1988 to be the associate pastor to a group of 12 United Methodist Churches known as the Bayview Cluster, located in Talbot County on the Eastern Shore of Maryland. The grouping was an experiment in cooperative ministry. I worked with 6 senior pastors and their congregations in the basic geographical areas of Royal Oak, Saint Michaels, and Tilghman Island.

My role was to help these churches work together. Much of my time was spent in assisting in their fund-raising projects and Christian education programs by creating original posters, banners, and brochures that were used in promoting their activities. These projects were done on an IBM computer using the desktop publishing software program. I preached expository sermons in the conservative evangelical tradition and led worship services whenever any of the senior pastors took some time off or became ill. I participated in a weekly Bible study group at Royal Oak Community Church in Royal Oak, Maryland. I assisted in the teaching of vacation Bible school during the summer months using a preplanned curriculum and lesson plans. I also taught a 12-week confirmation class for those youth and adults who were interested in becoming members of the United Methodist Church, likewise employing a preplanned curriculum and study guide. In order to help students better understand the gospel of Christ, I design graphic illustrations and other supplemental materials to be used in the confirmation classes.

With the assistance of the senior pastors and the laity, I made visits to the local hospital and nursing homes in the area, as well as engaging in various events within the several churches. As a cluster, we came together for special worship services during the liturgical church year at Thanksgiving, Christmas, Lent, and Easter.

My pastoral appointment took place in a large rural region. I had never owned a car due to lack of employment. There were no agencies in that area for teaching me to drive a car. Public transportation was limited to buses on fixed routes and short schedules. It was the laity of the congregations who picked me up from my apartment in their cars and transported me to my church job. There was a spirit of cooperation among the pastors and laity of the Bayview Cluster that made my job the limited success that it was.

When this church position ended on July 1, 1990, I was placed on involuntary retirement and removed from the pastoral appointment list. It was in February of 1990 when I presented myself for the oral examination by the conference's Board of Ordained Ministry for the office of elder that I was given the surprising announcement. There was no prior warning. It came as a shock, a totally unexpected action. At that time, I had thought that my professional career in the ministry was beginning after so many delays. My time of service within the Bayview Cluster has gone reasonably well, so I thought. The status of involuntary retirement has brought my career in ministry to an end, before it had a chance to begin. Both the bishop and the district superintendent compounded my dismay by concurring with the decision. The forced retirement chokes the life out of my chosen career.

Oddly, I was nevertheless ordained as an elder, but I have not been allowed to serve as one; nor have I been paid any salary. Since that time no church official has proposed any other pastoral appointment with me, or suggested paid employment of any sort within the church system. Immediately, all financial support was cut off, and I do not receive a pension for my years of service in the church. If this treatment of disabled persons, such as I have endured, becomes standard practice within the ordained ministry, persons with disabilities will have no ministerial future. A laborer is worthy of his hire. If there is no hiring, service cannot be rendered.

My supposition is that my disability was the chief factor in the Board of Ordained Ministry's action. At a later date, a church official told me that I would not have been ordained an elder in the first place unless I was retired at the same time; that was a highly unusual procedure. This shows me that the conference officials never intended for me to have a professional career in the ordained ministry. The district superintendent who had pushed for my appointment in the first place died of AIDS during my internship. Since the Peninsula Conference apparently no longer needed my services, no church leader has served as my advocate within the denomination.

For over 20 years, I have endured the Conference Board of Ordained Ministry's mistreatment of me. I was deeply hurt by the ruling and its aftermath. Today, it still stings.

Judge Me if You Must, but Not by My Deafness or Blindness
By Robert L. Walker, D.Min.

It hurt: "You're dumb," said teachers, kids alike
With gibes and scowls, then turned aside or ran
While tears were hid in heart where none could strike;
Yet haunt it does that child in me, a man,
For ears that hear, for eyes that see, I lacked,
And suffered taunts from those too deaf, too blind
To see my mind, to hear my heart that cracked
Those heartless walls they raised around their kind.
When walls are shattered, love and wisdom flow
To temper scorn and hate till born is care
For hearts and minds, but deaf and blind, to grow
In wisdom forming love in lives to share.
Oh child in me, your yearnings ne'er depart
Till all will see by mind, and hear in heart.[15]

Light Bulb Ablaze!

In the late 1980s, my former bishop, by then assigned to another United Methodist Conference, attended a workshop on handicapping conditions facing lay and clergy persons. The workshop leader was a staff member of the Health and Welfare Department of the United Methodist

---

The poem is titled "The Child in Me," an Elizabethan styled sonnet written in 2009 by this chapter's author.[15]

Church's General Board of Global Ministries on whose board of directors I served from 1980 to 1988.

At the close of the workshop, the bishop told the leader that in his former conference he had a minister who didn't see or hear well, and he never knew what to do with him. The leader—who was also a friend of mine—asked the inquiring bishop if I was the minister of whom he spoke. The surprised bishop said yes. My friend next asked if I was a competent minister. "Yes," said the bishop, "very competent." "That," said my friend in a moment of irony, "made it even more difficult, didn't it?"

All too often the prevailing, but bogus conventional wisdom in our culture is that bodily-challenged people by definition cannot fulfill a vocation of value.

Sad to say, that same bogus conventional wisdom has misled many church officials to center their attention narrowly on one's so-called disability, all the while remaining deaf and blind to the whole person living adequately—even superbly in some instances—beyond the physical challenge. Put it bluntly, someone's disability is not his or her problem; it is the prejudicial officials' problem in that he or she sees an individual's handicapping condition instead of his or her gifts and graces for either an ordained or lay ministry.

From where I stand, my former bishop's puzzlement over what to do with me as a "deaf-blind" ordained minister was his problem, not mine. That significant insight came to light in me in a January, 1970 light bulb moment. As most readers will recall, when past and present cartoonists displayed a character's unexpected enlightenment, a blazing light bulb was drawn over the character's head. I was 39 years old when that light bulb moment displayed the truth that not I, but others in power were creating barriers to my vocation as an ordained minister because I was hard of hearing and slowly losing my visual acuity.

That blazing moment came in the midst of a conversation with members of the Black Panther Organization in Kansas City, Missouri. What placed me in that city was a persistent fear that I had overheard a close friend's call to ordained ministry, but never mine. Several realities haunted me. The important work of preaching never came easily, no matter how diligently I labored over writing and delivering every sermon. Being hard of hearing and slowly losing my eyesight had long accompanied me, but the darkness fashioned by blindness was frighteningly increasing and made every aspect of pastoral work harder. I could no longer drive a car at night. A conflict with a small group of social conservatives in the Paradise, California Methodist Church had convinced the district superintendent that I, as the church's pastor, had to be removed. All of those and other moments of angst weighed in against being in my chosen vocation.

Mired in the throes of self-doubts, an opportunity came for my wife, our first two children and me to return to the Pacific Northwest Conference for an emergency appointment to a troubled two-point charge in Spokane, Washington.[16] That move, however, did not quiet my daily lament that ministry was not my true vocation; not even the subsequent plaudits of the majority in the Paradise Church in contrast to the small, but dominating group of negators, along with the appreciation voiced for me in Spokane could banish my fears.

Three years after our move to Spokane, I shared my depressed feelings with the newly-appointed district superintendent. He insisted that I should not leave the ministry. He then arranged for the conference to provide me with a scholarship to join six other Ministers in our conference attending the January, 1970 "Renewal Seminar" offered by the Saint Paul School of Theology in Kansas City.

The first week was devoted to what the seminar leaders called an "exposure" into different elements of the U.S. culture. That included the aforementioned visit to members of the Black Panthers, linked to the "Black Revolution" inspired by the Rev. Dr. Martin Luther King, Jr., in their downtown storefront headquarters. Their goal was to end once and for all the national prejudice leading to widespread and diabolical discrimination against U.S. citizens who were African-Americans.

---

[16] My journey into ministry had begun in 1952 while I was a student at the University of Washington in Seattle; hence, the 1966 move to Spokane was a return to the Pacific Northwest Conference of the Methodist Church.

In the course of our ministerial group's discussion with the Black Panthers, one of them offered an observation that resonated within me in my ongoing angst. Looking firmly, but without hostility at all of us white male clergypersons, he said that white people liked to claim they are solving a "black problem." We," he said, "are not the problem; you whites are the problem because you cannot accept the equality of us black people who are locked into a color that we did not choose."[17]

That insight was the cartoon light bulb blazing above my head. Like those men and all people of color, I did not choose to be locked into my irremovable hard of hearing condition, all the while losing my eyesight in an irreversible journey into what I later discovered had a title; namely "Usher syndrome." Incidentally, that month in Kansas City provided me with a gift of renewed mind and heart, and from that time on I no longer denied the legitimacy of being an ordained United Methodist minister.

What on Earth is the Usher Syndrome?

On Thanksgiving Day in the year of 1931, I was born hard of hearing and slowly becoming blind. My brother, older than I by two years, was also born hard of hearing, but was on a speedier journey than was I into blindness.

I do not know when our parents discovered that their sons did not hear or see well. Perhaps I would have soon enough learned of their awareness had not my mother tragically died when she was 28 and I was two years old. I have my mother's last letter sent to her parents and siblings a few days before her Palm Sunday hospitalization, followed by her Easter Sunday death in Hillsboro, Oregon. In that final missive she spoke fondly of her two "babies"—nicknamed Jimmy and Bobby—but makes no mention of a suspicion of our deafness and blindness.

Three weeks after my mother's death, my distraught father, an ordained minister in the Oregon Conference of the Methodist Church,

---

[17] The quotation is a paraphrase, but the written intent of the Black Panther member's witness is accurate.

transferred to the Idaho Conference, and was appointed to the local church in Burley, Idaho. It likely was there that my father reached the conclusion that his two motherless sons did not hear well, because in our subsequent move to Buhl, Idaho, and as a five year old first grader not turning six until late in November, I remember his request that I be seated in a front row desk so as to hear my teacher better.

If my father was also cognizant of his young sons' declining eyesight, it wasn't until our 1940 to 1946 sojourn in Nampa, Idaho that I heard him telling others that Jim and I were "night blind." None of us understood the oncoming nature of disappearing eyesight, but "night blindness" is an early marker of *retinitis pigmentosa* that names the shrinking periphery of the eye's retina.

Meanwhile, my brother and I had to contend with the frequent and cruel consequences of those sensory losses. It was in my Buhl, Nampa and Pocatello, Idaho schooling that I experienced the hurts voiced in my sonnet placed at the beginning of this chapter. My father, wishing to protect my feelings, waited until I was several years older to tell me that my teachers had informed him that I was "slow." In that era, "slow" was a euphemism for being mentally retarded at worse, not very bright at best.

I blame those teachers' erroneous evaluation on their uneducated awareness that my reduced hearing ability caused me to pause long enough to be sure that I understood the question or assigned lesson before responding. Even the use of my first bulky and often balky hearing aid at the age of 11, could not overcome every sound barrier confronting me.

Consequently, the several misunderstandings of what I heard led teachers to grade my class work negatively. None of their erroneous conclusions, however, prevented my pursuit of an education, demon-strated in being an early reader, frequently winning the classroom spelling bees, evidence of a good IQ when tested before entering college and seminary, placed in the top level of English literature and composition classes in my freshman college year, earning a Bachelor of Arts degree with a major in journalism and a minor in sociology, a Master of Divinity degree from Garrett-Evangelical Theological Seminary in Evanston, Illinois, and some years later a Doctor of Ministry degree in the theology of preaching from Saint Paul School of Theology in Kansas City, Missouri.

What hurt even more was the taunting often hurled at me by classmates from first grade on into my high school years: "Can't you see where you're going?" "Are you deaf and dumb?" "Clean the wax out of your ears." Especially tormenting were demands to pronounce words containing sibilant consonants such as s, c, z, sh, ch, st and the like; hurtful were the tormentors' uproariously laughing over my faulty speech.

Speech impediment is a harsh side effect of being hard of hearing. By the time that I was a student for one year at Idaho State University in Pocatello before transferring to the University of Washington in Seattle, a new speech correction science had become part of the curriculum, both for graduating more therapists and providing its aid to needful students. Paradoxically, the huge number of mentally or physically wounded World War II's soldiers needing to relearn the art of speech gave rise to that new science.

That was the case at Idaho State University. The lone professor of speech therapy happened to be a member of our Pocatello Methodist Church, and that helped my brother and me to seek her services. I was greatly helped, but ongoing years showed me that I needed still more therapy. In the late 1960s I received excellent help from Gonzaga University in Spokane, Washington. The school had a Department of Speech Therapy, and welcomed clients with whom their students could work.

A young woman was assigned to guide me, and for homework I was handed several lists of troublesome words to rehearse daily. Our youngest child, by then three years old would find one of her children's books, climb onto the sofa next to me, and laugh companionably as I repeated words and sibilant letters.

Another gracious helper in my effort to speak clearly was Mardy, my cherished and always loving wife of 49 years. She was undeterred by my increasing loss of eyesight in addition to my ever present low level of hearing. Mardy died on July 7, 2003, due to non-Hodgkin's lymphoma.

What, then, is the cause of my deafness and blindness? By the time I was a student at the University of Washington, an ophthalmologist

232

let me know that research was beginning to show the connected afflictions of these two sensory organs in the human body. He did not, however, know of any name or cure for the condition, let alone what caused it.

The eventual naming and defining of the condition came in my late 40's, provided by the former husband of one of my cousins. He was a Vocational Rehabilitation counselor in California, and had attended a training conference at Gallaudet University in Washington, D.C., to enable him to work with people who were blind. Gallaudet is the nation's only University created for Deaf, late-deafened, hard of hearing and deaf-blind students. In the course of the seminar, my friend came across a document dealing with the Usher Syndrome. He leafed through it and immediately saw that the description of that genetic disorder fitted my brother and me. He was correct.

In the year 2000, a test of my blood by an Usher syndrome research laboratory in Omaha, Nebraska, established which of three types of Usher syndrome I have. Type one names the baby born deaf and slowly becoming blind, type two names the baby born hard of hearing and slowly becoming blind, and type three has the child at the approximate age of ten years suddenly deafened followed by gradual blindness. I have Type Two, having been born hard of hearing with the creeping blindness reaching its zenith in 2001.

The Usher Syndrome, named for the medical scientist who discovered the gene, is inherited from both parents. The syndrome is incurable, but it can be bred out if at least four generations of progeny elapse without a recurrence. Our three children do not have the syndrome since Mardy was not a carrier; however, they are carriers of the faulty gene. Three of my four grandchildren do not have the condition, but likewise they are carriers. My first grandchild was adopted; hence, she is not a carrier.

The syndrome's deterioration of the eyes is the previously mentioned *retinitis pigmentosa*; starting at the periphery of the retina, its visualizing cells die, and in time the retina no longer functions. By early 2001, I could no longer see anything, except for an occasional non-illuminating glow from an unseen source of light. My hearing loss is essentially stable in that I have had for many years an 80 percent loss in one ear, and a 90 per cent loss in the other ear. Strong hearing aids, a small and portable amplifier called a "pocket talker", and the use of the Assistive Listening System in churches and other public facilities keep me tuned in to speech and music.

Of course, I am greatly affected by my lost eyesight and reduced hearing; however, conventional wisdom to the contrary notwithstanding, the two losses could not and still cannot prevent me from being a whole person. That is, I say that I am capable of contributing to the ongoing work of a divine grace-empowers transformation for a truly compassionate worldwide culture that benefits everyone, deserved or not.

Judge Me if You Must, but Only by the Fruits of my Life and Labors

It ought to be clear by now that my undergirding message is that societal and religious evaluations of persons should be based not on one's handicapping conditions, but on each physically-challenged person's gifts and graces for life's betterment and full enjoyment. The author of the Gospel According to Matthew underscores that point in a saying attributed to Jesus and spoken against prejudiced judgments; namely, let everyone be seen and heard by his or her "fruits," not by a bodily or mental faults.[18] The bishop who narrowed his vision of me to my deaf-blind condition was a fine and compassionate leader; after all, he once recruited me to deliver the sermon for the opening communion and memorial service at an Annual Conference session. Nevertheless, he feared that few local churches—especially the larger ones—would welcome me as their pastor.

That belief was not held by most of the members in the pastoral appointments that I served in California, Washington and North Idaho. Instead of seeing me as a handicapped person, they viewed me as a pastoral guide and fellow servant for the church's local and global ministry and mission. In my penultimate appointment, our district superintendent was told at a Charge Conference that I was the least handicapped minister they had ever had. That was an unsolicited, but prized honor.

---

[18] See Matthew 7:15-16 in the New Revised Standard Version (NRSV) of the Bible.

It can also be said that despite the hesitancy of some bishops and superintendents to assign me to a local church, I acquired a reputation for being a healer of wounded bodies of Christ; sadly, that label fell on five of my eight full-time pastoral appointments, some more seriously broken than others.

I confessed to being self-biased; nevertheless, I insist that— despite my never having a supernatural call to ordained ministry—I was rightly engaged in that sacred and earthly task. Evidence for the claim lies prior to as well as after my tormenting fear that I had overheard my good friend's call to ministry. His call was truly his, and mine just as truly mine.

The proof is in my pastoral journey in the churches I served, the membership and leadership for secular social justice agencies in those communities, assignment as a member or chairperson for United Method- ist District committees, several deanships at California-and Pacific Northwest Nevada Conferences Youth Camps, various conference boards, including chairing the Pacific Northwest Conference Board of Ordained Ministry, membership and leadership tasks in the United Methodist General Board of Global Ministry, membership after my retirement on the United Methodist Committee on Ministry with Deaf, Late-deafened, Hard of Hearing, and Deaf-blind People, contributing author for the second edition of "Signs of Solidarity," co-author with Bishop Peggy A. Johnson of "Make a Joyful Silence," to name some of many responsibilities asked of me.

Above all, I see and hear the proof of my ministerial calling in heeding and proclaiming the grand news of God's amazing grace that leads us to a life of gracious service amidst today's huge social problems. That sacred calling is modeled for us by Jesus, God's anointed servant as "messiah" and "Christ" mean, and by the remarkable teaching and preaching of John Wesley, our church's 18th century founder. As often as I could, I preached the essence of Wesley's declaration that "the grace or love of God, from whence cometh our salvation, is free in all, and free for all." Therefore, he declared, gratefully "Do all the good you can, by all the means you can, in all the times you can, for all the people you can, as long as you ever can."

I end with the last two lines of my sonnet:
Oh child in me, your yearnings ne'er depart
Till all will see by mind, and hear in heart.

Paul Crikelair

By Pastor Paul R. Crikelair

Editor's note: this chapter was originally published in 2002 by the author as a booklet. It is reprinted here with a few changes.

Does the clay say to the potter, "What are you making?"
Shall what is formed
say to him who formed it, "Why did you make me like this?"

Isaiah 45: 9
Romans 9: 20
(Scripture References in this chapter are from the
New International Version.)

No Man's Land: Living Between Two Worlds

It's gone now, but it was still there on that fine day in May 1988 when my father and I arrived. We had taken the train overnight out of Frankfurt, Germany, and during the night we had encountered the barking Communist guards and watched the search dogs plodding and sniffing silently down the length of the roof of the train. In the morning, we had come upon rows and rows of colorful pansies splashing in the bright sunshine among the bustling shopping streets of West Berlin. But in the afternoon, having survived Checkpoint Charlie and the somber dismantling of our tour bus, we were face to face in East Berlin with the infamous Berlin Wall.

It was ugly, monstrous, grotesque, rising up gray and bleak, despite being covered every square inch with graffiti. But what I had not fully realized from the textbooks was that the Berlin Wall was really not one but two walls, actually a double wall, separated by perhaps 20 or 30 yards of open space crammed with barbed wire and pocked by watchtowers. I stared in captivation at this stark and imposing no man's land. How many were there who had been seeking desperately to breach this wall and escape to freedom, who had suffered and even died in its confines?

Little did I realize at the time that Kruschev's doomed monument would supply an apt symbol for my own life. For I live in a no man's land. On my one side lies the hearing world, a world in which sound and speech and communication flow easily and effortlessly. On my other side lies the deaf world, with its own language, its own ways, its own culture. I seem always to have been a part of this first world, and never to have been a part of this second world. But I have come to realize that while this is true, in the deepest sense, as one who is profoundly hearing-impaired, I do not fully belong in either of these worlds; I am truly in a no man's land.

It is also true that to some extent, everyone who knows me or even casually interacts with me is compelled to enter this region, or at least to peer into it. And while there have always been those who have chosen to skirt this terrain by remaining ignorant or oblivious to it and me, the fact is that much of what I have been able to accomplish is a tribute to the untold number of those who have been willing to venture with me into this territory.

As I speak with God on these pages, perhaps you can eavesdrop a bit. Since statistics indicate that as many as ten percent of Americans have some degree of hearing loss, there are many who may benefit from this chapter.

In the past God spoke to our forefathers through the prophets at many times and in various ways, but in these last days he has spoken to us by his Son.

Hebrews 1: 1

O Lord God, I would speak with you. I would speak with you, though the world should smile and smirk, as much as to say, Why, look you, he means he would speak TO you, for that is all we can do, we puny mortals who are so foolish as to speak while you remain eternally silent.

Nay, Lord God, I say I would speak WITH you, for you are not silent – you are the God who speaks. You are the God who spoke at creation, and who by your mere word brought all of the universe into being. You are the God who spoke in visions of old to Abraham and the patriarchs, to Moses at the burning bush, and to your prophets with such power that they could do naught but cry forth, "Thus says the Lord!" You are the God who spoke by your Son Jesus Christ, the Living Word. You are the God who spoke through human agents to record the Scriptures, the Written Word. You are the God who speaks today through your Holy Spirit, quickening my mind and stirring my heart to worship you with a speaking that is beyond all words.

Truly I would speak with you, for you have spoken first, and if you had not first spoken to me, then I could never speak to you. I would speak with you, for only in speaking with you is my soul satisfied and my heart content.

> The righteous cry out, and the Lord hears them;
> he delivers them from all their troubles.
> Psalm 34: 17

O Lord God, I would you would hear me. I, one tiny voice inaudible amidst the unceasing clamor of this world, I would you would hear me. Are you in fact the God who hears all words, who hears all thoughts, who hears all yearnings and longings?

Yea, Lord God, I would you would hear me, for you are the God who hears all. You are the God who heard Hagar near the spring in the desert. You are the God who heard your people groaning in Egypt, heard them crying out in their distress. You are the God who heard Jonah cry out, through the engulfing waters, from the miry depths of the grave. You are the God who heard the prayer of old Zechariah, heard the song of young Mary, heard the decree of Caesar Augustus, heard the chorus of angels on high, heard the cry of the Baby in the manger. You are the God who heard the One who spoke as no man had ever spoken, heard the cry of anguish from Calvary, heard the angel's announcement at the tomb, heard the sound like the blowing of a violent wind from heaven filling the house.

And do you hear my crying out? Do you hear my whispers? Do you hear the child you have made? Yes, you have spoken. Yes, you have heard. O Lord, you have searched me and you know me … before a word is on my tongue, you know it completely, O Lord.

> For you created my inmost being;
> you knit me together in my mother's womb.
> Psalm 139: 13

Ah, Lord God, so you've taken up knitting. The Scripture says, "You knit me together in my mother's womb." Ah, Lord God, so you're a weaver. The Scripture says, "When I was woven together in the depths of the earth, your eyes saw my unformed body."

Ah, Lord God. So you knit me together. So what happened? Why did you knit in some of the hearing, just enough to give me a taste, and leave the rest out? Did you lose the pattern when you came to me? Were you running out of yarn when you were finishing me? Couldn't you find somewhere, anywhere, just a few more millimeters to finish that auditory nerve, to complete what you started? Or were you fancying yourself old Madame Defarge, knitting and secretly glorying in the long ominous shadows of the guillotine, and I your Charles Darnay, encoded and condemned in the stitches of your knitting? Did you fancy this a guillotine to make me die a thousand times before my death?

Or did you really mean to knit me together just as I am? Is it really true there are no accidents with you, that you do all things perfectly, that you had a purpose and a plan in making me just this way? Is it really true that I am fearfully and wonderfully made, that your works are wonderful, that nothing was hidden from you? Is it really true that all the days ordained for me were written in your book before one of them came to be?

> The Word of the Lord came to me, saying,
> "Before I formed you in the womb I knew you,
> before you were born I set you apart;
> I appointed you as a prophet to the nations."
> Jeremiah 1: 4-5

Shall I "out-Jeremiah" Jeremiah?
Ah, Sovereign Lord,
I do not know how to speak;
I am only a partially deaf child.

O Lord, you deceived me, and I was deceived.
The pot you were shaping from the clay
was marred in your hands.
I am ridiculed all day long;
everyone mocks me.
My speech and hearing impairments have brought me
insult and reproach all day long.
I have heard many whispering, taunting, shouting:
"Stupid! Moron! Retard! Imbecile!"
"Cleft palate? Psychotic? What country you from?"
Cursed be the day I was born!
Why did I ever come out of the womb?

Ah, Sovereign Lord, you have made the heavens and the earth by your great power and outstretched arm. Nothing is too hard for you. O great and powerful God, whose name is the Lord Almighty, great are your purposes and mighty are your deeds. "For I know the plans I have for you," declares the Lord, "plans to prosper you and not to harm you, plans to give you hope and a future."

Who has measured the waters
in the hollow of his hand?
Isaiah 40: 12

Measure it, measure it, measure it. It is one thing for God himself to measure the waters of the earth or for the psalmist to proclaim that he knows not the measure of God's salvation. The fact is that when we come to human things, they must be measured. The tabernacle and the temple and the city must be measured, the grain and the gold must be measured.

And the hearing too must be measured. There is a place that has been my place of reckoning, a place that has stripped all away to the bare naked truth, a place that has uncovered and exposed and revealed without mercy. It is a place I have visited all my life, a place where I have

241

screamed and sobbed, a place where I have lived and died. It is the place where I have gone to have my hearing and speech perception measured.

The headphones fit so snugly. The window into the audiologist's booth is so clear. I strain and listen for the beeps, the faintest beeps, the lowest beeps, the highest beeps. I search the audiologist's eyes for the remotest clue, but they are unyielding. Then the words begin to come, blocked from my view by a wretched piece of cardboard covering her mouth. The words float into my headphones, simple words, easy words, kindergarten words, and I am completely defenseless against them, they fall on every side, unsolved, unreturned. And the blood pounds and the tears burn hot and fierce within.

Every valley shall be raised up,
every mountain and hill made low;
the rough ground shall become level,
the rugged places a plain.
Isaiah 40: 4

An audiogram is a graph recording hearing. As one moves from left to right across the horizontal axis, the frequency level increases, which means the sounds get higher and higher. As one moves from top to bottom down the vertical axis, the decibel level increases, which means the sounds get louder and louder.

As I look at an audiogram recording normal hearing, I see a horizontal line going straight across the top of the page: as the sounds get higher, they do not need to be made any louder in order to be heard. This line is flat: flat as a Kansas prairie, flat as a buckwheat pancake, flat as a lazy river, broad enough to encompass every glorious sound one could want to hear.

But as I look at the audiogram recording my own hearing, I see a line which is practically vertical, going down, down, down as it cuts across the page: as the sounds get higher, they need to be made louder and louder in order to be heard. This line is steep, steep as the Matterhorn; so steep that it cuts off people talking, pianos playing, telephones ringing; so steep that it leaves only dogs and trucks, lawnmowers and jackhammers, firecrackers and rock bands, guns and airplanes.

Lord, I don't want the steep line; I want the flat line.
Hannah was praying in her heart,
and her lips were moving but her voice was not heard.
1 Samuel 1: 13

Oddly enough, there was one element of familiar comfort in this unfamiliar place, and that was a big yellow box of Cheerios which sat on the shelf. I had come into this strange city, into this dark building, into this quiet room, to learn to lipread. To do with my eyes what I could never do with my ears. And to snack on Cheerios.

Missing the higher frequencies, I was stripped of all the consonants, the vital identification points of speech. Imagine being sent into a room full of friends. The lighting isn't the greatest, and there's a bit of a fog … and everyone has a black ski mask over his head. "But their faces!" you scream. "I need to see their faces! How can I identify them without seeing their faces?"

And so the eyes are trained to take over for the ears, to put the faces on the bodies of the words. Watch the lips. The tongue. The teeth. The mouth. The cheeks. The face. The eyes. The head. The hands. The body. lipreading is as narrow as the skin of our teeth, as broad as our whole body language. It's an art. It's a science. It's focus and concentration. It's bold and daring. It's a blessing. It's a curse. Have some Cheerios.

"The eye is the lamp of the body. If your eyes are good, your whole body will be full of light." Ah, Lord Jesus, were you a lipreader too? I like to think that you were. The eyes have it, yes, it's all in the eyes.
Your voice will come ghostlike from the earth;
out of the dust your speech will whisper.
Isaiah 29: 4

They say that everything we learn, we learn by a process of association, relating the known to the unknown. And when it comes to learning speech, learning how to form the sounds and words of language, we learn simply by imitating and reproducing what we hear. Ergo it follows that not being able to hear most of the sounds produced in the speech of others, I would not naturally be able to learn these sounds for my own speech.

243

And so it was that in the beginning, there was speech therapy. There was year upon year of speech therapy. And at home, by night, there was practice and patience, persistence and perseverance. I loved it and I loathed it. I thrilled to it and I dreaded it. I was drawn to it and I was repelled by it. I lived by it and died by it.

Watch the lips, the tongue, the teeth. Make it look like this. No, like this. Put your hand here, feel the air coming out. Feel that spit. Higher, higher, put it higher. Back, back, put it back. Look at this picture, here's where you want the tongue. Up behind the teeth. Feel my vocal cords vibrating. Remember how that feels. Do it again. Do it again. Yes, better. Ah, yes.

"O Lord, I have never been eloquent, neither in the past nor since you have spoken to your servant. I am slow of speech and tongue." ..."Who gave man his mouth? Now go; I will help you speak and will teach you what to say."

You rule the raging of the sea;
when its waves rise, you still them.
Psalm 89: 9

Rage, my child,
rage, rage, rage.
Rage at the sounds drifting unclaimed,
rage at the words unconquered, unvanquished,
rage at the teasing, taunting, tearing.

Rule, my Lord,
rule, rule, rule.
Rule the waves of sound and water,
rule the rising billows, the breaking surf,
rule the foam and frothing and fearing.

Rage, my child,
rage, rage, rage.
Rage with a scream beyond all knowing,
rage with an anger unsubsiding,
rage with a fury unrelenting.

Rule, my Lord,
rule, rule, rule.
Rule the clenching fists and grinding teeth,
rule the pounding blood and flashing eyes,
rule the groping, grasping, grieving.

Rage, my child.
Rule, my Lord.
Rage, my child.
Rule, my Lord.
Weeping may remain for a night,
but rejoicing comes in the morning.
Psalm 30: 5

Weep, my child,
weep, weep, weep.
Weep for the sounds unheard,
weep for the syllables unfathomed,
weep for the words unrealized.

Weep, my Jesus,
weep, weep, weep.
Weep as you did at the dusty tomb,
weep in your infinite understanding,
weep in your measureless compassion.

Weep, my child,
weep, weep, weep.
Weep in the depths of the night,
weep in the silence and the stillness,
weep in between the days of frustration.

Rejoice, my child,
rejoice, rejoice, rejoice.
Rejoice that you are called to suffer,
rejoice because I am making all things new,
rejoice at the promise of a bright new morning.

Weep, my child.
Rejoice, my child.
Weeping Jesus, rejoicing Jesus.
Weep. Rejoice.
I can do all things through Christ
who strengthens me.
Philippians 4: 13

Shiny and splendent metal, pinned with utmost care to my shirt pocket. Dull and dirty wax, pressed with tender love into my ear. Slight and slender wire, snaked with artistic grace between the two. It all proclaimed to the world that I was different.

Kindergarten had begun, and the world was before me at St. Catherine's. Fathers and Sisters in black, appearing and disappearing mysteriously. Rows of blue and white and plaid in the classrooms. Ammonia in the hallways. Glory at the altar. Terror in the confessional.

We are deaf. We are blind. We are paralyzed. We are crippled. We are deformed, deficient, defective. We face the world nonetheless, and we face it recklessly and boldly, leaning in humility upon countless numbers of people who are willing to walk with us, even as we encounter a world none can conceive. We do it on sweat and guts, on sheer nerve and wits and chutzpah. We exult and we despair, we laugh and we weep, we quit and we persevere, we have all things and we have nothing.

And we do it, some of us, with Jesus. Praise God for the rich and sustaining grace of Jesus, for the precious gift of knowing the One who loves us with a compassion beyond measure, the One who has given to us far beyond anything we can ask or imagine, Amen.

"I can do all things through Christ who strengthens me."
My soul is in anguish.
How long, O Lord, how long?
Psalm 6: 3

My soul is in anguish.
How long, O Lord, how long?
45 years, 3 months, 17 days.
How long, O Lord, how long?

246

Will you hide yourself forever?
Will this deafness always prevail?

How long, O Lord, how long?
Will birds never sing?
Will sound never carry?
Will words never flow?
Will radio never come alive?
Will telephone never be simple?
Will child never be understood?
Will Mozart never be unimpeded?
Will discussion never be followed?

How long, O Lord?
Will you forget me forever?
How long will you hide your face from me?
How long must I wrestle with my thoughts
and every day have sorrow in my heart?

You are God my Savior,
and my hope is in you all day long.

God chose the weak things of the world to shame the strong ... so no
one may boast before him.
1 Corinthians 1: 26 – 31

And could it truly be that you would call even me to serve you in the ordained ministry? Oh no, my Lord, this could not be. So many others are so much more capable; so many others can hear, can speak, can serve. Call them!

Brothers, think of what you were when you were called. Not many of you were wise by human standards; not many were influential; not many were of noble birth. But God chose the foolish things of the world to shame the wise; God chose the weak things of the world to shame the strong. He chose the lowly things of this world and the despised things - and the things that are not – to nullify the things that are, so that no one may boast before him. It is because of him that you are in Christ Jesus, who has become for us wisdom from God ... Let him who boasts boast in the Lord.

But could you not be pleased to remove my handicap, take away my limitation, so that my effectiveness for you might be increased?

But we have this treasure in jars of clay to show that this all-surpassing power is from God and not from us ... Three times I pleaded with the Lord to take it away from me. But he said to me, "My grace is sufficient for you, for my power is made perfect in weakness." Therefore I will boast all the more gladly about my weaknesses, so that Christ's power may rest on me.

And I heard a sound from heaven ...
like that of harpists playing their harps.
Revelation 14: 2

Why, O Lord, did you grant to me such a love of music, not having granted me to hear all sounds? You made me love melody and harmony, rhythm and tempo, choir and band. You placed in my path an abundance of opportunities and inspiration: talented family and friends and teachers, instruments on every hand, mountains of fake books. You gave me the clarinet, brought forth from the reed the soul of Duke Ellington and Hoagy Carmichael. You gave me the baritone voice, brought forth from the cords the music of cathedral and stage. You gave me the guitar, brought forth from the strings the strains of Paul Simon and John Denver. You gave me the piano, brought forth from the keys the incomparable glory of Bach, beauty of Mozart, passion of Beethoven.

Truly I have delighted in these gifts, lost myself in them, found release in them. And yet too I have cursed them, cursed the reeds, the voices, the strings, the keys that venture beyond my range. In my mind a thousand times I have burned all reeds, cut all strings, split all pianos with a mighty axe at the point of no return, where the tones give way to emptiness and to nothingness.

And they sang a new song before the throne ... No one could learn the song except those who had been redeemed from the earth. Therefore the redeemed of the Lord shall return, and come with singing into Zion, and everlasting joy shall be upon their heads.

As he passed by, he saw a man blind from birth ...
"...that the works of God might be displayed in him."
John 9: 1 – 3

Savior Jesus, Savior Jesus,
See this man, blind from birth.
Speak. Spit. Send.
Goes out blind, comes home seeing.

Savior Jesus, Savior Jesus,
Display the works of God in him.
Open the eyes of his heart,
let him tell them who you are:
"... the man they call Jesus ..."
" ... a prophet ..."
"... this man from God ..."
"...the Son of Man ..."
"Lord, I believe," and he worshipped him.

Savior Jesus, Savior Jesus,
Look on me, deaf from birth.
Will you speak? Will you spit? Will you send?

Savior Jesus, Savior Jesus,
Display the works of God in me.
Open the ears of my heart,
Bring forth from my life
The testimony of the truth, who you are.
Display the works of God in me.

Savior Jesus, Savior Jesus.
Speak. Spit. Send.
Then some people brought to him a man who was deaf and could
hardly talk, and they begged him to place his hand on the man.
Mark 7: 32

Out of Tyre and Sidon, across the Sea,
far away to the wild Decapolis.
Lost and lonely place.
Deaf in the ears, mute in the tongue,

driving the people to a wild desperation.
Lost and lonely man.

Take him aside, away from the crowd,
one-on-one, undivided attention.
Wise and wonderful Savior.

Fingers in ears, spit on tongue,
eyes to heaven, command to open.
Cosmic struggle on high is joined.

Ears opened, tongue loosened,
sounds heard, mute man speaking plainly.
People overwhelmed with amazement.

Take me aside? Away from the crowd?
Fingers in my ears? Spit on my tongue?
My ears opened? My tongue loosened?

You have done everything well.
You even make me hear your voice,
you even make me speak your word.
The whole town gathered at the door,
and Jesus healed many who had various diseases.
Mark 1: 33 – 34

Nobleman's Son Lives
Invalid Gets Up at Pool
Man Born Blind Sees
Lazarus Raised From Dead
Demon Comes Out of Man
Fever Leaves Woman
Leper Touched and Healed
Paralytic Walks
Shriveled Hand Restored
Servant Near Death Restored
Many Demons Cast Out
Jairus' Daughter Raised
Bleeding Woman Healed
Demon Thrown From Boy

250

Mute Demon Driven Out
Crippled Woman Straightened
Ten Lepers Cleansed
Blind Bartimaeus Receives Sight
Malchus' Ear Restored
Two Blind Men See
Mute Man Speaks
Woman's Daughter Healed
Blind Man at Bethsaida Sees Clearly
Man with Dropsy Healed
Deaf and Mute Man Hears and Speaks

"He has done everything well.
He even makes the deaf hear and the mute speak."
What good will it be for a man if he gains the whole world, yet
forfeits his soul? Or what can a man give in exchange for his soul?
Matthew 16: 26

What good will it be for me
if I gain the whole world of physical hearing,
yet forfeit my soul by losing my spiritual hearing?

What good will it be for me
to hear all human voices, all earthly words,
yet no longer hear you, my God in heaven?

What can I give in exchange for my soul?
And if I hear all sounds of earth,
but hear not the sounds of heaven,
if I possess all hearing, yet hear you not,
I am nothing,
I am most utterly deprived and denied.

No eye has seen,
no ear has heard,
no mind has conceived
what God has prepared for those who love him –
but God has revealed it to us by his Spirit.

Whom have I in heaven but you?

251

And earth has nothing I desire besides you.
My flesh and my heart may fail,
my speech and my hearing may fail,
but God is the strength of my heart
and my portion forever.
Then will the eyes of the blind be opened
and the ears of the deaf unstopped.
Then will the lame leap like a deer,
and the mute tongue shout for joy.
Isaiah 35: 5 – 6

And shall the desert and the parched land be glad? Shall the wilderness rejoice and blossom? Shall it burst into bloom, glory, splendor? Shall the feeble hands be strengthened, the faltering knees steadied, the fearful hearts calmed? Shall the blind eyes be opened, the deaf ears unstopped, the lame legs leap like a deer, the mute tongue shout for joy?

We know that the whole creation has been groaning as in the pains of childbirth right up to the present time. Not only so, but we ourselves, who have the first fruits of the Spirit, groan inwardly as we wait eagerly for our adoption as sons, the redemption of our bodies ... The body that is sown is perishable, it is raised imperishable; it is sown in dishonor, it is raised in glory; it is sown in weakness, it is raised in power ... Listen, I tell you a mystery: We will not all sleep, but we will all be changed – in a flash, in the twinkling of an eye, at the last trumpet. For the trumpet will sound, the dead will be raised imperishable, and we will be changed ... He who was seated on the throne said, "I am making everything new!"

"Hear him, ye deaf; his praise, ye dumb,
Your loosened tongues employ;
Ye blind, behold your Savior come;
And leap, ye lame, for joy." (Verse Six of Charles Wesley's
"O For a Thousand Tongues to Sing")

Index

Made in the USA
Charleston, SC
08 August 2015